Together

A Reporter's Journey into
the New Black Politics

By L. H. Whittemore

Non-fiction

TOGETHER: A REPORTER'S JOURNEY
  INTO THE NEW BLACK POLITICS
COP!: A CLOSEUP OF VIOLENCE AND TRAGEDY
THE MAN WHO RAN THE SUBWAYS: THE STORY OF
  MIKE QUILL

Fiction

FEELING IT

Together

A Reporter's Journey into the New Black Politics

By L. H. Whittemore

1971   William Morrow & Company, Inc., New York

Contents

MAIN PARTICIPANTS (Alphabetical Order)

RICHARD AUSTIN	— Candidate for mayor of Detroit, 1969; elected secretary of state for Michigan, 1970.
JULIAN BOND	— State legislator, Georgia.
JOHN CASHIN	— Candidate for governor of Alabama, 1970; chairman of the National Democratic Party of Alabama.
JOHN CONYERS	— Congressman, Michigan.
CHARLES EVERS	— Mayor of Fayette, Mississippi.
KENNETH GIBSON	— Mayor of Newark, New Jersey.
RICHARD HATCHER	— Mayor of Gary, Indiana.
ZELMA WYCHE	— Police chief, Tallulah, Louisiana.
ANDREW YOUNG	— Candidate for Congress, Georgia, 1970.

OTHERS (Partial Listing)

HUGH ADDONIZIO	— Former mayor of Newark, New Jersey.
FERDINAND ALLEN	— Alderman, Fayette, Mississippi.
IMAMU AMIRI BARAKA (LeRoi Jones)	— The black militant of Newark, New Jersey.

THOMAS BRADLEY	— Candidate for mayor of Los Angeles, 1969.
EDWARD BROOKE	— U. S. Senator, Massachusetts.
JEROME CAVANAUGH	— Former mayor of Detroit, Michigan.
KENNETH CLARK	— Professor of psychology, City College of the City University of New York.
ALPHONSO DEAL	— Public safety administrator, Fayette, Mississippi.
RONALD DELLUMS	— Congressman, California.
FRANK DITTO	— Director of the East Side Voice of Independent Detroit.
CARROLL HARVEY	— Assistant to Mayor Richard Hatcher, Gary, Indiana.
ANTHONY IMPERIALE	— The white militant of Newark, New Jersey.
LONNIE KING	— Candidate for Congress, Georgia, 1970.
JOHN LEWIS	— Civil rights leader, Atlanta, Georgia.
WILLIAM MCCALLISTER	— President of the City Council, Gary, Indiana.
MELVIN ROBINSON	— Candidate for sheriff of Shelby County, Tennessee, 1970.
MRS. PAULINE SCHWEGEL	— Chairman of the Glen Park Information Committee, Gary, Indiana.
CARL STOKES	— Mayor of Cleveland, Ohio.
WILL TURNER	— Alderman, Fayette, Mississippi.
MRS. MARIE WALKER	— Editor and publisher of the Fayette *Chronicle,* Fayette, Mississippi.
COLEMAN YOUNG	— State senator, Michigan.

The white folks were mean to us. They kept us poor and ignorant, and they kept us from registering. But now we see that the white man's trump cards are economics and the vote, and now we're beginning to use the same trump cards. . . .

Well, white folks, we are not going to hate you. We're just going to keep on winning elections, keep on praying for you and keep on watching you, too—to make sure we don't go back where we came from.

—Mayor Charles Evers
Fayette, Mississippi

One

1.

I began by going to Detroit in the late summer of 1969, two years after the uprising in the slums. A decent, gentle man named Richard Henry Austin was trying to become the first black mayor of this "polarized" city, and it turned out that he was probably too decent and too gentle for his own good. At any rate, I went to his campaign headquarters and introduced myself, saying that I was hoping the book I was writing could include something about the election of a black man as mayor of America's fifth-largest city. Austin, a fifty-six-year-old, bespectacled accountant, sat on the edge of a desk and spoke about the chances for such a victory, his voice wavering between tones of elation and despair. He was the kind of fellow you could like right away, mostly because of his warm smile and the way he approached this whole ordeal of being a politician almost as if he were a young kid discussing the World Series. ("Have you seen my billboards?" he asked with excitement.) There was a bald spot on the back of his head, and the thin moustache was turning light gray like his receding hair. He wore an olive-green summer suit, and his legs dangled from the desk top, not quite reaching the floor.

More than 40 percent of Detroit's 1.5 million population was black, he noted, and therefore it was logical, if not inevitable, that they should get a mayor who would represent them. "Of course," he added, "I want to represent everyone, black and white. Detroit is in such racial trouble, race is our main problem—and we need someone who can bring us all together again." As he spoke, the soulful blast of Aretha Franklin's singing voice seemed to threaten the insides of someone's small transistorized radio. The loud wildness of the music nearly drowned out Austin's words; Aretha's throbbing wails seemed to clash with his low-keyed style, and for a few moments we both listened to this insistent reminder that a new generation of blacks had come on the scene.

Austin sighed, slid off the desk, and suggested that we go to a delicatessen next door for some food. Over sandwiches and tea served to us in a booth, he tried to explain to me something of the dilemma in which he had found himself. "If it weren't for the racial issue," he said, "I'd be the next mayor of Detroit. Of that there is little question." Being fundamentally a modest sort of man, Austin had managed to make such a statement only after a long period of deliberation during which he had fiddled with his tea bag and lighted up a small cigar. "The biggest single qualification I have," he added, "is that I've been able to unite the black community behind my candidacy. And that step was essential for any candidate trying to unite Detroit as a whole." With solid black support, he went on, all that remained to be done was to obtain 20 percent of the white vote. "Just 20 percent," he repeated, staring off into space as if he could see a vision of the white population as a huge pie, with a portion representing one fifth carefully being extracted from it on a spatula.

Well, he mused, it had happened before, so why not now, here in Detroit? Certainly it was true that blacks were making tremendous political gains in the nation's cities. Already there were some forty-eight black mayors and hundreds of black councilmen in the United States; in recent months, people in Chapel Hill, North Carolina, and Fayette, Mississippi, had elected black mayors, and the list of large cities with black chief executives also included Cleveland, Ohio, and Gary, Indiana. If Austin could win in Detroit, which was twice as large as Cleveland and four times the size of Gary—well, the importance of such a victory was immeasurable.

Pressing heavily upon Austin's mind at this point, however, was the unfortunate experience of Thomas Bradley, a formidable black candidate for mayor in Los Angeles back in the spring of this same year. Bradley had won the primary election only to be defeated by a slim margin in the runoff by incumbent Mayor Sam Yorty. Austin had tried to come to grips with the possibility that, like Bradley, he would face a flagrantly racist campaign in the runoff and be swamped at the polls by white voters afraid that a black mayor might unleash some terrible chaos upon their city. Sitting there with his tea bag and cigar, Austin looked about as radical or militant as Saint Francis among the birds, and it occurred to me that he probably would find himself unprepared and defenseless—an innocent but vulnerable victim—if such an attack were to be mounted against him. To begin the reporter's journey with this man was either a foolish mistake or a stroke of good fortune. It was difficult to tell, for while Dick Austin could not be classified as one of the "new breed" of black politicians, he held within himself most of the crosscurrents of thought and emotion that blacks seeking elective office were experiencing these days. He was caught between two conflicting tidal waves of social movement: On the one hand, there was the tremendous backlash from within Middle America, a fear of rising crime and a heightened resentment of blacks in general; and on the other hand, black anger and militancy were growing to frightful proportions. In his vision of himself as the new mayor, Austin considered that he could act as a buffer and mediator between the two forces, that somehow he could resolve black anger and white fear within himself and forge some kind of new direction for the entire community.

"I guess you could say that I'm walking a tightrope," he said, and for some reason the thought made him chuckle, as if he somehow enjoyed the danger involved.

2.

In a small hotel in a black neighborhood of Detroit, some local businessmen were having lunch. It was their regular Thursday luncheon meeting. Perhaps two dozen members of the group had shown up. They were mostly store owners and operators of modest companies—black merchants who did business primarily among other blacks. A tall man stood up at the head table and gained the attention of those in the dining room. He made some announcements and then indicated that he had more to say, but he was struggling to find the right words. "Tell it straight, Brother," came a voice from the floor, and suddenly the man relaxed and said what was on his mind:

"For years and years, we've been giving! We don't think we've been giving maybe, but we have. We've been buying automobiles that the white man has manufactured. Furniture that the white man has made. Clothing! Well, *we* sell a few things, too. And he hasn't been buying from us! So we ought to have some reciprocity! General Motors, Ford, and whatnot ought to start buying some flowers from our flower shops. They ought to start dealing with our travel agencies. Patronizing our restaurants! Anything else we can exchange! They should be giving us *those* kinds of dollars, not charity. And we can *also* get a little reciprocity from 'em in *politics*! They owe us a *whole lot* of reciprocity when it comes to politics. They've always said, 'Some day you Negroes'll be able to put up a candidate for office.' Well, now we've *got* that candidate. We got a candidate for *mayor*! We got a *contribution* to make to the city of Detroit! Dick Austin is one of the outstanding black CPAs in the entire nation, and I say that some of us ought to tell our white friends, 'Look, Brother, *here at last,* we're able to make you a significant contribution! God knows, the city needs a hard-headed, good-thinking, true businessman to get it out of its trouble. And we have the *only man* on the ballot with those qualifications and that ability! And we are *damn proud* that we have been able to pull out of the ghettos of Detroit a little black boy who has the kind of information you need, to lead you white people as well as us black people out of the wilderness!' "

His voice cracked a little. He hadn't meant to make such a speech, or at least not one with such emotion. He sat down and wiped his eyes.

3.

In a room on the second floor of the old, elegant Harmonie Club building in downtown Detroit, a hundred white businessmen sat finishing their lunch at round tables, gobbling green sherbet amid the tinkle of silverware and the murmur of light conversation. One of their members went to the podium and introduced Richard Austin, the only person in the room with a black face. The man at the podium pointed out that Austin was one of twenty-eight candidates competing for the office of mayor in a nonpartisan primary campaign. He didn't mention that Austin would become the first *black* mayor of Detroit if he should win both the primary and the runoff election, but that was understood.

There seemed to be little question that Austin was the most qualified man in the race. He was known as a tireless worker, a man who had virtually made a separate career out of public service. He had been involved in a myriad of civic activities over the past fifteen years or so, serving as chairman or president of literally dozens of committees, boards, foundations. It was almost impossible to begin a tax study or fiscal investigation in Detroit without Richard Austin. He had worked with governors and state politicians, down the line, earning respect and admiration and a reputation for honesty, integrity, and every other quality listed in the Boy Scout handbook. The trouble was, he was black.

Austin was still wearing the olive-green summer suit, and he looked somewhat younger than his fifty-six years, perhaps because his attitude was so cheerful. He stepped up to the podium and folded his hands atop it for a moment, then thrust a hand into one of his pockets and began to jiggle some loose change. He was considering the right way to approach this audience, I suppose, for gathered here were a hundred white businessmen in a city whose white business leaders were among the most powerful in the world. They seemed to lean back as if waiting to be jolted out of a mood as cold as the sherbet, their arms folded and faces blank.

"As you know," he began, "my name is Richard Austin. I've lived in Detroit for forty-four years. I attended grammar school here and high school and college. I became Michigan's first Negro certified public accountant in 1941. With the young fellows who worked with me, we built a practice, and we organized a partnership. In 1966, with your help, I was elected one of the three Wayne County auditors, and I want to tell you that it's been a pleasure to be serving you in that capacity. It's in the field of government finance, money management, and business management that I claim the most expertise. And many of you are aware that I have spent hours, hours on top of hours, working in civic affairs, trying to solve the human needs of the people in this city. . . ."

No, we were not on the brink of black revolution in this room. This was not Stokely Carmichael speaking. Austin was cautious, mild, soft-spoken, so sincere and logical that it was fashionable to say he was uninspiring.

"The central issue in this campaign, from my point of view," he went on, "is that too many people no longer think that this city is the best place in which to live."

Vapid eyes stared up at him. A red-faced man with a cigar hanging from his mouth was sitting almost directly in front of Austin, and one could only guess what visions were passing across his mind. Austin had just made one of the understatements of the year, for Detroit not only had lost its image as a fit place to live but was on the brink of final collapse. A little more than two years ago, the city was swept by burning, looting, and killing—the worst black riot in the nation's history, leaving forty-three dead and as many millions of dollars in damage—and since then the animosity between blacks and whites had grown to frightening proportions. The first people I had met in Detroit had been a cab driver who showed me his gun and an elderly hotel porter who told me how he had been mugged and robbed. The cab driver explained that he would move out of the central city like all the white liberals, if only he could afford to do so, and as far as the election was concerned, it was okay with him if Austin became mayor: "We've messed up the city so bad, we might as well let the niggers have it. We're just lettin' them take over here, anyway. We're just *giving* 'em the fucking city. At seven o'clock, the white people start pulling into their holes and hiding. After that, it's all colored." And the public relations over at City Hall had offered hardly any more cheerful words of welcome. A message to visitors had instructed: "When you travel about the city, day or night, try to travel in the company of one or more persons. When approaching alleys or recessed doorways, walk near the curb so you cannot be surprised. Before getting into your parked

car, check the rear floor. At night, use a flashlight." Even the
newspapers, whose editorial writers often warned "outsiders" to
stop "badmouthing" Detroit, were reluctantly printing the worst.
The Detroit *News* had observed: "People are shooting themselves,
and each other, at a fantastic rate here these days. Detroit has become an armed camp. Nobody has any idea how many guns there
are in this city, but one for every household would be a fair
estimate." After raising the dirty blinds on the window of my
hotel room, and after gazing out at the river, the factories, the
smoke, it was not difficult to wonder why in hell I had come.
After checking my bags, I had wandered about the Motor City
and visited the insides of some long, low-slung, ugly buildings,
the automobile plants where men on assembly lines used the
machines of white technology to churn out air-polluting, lung-
poisoning, junkyard-heading vehicles of American mobility and
death. Outside, I saw vast displays of shiny, colorful cars, block
after block of them lighted up in the night under strings of flut-
tering little banners, and elsewhere I passed across acres of
desolate parking lots. I roamed through sodden, sagging ghettos,
gaped at the hulks of burned buildings, the blackened brick walls,
and I could almost smell the mood of dull anger and despair.
Still later in the night, I had walked the deserted streets of midtown, a kind of gray cavern of stillness, hearing the echo of my
own footsteps amid the rattle of garbage blown by the wind. And
although I detested the use of the phrases "law and order" and
"crime in the streets" to obscure the diseases of racism and neglect,
I found it annoyingly difficult to stop glancing behind.

And so, Richard Austin was not even *trying* to inspire the white
businessmen. For a moment I imagined that he was attempting
to tiptoe across the top of a huge eggshell without breaking it.
He was citing his qualifications, trying to convince them that the
color of his skin would have no bearing upon his ability to perform as mayor. He had already earned their respect in the past,
but now he wanted their consideration of him as a political leader,
and you could see the pleading in his face. In a rather high-
pitched voice, choosing his words carefully but without notes, he
said that people were leaving Detroit, giving up, for many reasons.
He mentioned the shoddy public schools, the filthy streets and
alleys, the fear of inadequate police protection (Austin's way of

phrasing what was actually a dread of black militancy and crime), the pollution in the air, the lack of decent housing. Meanwhile, the white businessmen continued to stare up without expression at his black face.

"Some of our people have left," Austin said, his voice beginning to tremble slightly, "because of the racial tension."

He had said "racial tension" like a doctor using the word "cancer" and still attempting to sound reassuring. The room had become eerily quiet. Although he had approached the subject with extreme gentleness and delicacy, it seemed that he had come down upon a fragile nerve with yet too great a force.

"And some people," he continued on into their collective white mind like a dull but persistent chisel, "have left simply because they don't like black neighbors."

No reaction. There was only the faint sound of chairs scraping the floor as the businessmen adjusted their sitting positions.

"The fact that so many who have left our city are in the middle- and upper-income brackets means that we are being left with an older population, with less-affluent people, and—and with a larger black population."

Silence. Austin went on to outline some of his proposals for reversing the city's economic plight, but already he had lost them. By the time he came to the end of his speech, when he made a final appeal for unity and racial harmony and for joint efforts to save Detroit, he might as well have been talking to himself.

4.

The black businessmen had loosened up a bit following the emotional speech by the tall fellow at the head table. Now another man stood up, his napkin falling to the floor, and he addressed his friends at the other tables in a loud, booming tone of voice, pacing around and gesturing to them whenever he felt that a point needed emphasis. "Somehow or other we holler like hell to get up to the starting gate," he hollered, "and then we get *mad* because it looks like it might *open* for us!"

"That's right," said another black man, nodding his head in agreement.

"And we start *backing away* from it!"

"You said it."

"Negroes have been hollerin' all these years about how good they could do if they were just *white*. Now, they got an opportunity to do something because they're *black*! And yet they're still busy selling themselves the idea that it can't be done!"

His listeners bowed their heads slightly as if out of shame. Then another man took the floor and said, "We've got to *arouse* our people! To get them to the polls! This is an important occasion! We've got to raise our level, economically and politically! This is one of the first times in our history that we're gonna be able to do something *fundamental*, in politics. We're gonna be able to elect a good man! To the top governmental office! *We got to do it!*"

Dessert and coffee came after the impromptu speechmaking, and at one of the tables, three black men leaned toward each other in conversation. "Austin," one was saying, "is the only candidate who can save the white man's investment in this city. We gotta make the white man see that."

"That's right. The whites gotta see that *they* have a stake in Dick's election, just as we have."

"Maybe they have *more* of a stake," the third man said. "Their future here depends on whether we blacks can make Detroit a good place to live again."

"Look," said the first man, "my heart is in Detroit. My *roots* are in this city. And I see progress in the fact that every part of Detroit has *some* blacks in it, now. And I'm determined to stay here and fight for Detroit."

As I listened to them talk, I remembered how I had come to Detroit expecting to find among black people almost total disillusionment with politics. Indeed, there was a tremendous amount of hatred and despair, but the prospect of electing Dick Austin, of seeing a whole new direction in city government, had helped to heal some of the wounds, at least for a while. The message of blacks in politics, here in this room, was one of hope and determination. Austin had come out of the great black middle class, and as such he was not only a symbol of what individual black men could achieve, but a hope for the future in terms of the dominant minority group ultimately becoming a part of the

System. In his personal career, Austin had opened doors which had been closed to the rest of his people, and in doing so he had become a kind of pioneer. Now he was on the frontier of politics in behalf of his people, and the men in this room, while relatively inexperienced in this realm, were entering democracy with the same kind of enthusiasm that had spurred the Founding Fathers. It seemed such an irony that blacks—who had been shut off from the System and oppressed and exploited all these years—were now the most eager to make it work. It occurred to me that, for most white men, politics was more a matter of personal ambition, while for most blacks, the game was rooted in a cause that went far beyond their own success or failure. Austin's pursuit of political power encompassed the aspirations of all who identified with him. His pursuit represented the struggle of a separate Black Nation in Detroit to join the total city. For how else could the city's black population assume its proper role in society and overcome its feelings of powerlessness and lack of self-respect if not by exerting power over decisions which directly affected its own members? By its very nature, Austin's was an extremely emotional, deeply rooted pursuit. In fact, a new black political enthusiasm was infusing some long-needed vitality into the corrupt carcass of the System, for no longer could a black politician be motivated merely by personal gain. No matter who he was, the black candidate for mayor had no choice but to pursue a mission of great urgency and commitment to the health of the entire community. Austin was the symbol of this mission, but below him were the strands of hope extending into all segments of Detroit's black community, and all the divergent and sometimes conflicting goals of the blacks, all their separate hopes, reached up and came together in the person of this modest, humble man. His personal success would make history, true, but with him stood more than 500,000 blacks on the threshold of the democratic process. At this moment, Richard Austin was possessed of more passion for what America stood for than any ten law-and-order candidates put together.

5.

He sat down to only the barest amount of applause, and the white businessmen turned their attention to the next candidate, a woman, Miss Mary Beck, who had been a member of the City Council for something like twenty years. Now in her sixties, she was the chairman of an organization called the Busy Broom Brigade. "People ask where is my broom," she told the businessmen. "Well, I haven't yet the authority to wield that broom, but that is what I hope to secure on election day. My goal is to sweep this place clean of crime, corruption, and pollution, and to maintain law and order with justice."

The businessmen gave her a big hand.

Next came Sheriff Roman S. Gribbs, forty-three, Austin's leading opponent. He made his way to the podium, flashy in a blue suit and lighter-blue shirt, a pale-blue handkerchief, a blue-and-yellow tie, and shiny black pointed shoes. He was a TV-handsome figure of a man up there, and his light-brown, graying hair was swept back neatly into place, glistening under the lights.

Gribbs had a way of becoming quite passionate over nothing. As his words became more empty of content, he seemed to compensate for the void by getting physically worked up. He gripped the podium, leaned forward, and said he was optimistic as hell about the city's future. He might have added that he seemed optimistic as hell about his *own* future as well.

Somehow, Roman Gribbs was the leading candidate in the race for mayor. Dick Austin had announced his own candidacy in early June, throwing the white rulers of Detroit into a virtual panic. It was obvious that not in a long time had such a qualified person appeared on the political scene, but, dammit, he was black. The sophisticated white rulers, many so-called liberals among them, could not bear the thought of a black man as the chief figure in their city. Austin had a clear field, largely because incumbent Mayor Jerome Cavanaugh had declared that he wasn't going to run for a third term. So what to do? The white rulers suddenly found themselves with a black candidate, and their silence on the matter was becoming more embarrassing by the day. Mary Beck was okay, but after all, she was a woman, and besides, her overt appeals to racism and fear were distasteful to many white folks. A more subtle approach, a less obvious, less *crude* alternative to Richard Austin, was needed. Mary Beck and her Broom had a strong following, but she was too honest, too open, too— again—embarrassing. The sophisticated white rulers needed someone whom they could support without feeling guilty. Mary Beck had become sort of a female version of George Wallace, and white liberals in Detroit were more, well, *civilized* than that. Better to have a white fellow who wouldn't come right out and say what was on everyone's minds.

So they came up with the sheriff of Wayne County, a man who happened to be a Democrat, like Austin. He was a "moderate" on the issues, so moderate that it was impossible to tell what he stood for, and yet at the same time he was a former assistant prosecutor who had systematically used his peremptory challenges to keep blacks off the jury. In other words, he was anything you wanted to make of him. He made it comfortable, painless, for white liberals to turn away from Austin. And as soon as the hand-some six-footer came on the scene, both city newspapers declared him the front-runner. He had come out of nowhere, really, just before the filing date for the primary, but his arrival was no acci-dent. Mayor Cavanaugh made this about as clear as he could in a conversation I had with him: "I think the newspapers were very instrumental in Gribbs's running, in urging him to run." The papers, of course, patted themselves on the back for having avoided the prospect of a nasty, racially divisive campaign be-tween Dick Austin and Mary Beck. But what they really had done, and were doing, was to put forth a white alternative to the most qualified man who happened to be black. For all those who still weren't ready for black political power in high places, Roman Gribbs was the conscience-soothing answer.

The white businessmen obviously liked the sheriff's style, empty as it was of substance. Like Mary Beck, he was very big on law, order, and justice, the latter word falling out as a kind of bother-some addition to what had become a clear and concise call for putting unruly blacks in their place. The businessmen liked him, and indeed, nearly all of the white rulers had rushed to Gribbs's side. Many of the city's biggest liberals had gone to Gribbs secretly with money for his campaign. Those with heavy financial stakes in the city, those concerned with holding on to their economic power, those who were more concerned with the "image" of Detroit than with the quality of life for its poor and downtrodden citizens—they all went to Gribbs and pledged their financial sup-port. (One very outspoken white candidate, Walter Shamie, put it this way: "I've a great deal of respect for Dick Austin, for his ability, for his sincerity, and integrity. He's a good man. He's a beautiful person, a beautiful human being. But regretfully, he's being used. And I'm sure that in his heart he must know this. I'm convinced beyond any doubt that this good man is being used by the power structure, the officials and the tycoons of the utilities and the news media of this city, who are venting their consciences in the usual manner of playing the role of supporting a black man, but behind the scenes they're really supporting Roman Gribbs, the man they brought into the whole act in the very final moment, as if it were an afterthought.") Supporting Gribbs financially were the management and executive types who lived in the suburbs, outside the city altogether, people for whose convenience and safety the freeways had been built; the list included lawyers and higher-ups from Detroit Bank and Trust, Cadillac, the National Bank of Detroit, Michigan Bell Telephone, the Bank of Commonwealth, General Motors, the white craft unions and, topping all contributors, the mostly white Detroit Police Officers Association.

After Gribbs spoke, two more white candidates offered themselves upon the altar of public service, one telling the businessmen that it was "almost too late" for a city so plagued by crime and bankruptcy and racial strife and general woe. The next fellow, apparently trying to top all the previous rhetoric, declared, "In regard to law, crime, order, and so forth, I wish to set the records clear. I am the *original* and *only* law-and-order candidate in this campaign." What it had come down to, I suppose, was a contest of the most shallow and almost comical sort. This final speaker even went on to recite a poem to the businessmen: "Our city once great / now seething with hate, / Lord help us to face an uncertain fate."

6.

By the end of the white businessmen's luncheon, it was nearly impossible to remember what Richard Austin looked like, much less what he had said. The white candidates had drowned him out with rhetoric. It was amazing that white leaders, who had created the conditions breeding poverty and unrest in the first place, now shouted the loudest about how they were most qualified to save the city. By what logic? The whites in Detroit were facing a choice whether to hold on to their political control for a short while longer or to extend an arm of cooperation now, while they still had an arm to extend. Detroit was one in a long list of major American cities whose emerging Negro majorities were inevitably moving toward political control. The white exodus to the suburbs had caused a drop in population from nearly 1.7 million to less than 1.5 million, and the black population had risen to nearly half. This was the last chance to work together, for next time City Hall would pass from white to black hands anyway—not through new channels of brotherhood but simply because the numerical balance would have shifted. Then, in 1974, the wreckage would be dumped in the laps of the black leaders, who would have to start rebuilding Detroit from the cinders up. The question now was, why wait? Richard Austin offered the last chance for democracy to work on a basis other than sheer numerical strength.

7.

Before my conversation about the campaign with Mayor Cavanaugh, his press officer had set the mood with these words of greeting: "Nothing but grief, torment, turmoil. Half the population's always against you. If you appoint a black man, the whites say, 'Oh, he's always doing something for the blacks.' The same thing if you appoint a white man. They're *all* mad at you. Nobody appreciates anything you do, anymore. A guy can take just so much of it."

Mayor Cavanaugh was seated behind his desk, high up in his blue-carpeted office, still presiding over the demolition of dreams. The once-dynamic Jerry Cavanaugh sat there while a clock ticked loudly and slowly, as if the spaces between each second were becoming longer and more painful. One knew right away that he would be glad to leave.

In the beginning, at the start of the decade and when he had been only thirty-three, Cavanaugh had bubbled with new ideas and restless, seemingly boundless energy. He had become a national leader, and ideas hatched by his staff in Detroit were used as models for new programs drawn up in Washington. Now he was forty-one, still young but weary and almost beaten down. Since the riot, everything had gone steadily downhill. "In one short week," he sighed, "all the things we were building on seemed to come crumbling down. At one time we were interested in poverty programs, Model Cities, urban renewal, and so forth, but now it's all we can do to keep enough police on the streets and to keep the hospital doors open."

Part of the weary attitude conveyed by this large, friendly Irishman seemed deliberate, as if he were trying to communicate something of his experience without using phony-sounding words. I asked him about the primary campaign, and he said he felt that Austin was being more "definitive" than the other candidates. "And Dick also has hit at something more basic—the question of national priorities. He's spoken out against the ABM, for example, and against the war in Vietnam." Cavanaugh dwelled on this point for a while, repeating in various contexts that a mayor must not only articulate the needs of Detroit but also the "mistaken sense of priorities" in America. I thought of Martin Luther King's statement that racism, economic exploitation, and militarism were inextricable from each other, and that to attack one it was necessary to solve them all. Then I thought of Gribbs, who was being supported by white-racist homeowner groups, by General Motors, and by the police. Unlike Austin, the sheriff was saying that Vietnam had nothing to do with conditions in Detroit.

"I probably could have beaten Austin if I'd run for reelection again," Cavanaugh said. "There's a feeling, though, that I'm too soft with the blacks. Those who feel that way, they're not all bigoted people, but that's their view, their frustration. Underlying all this discontent is this fast-growing alienation between black and white in America. . . .

"A black man in this office couldn't really do any better, I don't think. And some blacks would even have a *more* difficult time running the city. Carl Stokes himself says there's no 'black' way to eliminate social blight, rats, slums. The provision of resources, the changing of our whole view of things, our values—the election of a black man can't change all that, and that's the guts of the whole situation. Some people think a black man can temporarily still the troubled waters, but I don't hold with that.

"Anyhow, a black like Austin should be considered on the basis of his quality and ability. That's the measure. And if you apply it, most of the black candidates *are* superior to those who run. It's their optimism, maybe. It isn't an unnatural thing. It's their enthusiasm in getting a share of the action, like the Irish and Italians and so on when they just started to get a foothold politically."

We discussed Austin's chances in the primary and in the runoff election, and Cavanaugh remarked, "Under certain conditions, Austin can win. I think if Mary Beck was to be nominated in the primary, he could win. But let's say he ends up running against Ray Gribbs in the runoff. Now, Ray is a moderate sort of a fellow, by political definition. A lot of whites, it wouldn't bother them at all to vote for Gribbs and not for Austin. But if you had Beck and Austin pitted against each other, that's something different."

Two

1.

Toward the end of the turbulent decade of the sixties, after so many dreams of racial progress and harmony had crumbled, after so many of our darkest nightmares had become reality, when it was now difficult, almost impossible, to believe that America could heal its wounds, when in fact our wounds seemed to be widening, deepening, and freezing solid, several hundred black men and women from all over the country traveled to the nation's capital, to the Washington-Hilton Hotel, where they began to discuss among themselves how to make democracy work in the new decade ahead. Aside from the color of their skin, aside from the experience of being black in a white-controlled society, these men and women shared at least one other thing in common: Each of them had been elected to a position of some influence, whether on a remote school board in Colorado or in the halls of Congress itself, and therefore each had arrived still holding on to some sort of faith, large or small, in the eventual workability of the American political process. No doubt the setting was incongruous, for many of them had come to the plush Hilton, with its swimming pool and tennis courts and huge ornate ballrooms, from crowded urban ghettos or from desperately poor rural slums. More than a few were made uneasy by the surroundings, for most of them represented predominantly black constituencies that were still struggling for a place in American life. And just as a good many were visiting Washington, D.C., for the first time in their lives, all were relative newcomers to the system of government that this town symbolized—indeed, many hadn't even been able to vote, much less run for office, only five years before.

Despite the gloom and frustration of the sixties overshadowing their meeting, these men and women could not suppress the hint of an enthusiasm unequaled since the Reconstruction period following the Civil War. Once again, blacks were moving into American politics, they were getting into positions of leverage, if not real power, in greater numbers all the time. It was hoped that the sad history of Reconstruction would not be repeated this time around, for even with these current gains, the hour was late.

The figures showed that nearly fifteen hundred blacks were holding elective public office in the United States, a large increase in recent years, although black elected officials still made up only .03 percent of the more than 500,000 elected officials across the country. Three tenths of 1 percent—even though blacks comprised some 11 percent of America's population. Even a doubling of elected black officials would leave them with less than 1 percent of the total number of elected officials. It would take the election of 55,000 black officials to give blacks a proportionate share of the pie. Within this context, the most commonly heard frustration at the Washington meeting was that the black public official was virtually unable to produce results for his constituents, caught as he was between their demands and the refusal of the white politicians, who held the majority of power, to cooperate. At the same time, the white politicians expected the black officials to "control" their black constituencies, a policy threatening to reduce the new black leaders' credibility to zero. The question for many was how to remain a "moderate" and "respectable" person who poses little threat to the white Establishment, while at the same time forcefully advocating a response to the needs of the poor. Like Richard Austin, many felt they were "walking a tightrope" between the white racists on one side and the black militants on the other. I met Austin at the three-day meeting in the Hilton. He told me that militant blacks wanted him to support forcefully a civilian review board for the Detroit police force, whose members were being accused of widespread harassment of blacks in the ghetto, and on the other hand that most whites were violently opposed to a review board. Needing black support *and* white votes, Austin was indeed walking a tightrope. His answer had been to support a *petition* for the review board, not the proposal itself, and in the hotel he came up to me and said, "How can I convince white people that I'm just as concerned with law enforcement as they are?" The question went unanswered, and it was almost pitiful to see how the game of political compromise could reduce a man to a position of such insecurity.

2.

The conference in Washington was called the Institute for Black Elected Officials. It was sponsored by the Metropolitan Applied Research Center, and as such it was not involved in partisan politics, nor was it concerned with the development of any ideology such as black power, black nationalism, or whatnot. Its main purpose was to enable all these people to come together and learn about each others' problems and experiences, so they could return home with perhaps a bit more knowledge of how to represent their constituencies with greater effectiveness.

The main speaker at the conference was Dr. Kenneth B. Clark, the black psychologist and educator whose social studies had helped persuade the Supreme Court to ban school segregation, back in 1954. Clark spoke in the big International Ballroom East while the delegates ate dinner, and as an intellectual, he viewed his function differently from the way most speakers would. Concerned with a larger perspective, he gave a speech that was both dull and forceful, criticizing extremists on all sides. He spoke of the "fundamental survival wisdom and realism of the folk Negro" and reminded everyone that the "commitment of the masses of American Negroes to racial integration remains intact." Despite the public media's "persistent overdramatization of black separatism," the facts indicated that the struggle against segregation was still "a profound and moving reality for the masses of American Negroes." And as far as Clark was concerned, "irresistible racial progress" was going on, all fashionable views to the contrary.

Clark's message, for me, was that the civil-rights movement could not be halted, that certain irrevocable forces were abroad in the land, more powerful than white racism or black separatism, and, moreover, that black elected officials had, in a real sense, become the new leaders of the Movement. "The civil-rights movement," he said, "far from being dead, has, all emotional rhetoric to the contrary, moved to new and necessary and realistic levels of implementation." Social implementation in a democracy is politics, and therefore the "agents of implementation" are public officials. Black elected officials were now the *only* civil-rights leaders with real effectiveness, and the challenge for them will be "to insist that they be taken seriously as public officials, and that they be listened to in the halls of power." The black political official must be prepared "for the realities and the problems of a politics of integration." He must be a cool, informed professional, capable of intelligent strategy, and also he must be a warm, compassionate human being, capable of genuine communication and identification with his constituency. He must prepare himself to help America "to save itself from its past racial and urban mistakes," and to "develop new and higher standards of political morality and performance." The leader of an oppressed minority "cannot be just another politician."

3.

During the conference in Washington, I spoke with a so-called black militant who happened to mention Richard Gordon Hatcher, the young black mayor of Gary, Indiana, who was scheduled to speak to the group. "Now, there's one guy," the militant said, "who has really articulated the goals and aspirations of black people." I waited for him to go down the list of other black mayors whom he admired, but *his* list abruptly ended right there.

Lately I had often been confronted with that strikingly small nonlist of one name, and at least twice had been told bluntly, "Hatcher is the *only* black mayor in America." Sometimes the list expanded a bit, depending upon who was drawing it up, but at other times, especially when one was searching for the realistic heart of the country's black movement, there were no *elected* leaders mentioned at all, Dr. Clark's speech notwithstanding. In fact, the focus of any discussion depended entirely upon one's perception of how current history was being made: by black politicians or Black Panthers? If one really believed that the civil-rights movement was dead, and therefore that the political realm was also inconsequential, then one had to go looking for black leadership in ghetto streets and storefronts, and among the legions of those disaffected, militant young who saw no hope short of physical confrontation and violent revolution. In fact, I thought, they may actually be at the heart of the struggle, at the front lines of current history, since the threat of violence sometimes seemed the sole method of maintaining concern in high places. And it may be, I thought, that the militants' frightening, bold rhetoric—and indeed, actions—comprised the most frontward edge of the attack, making it possible for quieter men, like Richard Austin, to speak up. Would Carl Stokes have been elected mayor of Cleveland if not for Stokely and Rap and Eldridge? It was possible that the Panthers and others like them had expanded the circle of dialogue, giving moderate blacks more room to move around, more free-dom to press for legitimate but controversial black goals through the circuits of our tired and undoubtedly reluctant system.

In any event, when I had been able to engage militant young blacks in political discussions, only two public figures were usually mentioned: Hatcher and Georgia State Representative Julian Bond. Like Bond, Hatcher was fast becoming a symbol of a new breed of black politician, especially among the street kids in our numerous urban slums and also among the latest influx of black college students. At this point Hatcher may not have had Bond's charismatic appeal to the white press, but the word on him seemed to be getting around.

Hatcher and Bond were sharing the same speakers' platform be-fore the black elected officials in Washington. Hatcher was sched-uled to speak first, and you had to figure that they regarded his act as a mere curtain raiser for Bond's, but it didn't turn out that way. He stood up there facing the crowd of at least three hun-dred black men and women, who were seated around dozens of dinner tables in one of the ballrooms, and he might have been a visiting student scholar from Kenya, or maybe even a member of the Yale debating team. Under the lights, and perhaps because of the contrast to the white collar lining his neck, one could not help but make note of the rich darkness of his black skin. He evoked the vision of a bold young leader of an emerging African nation, a bookworm with black horn-rimmed glasses who would look equally at home in a dashiki. He was so damned young-looking, younger even than his thirty-six years, a clean-cut kid with a high forehead that slanted slightly backward, the neatly trimmed hair continuing the slant for another inch and following the round shape of his head, and the sideburns ending just below the tops of his small ears. He was quite open, easy-going, personable; he exuded a feeling of physical relaxation or tranquillity. But there also existed in the man a hesitation that went beyond mere shyness or introversion, a hint that maybe beneath this whole demeanor of coolness lurked an angry demon that was kept carefully hidden from the rest of the world.

But above all he was young and acutely aware that he was facing the most formidable among his peers. He started slowly, in the voice of a schoolboy addressing the senior class, taking long pauses between phrases and going the humble route: "I think that I am at a loss for words, when I look about and I see individuals who've made such outstanding contributions to the struggle for freedom, dignity, and justice in this country." Collectively the audience seemed to sit back, pleased with itself, and some poured second or third cups of coffee.

Then he told them a joke about a man caught in the Johnstown Flood who went to heaven and was about to boast of his experiences when a kind angel leaned over and whispered in his ear, "I just thought I ought to tell you—there's a fella named Noah in the audience." It was a good anecdotal joke, delivered with fine rhythm and punch. First they laughed, quieted down a bit, and then inexplicably began laughing all over again. What had taken place, I think, was a double reaction whose exposures had occurred some five seconds apart. First they appreciated the style and wit of the joke itself, then they erupted at the recognition of their own response. The second round of laughter seemed born of something more deeply pleasurable and exciting—the kid up there was cool; you could feel the draught of fresh air and anticipation sweeping over the room.

"And I feel that way this evening," he continued. "I feel there are many Noahs in the audience."

Hatcher assumed the humble stance once more before he was

ready to become his own man. This time he turned gracefully to Julian Bond, who was seated to his right, and singled him out as a young man who "has demonstrated the kind of commitment and concern that is all too rare in these troubled times."

And now, having paid some dues, having displayed a capacity for poise and wit, and having earned the audience's attention, Hatcher underwent a quick transformation of the spirit and a sudden bold defiance leaped into his youthful throat: "I've been asked to speak tonight on the Negro in politics. And, of course, at the very outset, most of you recognize that such a speech would be somewhat outdated. Because today, to be very frank with you, there is no place for a *Negro* in politics!"

The audience applauded, now roused from its after-dinner dullness, riding on a strange field of energy and excitement mixed with respect and possibly even fear. Undoubtedly each person in the ballroom was scrambling his brain to discover the true meaning of his own enthusiasm. A handful could cheer with an easy conscience; some, I suspect, were applauding a romantic vision, perhaps rapidly switching their self-images from "Negro" to "black" in a moment's delusion of the mind; still others were unconsciously celebrating their own political deaths.

Slowly, Hatcher created a mood to suit his style. He dipped into some Charles Dickens, giving a panoramic view of why we lived in the best and the worst of times, and then gave a brief account of his own experience in Gary. There was the edge of the rebel in his voice, the tone of the fighter, but it was a controlled performance, laced with fine intelligence and good phraseology and enthusiastic reports of accomplishment back home. At times he seemed to mesmerize the audience, as much by the rhythm of his approach as by the substance of the speech, and near the end he was quoting both Martin Luther King *and* Eldridge Cleaver, reaching out for his listeners' best instincts of self-sacrifice and responsibility as elected leaders. The thing was, he was not just talking about the horrors of white America before a black audience but challenging the audience itself:

Our biggest problems in Gary were not with the white section of the political machine, but with its Negro lackeys who thrive on the oppression of their brothers, but whose sordid careers are doomed to end when that oppression ends.

A colonial power cannot exploit its colony without the support of some of the natives. In like fashion, blacks in this country couldn't be so colonized were it not for the soul brothers who sell their souls.

Black political power is essential, but in and of itself, it is not enough. The black movement must more and more doggedly direct its thoughts and energies to the problems of economic power. And by economic power I don't mean black capitalism, which is a travesty and a hoax. Since black people of this nation are, as a whole, the most deprived and oppressed, it must be black people who are the vanguard of the movement which demands that the system be radically transformed.

As we press for reforms, we must not lull the people to sleep. We must awaken them to the truth.

And we black leaders must also tend to an absolutely crucial problem, particular to our own people, our black brothers and sisters—the development of a healthy, vital black nationalism and black culture.

Black people have not yet gotten themselves together, and the white radical position is occupied primarily by youth. Given those conditions, blacks must continue to organize themselves as blacks. In unions, in bar associations, among doctors—and yes, even in politics. No, especially in politics. And that includes each and every one of us here today, no matter what the political party. We must organize black!

Hatcher wound up by calling on his colleagues to form a "national, independent, black political organization, whose purposes and deeds, swift and true, will give hope, spirit, and pride to black America and a decent and human society for all." Applause followed applause until, at the end, he quietly, unemotionally, repeated his campaign slogan of two years before: "For God's sake, for America's sake, let's get ourselves together." When it was over, when he sat down amid the ovation, his listeners seemed to realize that out of all the speeches they were to sit through during their stay, this was the one they had come to hear.

Three

1.

Richard Hatcher had been in office more than two years when I first went to see him in Gary in the late spring of 1970. Since he had become the city's first black mayor, he had begun a kind of nonviolent revolution in a most unlikely place. What I mean here by "revolution" is a movement of basic change from one fundamental condition to another, wholly different one and mainly a change that had begun to bring about a wider distribution of power to people who had been unrepresented, exploited, sold out. As an individual, he was a perfect example of the progression in the civil-rights movement that Dr. Clark had referred to in general. His roots were in the Movement, and now he had brought that kind of nonviolent struggle to a new stage of implementation, namely political action, and there was every reason to believe that if it didn't work out, the kind of revolution requiring a violent convulsion of some sort would surely take place.

Among those who worked with or for him, there were many descriptions for Richard Hatcher. He was a humanist—no, a *black* humanist. He was an intellectual—no, an intellectual who *recognized that he was black;* for God's sake, he was the *blackest* and *most* intellectual of politicians. He was, yes, an historical figure like Carl Stokes—no, he was *the first of the second-generation black mayors, born prematurely.* He was an honest mayor rooting out corruption—well, a *reform* mayor, if you will, a *lower-class* mayor.

He was cool—no, dammit, *super*cool. And with all of this romantic repetition pounding into the visiting writer's skull, there was the impulse to call him the Swinging Soul Mayor of the Steel City, or the Beleaguered Black Saint of Sin City, and to let it go at that. But Dick Hatcher in private was too calm, and, well, too *natural* for such labels.

He had almost none of the theatricality of a Carl Stokes or a John Lindsay. Whatever Hatcher was, in reality he eluded the deft phrase and came on as an inward, remote sort of man, very much alone. It was clear that he was driving toward some kind of perfect ideal, toward a vision of himself and society that must have gone beyond the wildest dreams that he could have had as a small boy. And the boy was still very much there, even though the people of Gary now called him Mr. Mayor. The boy inside him penetrated right through the double-breasted Continental suits when he strolled along the sidewalks of his downtown, a slight, not-so-tall figure bouncing on the balls of his feet like a hip young stud on the way to the pool hall. "There's Hatcher," said one small black kid standing on the corner, his lips slack and his eyes wide open with awe. Hatcher had given a whole generation of such kids an alternate identity, a self-perception that they never had had before, and a pride in themselves, too, that was probably at least equal to that which they derived from belonging to any of Gary's fifteen street gangs.

"Someone once asked me," Hatcher said, " 'What about the militants in Gary?' And I replied, sorta joking around, *'We're* the militants in Gary.' And to a degree, for a while, that was true." Now there were more combative voices than his to be found, but none had thus far accused Hatcher of not being militant enough.

"Being a black militant is a very dangerous business, these days," he commented to me. "You can get into the black-blacker-blackest game, sort of an escalating rhetoric, where one guy comes along and says, 'White people are bad, and we've really gotta do some-thing about them,' so the next guy thinks, 'Man, I can't be a leader unless I top that.' So he says, 'I tell you what we gotta do. We gotta *kill* whitey,' and it just goes on and on. It becomes a very irrational and unreasonable kind of thing."

By nature Hatcher seemed neither irrational nor unreasonable; he seemed to attempt a careful balance between emotion and intellect, realizing, undoubtedly, that he was in a position to try to accomplish through established channels what others were only able to scream about. "So the trick, if you can call it that," he said, "is to be militant where it counts, and to do the things that have to be done, without getting caught up in that bag of can-you-top-this kind of thing. And that's a difficult path to walk, these days. To try to maintain your own level of sanity and reason, and at the same time *not* sell out, *not* do things you really shouldn't be doing."

Since taking office, Hatcher had been an innovator more than anything else, and he had begun to turn around some basic things in order to head Gary in a new direction. Perhaps his biggest task had been to transform City Hall from a self-satisfying operation into one that was basically geared to serving people. His greatest claim, I think, was that the community now participated more in matters that directly affected it. This was especially so in the poverty program, which Hatcher had shoved out of City Hall and into the hands of a majority of poor people. With a deluge of Federal and foundation funds, Hatcher had set up job-training programs and had begun to tear down the slums. Public housing had gone up all over the city; none had been built in the previous ten years.

A large percentage of Gary's white population had, to put it mildly, an antipathy toward Negroes. The emergence of a black chief executive had produced in the whites an extreme case of the jitters and also a weird schizophrenia over some very basic things. Some people in the largest white section, Glen Park, feeling that Hatcher was not representing their interests (which was understandable, since many of their interests added up to an opposition to black aspirations), even wanted to "secede" from the rest of the city and to elect their own mayor—which was probably a high point in the politics of polarization anywhere. The schizophrenia grew out of several things, one being a feeling that Hatcher provided a kind of insurance policy against black riots, which was possibly true but only within narrow limits. Another development that seemed to confuse the whites was that, while Hatcher was the first black mayor, he was also the first *honest* one they had seen in a long time. Some tried to resolve this conflict by saying that they *admired* the past white mayors who could steal *and not get caught* —Hatcher just wasn't *smart* enough to do it, you see. Others convinced themselves that he was a Communist sent from either Moscow or Peking, and still others had decided that the reason they didn't like him was the way he collected their garbage. Whatever, the town now had a majority of blacks, and they were mostly in slums, and Hatcher was either going to get them out of that condition, or—well, it had all come down to a situation where no matter what happened in the future, Gary, Indiana, was being forced to come to grips in a very real way with the most volatile, most critical domestic issue of our time, and either the lid would blow off, or somehow, God knows how, a new kind of social order would emerge.

2.

Because he had assaulted his city's political system from the outside rather than worked his way up through its graft-ridden channels, Hatcher remained a loner, an antagonist, in a place that was a kind of paradigm of American apple pie and corruption. During many of my private conversations with him, I had the feeling that we were meeting secretly, like two members of the underground Resistance, so that Hatcher could confide some thoughts and attitudes that he dared not reveal in public. Not that he did make any such conspiratorial or treacherous revelations, but it was just the feeling of the mood—"Let's duck into this coffee shop so we can talk alone," that kind of thing—and that is the way I came to think of Richard Hatcher. He was the mayor, yes, but he was also still the young intellectual, a member of the opposition; he ran City Hall, but somehow he still seemed to be outside it, still plotting to storm its corridors and capture his own office. Perhaps this feeling came from the fact that he was still unused to holding power, that he still conceived of himself as fighting it—and indeed, he had learned that being mayor carried with it no assurance that he had now found the secret source of political or economic control. "I may be mayor of Gary," he had said, "but I cannot, by that token, guarantee that black people will share in the unbelievable profits of U. S. Steel, which dominates our city's economic life." The power was still somewhere else, still as elusive as ever, and therefore, although he was indeed the mayor, he had not lost his challenging stance.

Ever since the November elections in 1967, when Carl Stokes of Cleveland had become the first Negro ever elected mayor of a major American city and when Hatcher had risen to power in Gary at the same time ("the other one," he joked, referring to himself), there had been a tendency to speak of them both in the same breath. But after spending time in each of their cities, I came away with two completely different impressions. The distance from Stokes to Hatcher was much farther than the journey from Cleveland to Gary; it was a full 180-degree turn of the mind—although, paradoxically, it was a sure bet that the two men could sit down together and agree on virtually everything of substance. It was just that by age, temperament, background, and experience, Hatcher was in a position to realize himself, to allow his black identity to reveal itself, in more ways than Stokes was either able or willing to do.

There was hardly a recent public photograph of an unsmiling Carl Stokes; it was a smile for the cameras, and it sometimes appeared to have been grafted onto his face as a fixture that could not possibly correspond always to the mood of his inner life. He could be President someday with that smile, one feels. "Buoyant" was the word for him that keeps coming to mind. He strode through the lobby of the Sheraton-Cleveland Hotel, for example, his security man trying to keep pace, and he turned as a group of young waitresses came down the stairs from the mezzanine floor, and with his gaze he singled out the prettiest in the group, smiled that smile, and she blushed and giggled and nearly tripped down the rest of the stairs; when she recovered, he was gone. Everyone received the full blast of the Stokes personality, while Hatcher walked his own turf with a style that was almost monklike in comparison.

Stokes was the complete political animal, having made a career of it—having made a career of *being accepted*—while Hatcher's involvement in politics grew out of the frustration of not being able to change the basic conditions in the lives of black people. Stokes lived in an expensive house in an overwhelmingly white neighborhood; Hatcher resided in a modest house in an all-black section of Gary. Stokes bristled when journalists attempted to interview him as a "black" public official, while Hatcher made public statements like the following:

> It is beyond dispute that I am black—I am too abashed to add "and beautiful," though it is tempting. . . . My blackness has been the dominant fact of life's experience, as it is the dominant fact of the life of every black man in America, and perhaps in the world. . . . Being black has made me a stranger. Being black has dominated my life. I cannot, nor would I wish to, reject my blackness.

Stokes could sound like Martin Luther King before a black audience and then change his style completely in order to suit the tastes of, say, a group of bankers, but Hatcher wouldn't know how to juggle his personality around if he had to. They were not alike at all, and it went beyond the fact that one was light-skinned, the other dark, or that one presided over a large urban metropolis of 800,000 people, in a palacelike City Hall, while the other was mayor of an out-of-the way steel town a fourth the size, in a dingy City Hall which in comparison to Cleveland's could be taken for an outhouse, or that one was elected by a two thirds white population while the other, Hatcher, took office in a city nearly 60 percent black. It went beyond those things, but maybe it started with them all the same.

My impression of Stokes was that he was trying too hard to please everyone, although, admittedly, the impression was superficial. The fact remains, however, that unlike Hatcher he publicly rejected black-power leaders and supported President Johnson's war effort in Vietnam. I saw Stokes as a man in a kind of glorious parade in which he was sitting atop a convertible with the top down, waving to the crowds. He was continually "winning their hearts," so to speak, and shaking hands, clapping shoulders, becoming excited over whatever the moment had to offer. He seemed to be constantly *on top* of things, smiling even into the teeth of his enemies, looking *down* at them, smiling, dancing about like the Golden Gloves boxer that he was—he probably smiled like that when he went into the ring. And all this was fine, probably even necessary, for the big city of Cleveland, which was not cosmopolitan by a long shot but which, when compared to Gary, looked like the zenith of civilization. And it was fine in a city where whites still dominated and where the black mayor had *better* be a good smiler, dancer, swinger, actor, or whatever Carl Stokes did in order to maintain his effectiveness. But Hatcher—well, Hatcher was down there in a city which, until he came along, had never been in the public eye except when a mayor went off to prison in handcuffs. If Carl Stokes were the mayor of Gary, he'd—no, Carl Stokes would never *want* to be the mayor of Gary, and in turn, Hatcher could never be *elected* mayor of Cleveland, not as the black-white population there now stands. Stokes had the unique ability to build solid black support while still appealing to white liberals and others who simply felt he was the best qualified man. Meanwhile, Richard Hatcher, in my view, was down in the thick of some far more primitive, ideological struggle, moving about through the streets as part of the crowd and only seldom in the parade.

"The personality thing," Hatcher told me one afternoon, "that's not my bag. Carl is far more acceptable in the white community than I am. But he pays more, nationally, among blacks. Carl represents one thing, and I don't feel we should waste time talking about who is blacker. He's doing his thing, we all are. I just feel that there's also a need for somebody to say, 'Look, it's not as nice as that. Things aren't all that good.' To me, people never willingly give up power. You have to *take* it from them, so to speak. And I find myself doing things that I *know* will be less acceptable to people. For example, when Fred Hampton was killed by the police in Chicago, I went on radio and said it was 'murder.' I had talked it over with my staff, and we knew we'd have to pay a price for that, by responding that way. I guess I could have played it safe, but then, I couldn't."

3.

He had inherited a share of the nation's urban quagmire down at the farthest southern edge of Lake Michigan, at the very bottom tip of the lake's fingerlike thrust into the belly of America. Driving southeast from Chicago's O'Hare Airport, one gradually rediscovers the vast flatness of the Midwest. For long stretches of time, one continues to stare far ahead at the convergence of road, land,

and sky, and as the miles of concrete expressway pass beneath the car, you can sense the tension and conflict between man's technology and nature's creation. Sweeping stretches of grassy fields are disfigured by the sight of oil refineries, power-line derricks and wires, industrial plants, railroad sidings, and freight cars—as if the seeds of destruction have been spilled chaotically from the hatch of a jet plane whose pilot went mad. Occasionally the road glides upward slightly past a trailer camp or a subdivision of small, box-like homes, a sea of white rooftops and erratic TV antennae, hard-won fortresses of the silent majority. And on the edges of swamp lands or crop fields, broken by dirt roads, lie the wrecked battle-fields of the conflict—junkyards, billboards, grubby clusters of weatherbeaten shacks, abandoned cars, and clotheslines scattered over the backyards.

And then you see it—first the pink-white-gray-black smoke pushing over the horizon, and suddenly the skyline fills with a rash of steeplelike smokestacks and sinister, jagged engineering shapes, the steel mills of the Steel City: Gary, Indiana. They are an awesome presence, the power-line towers in the foreground, the smoke billowing upward, forming a ceiling of dust, and in the background the huge rust-colored buildings and machinery. First there is a voluminous cloud of pink smoke hovering under a blue sky, and later, against the backdrop of the red veil of sundown, all Rome seems to be burning to the ground, or maybe they have dropped the Bomb. Here, at the end of the journey, the road seems to curve down and into the mouth of the dragon, to be swallowed and lost forever in the darkness and fire of the devil.

I don't think I have ever seen—or smelled, for that matter—air pollution of such unrelenting persistence as that in Gary. Perhaps it was just that its source was so identifiable, for certainly other cities, like New York, can be much worse. The thing is, the steel mills and their grimy smoke are such a dominating presence, squatting there defiantly on the edge of the city, that one feels they would keep on churning full blast even if the manpower to run them were to disappear. It is just possible, one imagines, that here the people exist to serve the monster, that the mill *is* the city, the human inhabitants only an afterthought. There is a tendency to become overwhelmed—humiliated and angry even—when one stands at the edge of Broadway looking north toward the lake. One sees no water, just the gaudy little railroad station with its orange trim and orange-lettered sign, THE SHORE LINE, the freight cars, the power-line erections, and, a few hundred yards beyond, the specter of the mills. Their dark, zigzagging, angular forms fill the horizon from left to right, their collective breath seemingly suspended like a low cloud. Then the wind comes off the lake and blows the smoke and fumes inland, sometimes right over and through the main streets of downtown Gary, and there are moments when you have the impulse to hold your breath for as long as possible. In most other places one would think that a fire were raging just around the corner or that a truck had overturned its load of burning garbage. The city seems a slave to the mill, whose owners live somewhere else, and there is a sinking feeling that one has crawled at last into the deepest wound, the primary source, of the cancer that has in fact spread to every corner of the land.

"And so it came to pass," I read in "The Mayor's Report to the People," "that the meek have finally inherited, not the earth, but concrete and asphalt, sound and fury, foul air and fetid water."

The city had been born in 1906 as the child of United States Steel, receiving its name from the company's board chairman, Judge Elbert H. Gary, whose statue stands today outside Richard Hatcher's City Hall, and 65 percent of Gary's work force was still employed by U.S.S. alone. Early settlers were mill workers recruited in successive waves from Eastern and Central Europe, cheap labor, and today the city was a hodgepodge of more than fifty ethnic groups: Poles, Greeks, Italians, Swedes, Irish, Hungarians, Serbs, Croats, Mexicans, Lithuanians, Armenians, and so on, including white Appalachians. Negroes from the South were the most recent immigrants, first brought in as strikebreakers, and they now mingled—on the job, but not at home—with the other peoples.

The city reached into the flatlands, its streets extending in all directions out of the dull, bleak, dingy Midtown section and ending in a world of thick green vegetation and neat little houses on tiny, squared-off plots of grass. The contrast was a constant source of wonder. Most of Gary's forty-five square miles had a residential or even rural complexion, much in the shape of a thick T on the map. There were maybe 190,000 citizens, whites living on the extensions of the T and blacks, whose proportion of the population

rose from 39 to nearly 60 percent over the past decade, jammed
into the center and forced to occupy only 10 percent of the land.
It was typical of most American cities, the disease of pollution
overshadowed by the crippling sickness of racism. The blacks, and
not necessarily the meek, had inherited the ugliness, the decay,
the foulest of the air, the worst of the housing, the shame of the
ghetto.

4.

Still looming over this drab little steel town, still threatening to
push Hatcher from the halls of power, was the political counterpart to the mill, the Lake County Democratic organization, the
Machine, and its ally, organized crime, the Syndicate. In a weird
way, perhaps the people of Gary were more honest, or cynically
inclined, than most, since they seemed to speak of corruption in
government as if it were the most fundamental fact of American
political life, which it may well be. "If you thought the Chicago
guys were bad," said one local insider, "well, the Gary guys are
the ones who taught the Chicago guys how to do it." There was
more than a tinge of pride in their voices as they recounted the
city's colorful history, and they gladly listed a succession of mayors
who had been jailed or arrested, not to mention those who had
managed not to get caught. It seems that an ambitious chief executive was able to make up to six million dollars of extra income
in four years, and mayors who did get caught were only those who
had failed to report the graft on their income-tax returns. One
was convicted while in office back in 1962; another spent two
years in prison for a liquor conspiracy, came out and made a
hero's return to City Hall. On and on come the stories of the
Syndicate's stranglehold on the community—prostitution, gambling, dope pushing, and so forth, all feeding money into the
hands of elected officials—and of political corruption in the form
of payroll padding, favoritism, kickbacks, money passing. There
had never been a two-term mayor in Gary, probably because four
years on the take was considered quite enough for any one man.
"Don't be greedy" was the slogan used by the line of eagerly waiting successors.

Meanwhile, Dick Hatcher would engage in none of this, and that was one good reason why he was in such apparent political trouble at home when I went there to visit. The local press was giving a gloomy picture of his future as mayor; there was no mystique about Hatcher in the news media, far from it. Apparently he would be facing both white *and* black opposition to his reelection bid in the fall of 1971, and it seemed that despite all the progress made by his administration, the same kind of miraculous events that put him in office the first time around would have to be repeated all over again. He was like a football player running with the ball while both teams on the field, Republicans *and* Democrats, were trying to tackle him and wrest it loose. He had won election in the beginning by beating the Machine of his own party, and now he refused to bend to it or to continue in the old ways that used to make public service so privately profitable. Yet remnants of the Machine still had a pervasive influence in Gary; many of the Negro precincts still owed allegiance to it, and much of the Machine's opposition showed up in the City Council itself. There were nine members, six from districts and three elected at large; four were black, four were white, and one was of Latin descent. Seven were Democrats, and the two Republicans were white. But Hatcher's relationship with the councilmen could be traced, not by political party or by color but according to "honest" and "crooked" classifications. Not all the blacks were in the "honest" category, and in fact some wanted to be mayor. "It's much tougher to make a crooked buck now," said a City Hall aide, "but out of the nine council members, it's still five to four in favor of the crooks."

But if in truth the city had become slave to the monsters of corporate power, pollution, political corruption, and racism, perhaps it was fitting that a young black man, a child of a race of slaves, had come on the scene to set things right. He seemed to be playing much of his hand by instinct, betting on the growing independence and political sophistication of black folks and lower classes of every race. In his speech in Washington he had made what I thought was a significant point:

> In Gary we do not abandon to George Wallace the white working class; they are fearful, confused, battered by inflation,

barely making their mortgage payments. We point out to them the real enemy. We explain to them patiently, tirelessly, day in and day out, that the Establishment fears nothing so much as little black people and little white people getting themselves together. Because when that day comes, Brother, the system is going to change.

And it could be, I thought, that Gary, Indiana, maybe *because* it was such an unlikely place, would be the battleground from whose rubble a new race of men, both black and white, could be formed. For here was a city of working people, almost devoid of a middle class, whose mayor had assumed office not only as a black militant, whatever meaning can be accorded that amorphous term, but also with an agenda for a class struggle against a common enemy. He was going against the grain and had begun to confront, to push, and to turn around the weight of a dying spirit.

Four

1.

Julian Bond got up to speak following the applause for Richard Hatcher, and here again was a singular young man, also one of the new breed of black politicians in America, perhaps the leading figure in the so-called New Politics, somehow drawing together the youth, peace, and black-power movements wherever he went. Bond's appearance, his physical appearance, was startling. One noticed, before his turn to speak, that he gazed quietly out at the audience from beneath a newly acquired Afro and that people tended to stare at him as if he possessed some mysterious inner quality they could not quite define. He has the kind of looks—a certain regal nonchalance—that make white men stop and glare at him, as if by virtue of appearance alone he posed a threat to them, and women tend to want to catch his eye. He is very much aware of the response he provokes, and this awareness enables him to maintain a quality of aloofness and reserve that in turn only magnifies one's first impressions.

It came as little surprise to me when Richard Hatcher indicated that he admired Bond probably more than any other black politician. "I think he's a tremendous guy," Hatcher told me. "He's got talent that hasn't even been tapped yet. He hasn't even had a chance to show what he really can do. He's uniquely equipped to deal with contemporary problems. He's extremely articulate, but beyond that, he has an excellent historical perspective. He's not a superficial individual. He understands history, the events of history, and he's able to relate them to the present. And I think that's the real mark of a leader, in that he's able to understand the historical significance of what is taking place today."

And indeed, Bond's speech in Washington quickly took an historical turn. "Our history in the art we all practice, politics, is not a long one, but it has had some glorious chapters," he began, and went on to trace the course of black politics from 1868 to the present. In the process, he came out with some funny but bitter lines, such as, "Rutherford B. Hayes ended the first Reconstruction in Washington in the Wormley Hotel in 1877—and Richard Nixon is trying to strangle the short-lived second Reconstruction with a deal made in Miami Beach in 1968." There is something almost thrilling, if you will, about a young, well-mannered, black gentleman, composed as all hell, taking on the President of the United States without once raising his voice or dropping the deadpan expression on his face. The black movement, he said, must address itself to solving "America's white problem," to developing a new racial solidarity, and to "making democracy safe for the world"—the latter again delivered in deadpan style.

While he spoke, one could not help but reflect that Bond was only thirty years old, that the decade of his twenties had coincided exactly with that of the 1960's, a truly remarkable period of time for him as well as for the nation itself, and that now he was uniquely a product of the age. One almost had the feeling that in order to find out where America was going in the seventies, one should stick close to Julian Bond. Although perhaps that was too much to hope for; perhaps one was being too optimistic about the nation and placing too much faith in a single man.

On November 12, 1969, two months after Bond spoke in Washington to the black elected officials, he received a letter from one of his closest friends, John Lewis, the soft-spoken, gentle black man who had been the last chairman of the Student Nonviolent Coordinating Committee before Stokely Carmichael. Lewis, now head of the Voter Education Project of the Southern Regional Council, expressed in his confidential letter what many had come to feel about Bond's role in the decade ahead:

Dear Julian:

I don't quite know how to begin this letter because it might seem a little presumptuous on my part to write such a letter to a friend.

As you know, I have a deep interest in seeing what I like to call "good men" elevated to higher positions in the political arena. Those men who act on principles and their own convictions and not according to political expediency. Those who are willing to inject into the body politics a degree of the honesty and morality that we witnessed in the early days of the Civil Rights Movement.

Some of us have said many times in private discussions, interviews, and even speeches, that after the death of Martin Luther King and Robert Kennedy you arose as the political leader of many. Your presence filled a vacuum and you became the hope of millions who had previously identified with these two great men. Many Blacks and whites who were committed to humane political leaders in the past placed their future in your hands. On the other hand, there are hundreds and thousands of young people, both black and white, who are dissatisfied, disillusioned, disappointed, frustrated, and bitter who have given up on the political systems. Julian, you have an obligation to the youth of today to use your influence to let them know that there are some basic changes that can be made through the machinery of politics.

Now, the preaching is over! Let's consider the matter at hand. As you know, during the past few days and especially since the recent elections, there have been rumors and speculations about who will run for Congress from the 5th Congressional District [Atlanta, Georgia]. . . .

I have no idea what you have decided to do, for the last time I talked to you, I got the feeling that you were seriously contemplating a decision. Personally, I think you should seriously consider running and run like you have never run before! If you do decide to run, you cannot afford to let the luxury of being a political celebrity and in demand throughout the country keep you from tackling the "nitty-gritty" and difficult problems of planning and building a political organization.

Julian, you know for the most part that things just don't happen in the world of politics. One has to work and get the people behind him. I have a few suggestions that I wish you would consider.

(1) Spend more time in Georgia, and particularly in your own district speaking and just being visible;

(2) Become more involved in the Fulton County Democratic Party;

(3) Work more closely with the black community and neighborhood groups in your district and other parts of the city and state;

(4) Work with the students in the Atlanta University Complex;

(5) Accept more speaking engagements within the state—schools, colleges, both black and white, teas, clubs, P.T.A.s, churches, and other civic groups;

(6) Start developing your campaign platform and an organization for the next election.

Julian, out of all the possible candidates, you are the only one that could get 300 or more students to work in your campaign as volunteers. In addition, you are the only one that people throughout the nation would contribute the necessary funds to conduct such a massive campaign, and you would have the support not only of the black votes, but the white liberals and young people. Your position on the war in Vietnam and the Urban Crisis is clear. I am not sure where the other possible candidates stand on these issues. I am positive that the war in Vietnam and the problems of the cities will be the issues in next year's election.

Julian, if you decide to run, I don't think it is necessary for you to announce it early. However, during the period between reaching your decision and the announcement of your candidacy, you should have put together an effective organization and begun raising funds for your campaign. On the other hand, if you reach a decision and decide not to run for Congress, I don't think you should be quick to announce it. I just think you have to keep all the possibilities open.

I realize that you must be under a great deal of pressure, for I am sure you are receiving all kinds of suggestions and proposals from other people.

Whatever you decide to do, you have my support!

Sincerely yours,
John Lewis

Would he run for Congress? The idea seemed only natural for a young man who two years before, at the age of twenty-eight, had been put forth in convention as a nominee for the Vice-Presidency of the United States. Surely he couldn't be satisfied to remain a mere state legislator in Georgia—not, as Lewis had pointed out, when so many people, blacks especially, were starving for a leader to fill some of the void. The state of Georgia hadn't sent a black man to Congress since Reconstruction—in fact, it had been more than seventy years since a Negro from *anywhere* in the South had gone to Congress—and that, too, would certainly appeal to Julian Bond's sense of timing.

By the summer of 1970, however, the whole situation had changed. "Once again," he wrote to his constituents in June, "I am a candidate for reelection to the Georgia House of Representatives. I am pleased to be able to run again without opposition, but nevertheless, want to ask each one of you for your vote and support." In July, he outlined for them what he felt had been his major work in the legislature:

> It has been my privilege to serve you for the last five years. During that period, I have tried to stay as close as possible to the people of the 111th District and the problems we all share. . . . In the Legislature, I serve on three important committees: Insurance, Education, and State Institutions and Property. I have introduced and co-sponsored legislation to stop the death penalty, to end slum housing, to put Negro History in all of Georgia's schools.

There were attempts to portray his decision not to run for Congress as based on "personal reasons"—his wife Alice had just had their fifth child, they had moved into a new house in Atlanta—but the truth was political rather than personal. The Fifth Congressional District was 70 percent white, and white Southerners were not known to possess any overwhelming affection for Julian Bond. He couldn't win. As he told me without hesitation: "I just don't like to lose."

2.

Time magazine described Atlanta's Fifth District as having "all the elements that Vice-President Spiro Agnew wants to mix into Republican election victories . . . resentful white workers in automobile plants, middle managers worried about inflation, and old-time gentry upset over the erosion of their ancient values." Not exactly typical of the crowd that goes wild over Julian Bond. However, the Fifth also had "a black minority divided between slums as desperate as any city's and a middle-class area of preachers and teachers centered around the Atlanta University complex."

As soon as Bond took himself out of the running, several Atlanta blacks considered making the race, including State Senator Leroy Johnson, who had been the first Negro elected to a Southern legislature in modern times. However, Johnson was now regarded as an Establishment black leader—one with great power as a politician but also one who had abandoned his black brothers who were trying to "work within the System" at the grass-roots level. There were other possible candidates as well, but the most exciting prospect was that the Reverend Andrew Young, executive vice-president of the Southern Christian Leadership Conference (SCLC), would throw his hat in the ring. When he finally made the announcement in March of 1970 that he was officially going off the payroll of the SCLC in order to campaign, he said he had never even considered running for public office until Bond had urged him to do so. "After Julian decided that he couldn't run," Young said, "he came to me and said, 'You oughtta try.' I told him, 'No,' but he said, 'Well, all of the support I could get, you could get.' And then I decided that maybe it would be fun. I've run campaigns for all kinds of other people for these last ten years, and it might be fun to try to run one for myself."

If there was anyone in the United States who came close to embodying the spirit of the late Martin Luther King, that person was probably Andrew Young, who had been extremely close to him for years. In Young's own modest way of putting it, he would say, "Oh, I just sort of tagged along with Dr. King for about nine years." In fact, he had marched at King's side across nearly every civil-rights battleground of the 1960's—"Wal, I guess you *could* say I was in just about every major scuffle in the South." He was an organizer, negotiator, confidant, mediator, and behind-the-scenes man whose rare gift was the ability to bring enemies together in a climate of calm logic and reason. As one admirer expressed it to me, "Andy's gone through a lot of personal changes in his life, and he's come out whole. People can disagree on every issue, yet they all can agree on *him*. He just brings folks together. If he was in Congress, he could get other guys together and put together programs that they all could vote for."

He had been in charge of the demonstration the day in 1963 that Birmingham's Bull Connor had set dogs on the marchers; he had helped to construct the settlements of racial disputes in that city and in Selma; he had been a negotiator in the hospital strike in Charleston; he had been the mediator in Resurrection City, trying to unite blacks, Mexican Americans, and Indians. Following King's death, there were strong suggestions that Young replace the fallen leader, but he was too loyal for that. Crushed by the assassination of the man from whom he had learned so much, aware that he was the choice of much of the press and the public, he carefully remained in the background in order to allow King's chosen successor, the Reverend Ralph Abernathy, establish himself. But two years had now passed since the Memphis tragedy. The civil-rights movement had passed into a new phase, and Andy Young was going with it.

"I see my running for Congress as a continuation of what Dr. King was doing in the South," he said. "When we started out, we said we would try to redeem the soul of America, and one way of doing that was securing the right of the ballot for all of its citizens."

In fact, Andy Young had participated in the drafting of the Civil Rights Act of 1964 and the Voting Rights Act of 1965. Unlike many blacks in the North (and in the South, too, for that matter), Young was still fired with the power of human reason, persistence, endurance, patience; and unlike a large segment of the new student generation, Young, who was now thirty-eight years old, remembered how things had been before Dr. King had come on the scene. In reaction to those who preached violence as the only effective means to bring about change, Young spoke of the "powerful gentleness" that he had learned from King, and he remembered how the great leader had been able to "melt his opposition through love." All this may have sounded naïve to the young, militant blacks, but in the face of mounting despair Andy Young would still reply, "When people get cynical, they don't *do* anything." He had seen nonviolence work in the face of tremendous hostility and hatred. The "religiously oriented, nonviolent movement that started in the cradle of the Confederacy" had made "tremendous progress" over a thirteen-year period. How could the eighteen-year-old student of 1970, who had been only eight in 1960, know the reality of the progress if he had never seen, or experienced, the reality of the past?

Young had an easy, cool, almost lazy way of talking, and an underplayed sense of humor that derived much of its effect from the Southern Negro accent. But it also came out of his experiences with Dr. King. "We'd just kinda joke about things," he said. "When we were first going into Birmingham, Dr. King told us, 'We have to make up our minds that some of us might not make it outa here.' And then he turned to me and said, 'Now, I don't know. I tell you, Andy, if it's you, I'll be sure to preach you a good funeral, I'll make sure everybody remembers ya.' And I think that kind of humor was important. It was one of the ways we dealt with things that we were uneasy about."

There was a good deal of sentimentalism in my view of Andy Young, at least it appeared that way to me, but I found that the man in person really did carry within him the attitudes and dreams of the past decade. Hatred, despair, violence, division, chaos—Andy Young still deeply believed that these things would give way in the face of persistent reasonableness, commitment, love. It was difficult, really impossible to disagree with him on this point, just as I imagine it would have been difficult to argue with Dr. King. I felt about Young something of what Norman Mailer must have felt about Dr. King: "He [King] had the presence of a man who would deal with complexity by absorbing its mood and so solve its contradiction by living with it, an abstract way of saying that he comprehended issues by the people who embodied them, and so gave off a sense of social comfort with his attendance in a room." Something of that feeling came through when Andy Young was in the room, not all of it, but enough, despite his boyish appearance and the occasional hint of an insecurity and the sense of an ever-present, ineradicable loss. He had been there, one remembers, in the parking lot below, when King had stepped out of his motel room to lean on the balcony railing; he had heard the shot, had felt the dying pulse of the great leader. Who, indeed, would dare argue with Andy Young if he was still able to believe in the dream?

Explaining why he got involved in the race to begin with, he told me, "We saw that the thing that's wrong with America was that democracy was not allowed to work in the South. So that you developed a one-party system, and that enabled Southern committee chairmen to dominate the Congress. And that threw everything out of balance. The whole Congress of the United States being dominated by the one-party South, which is not only racist, but it's rural, too, and much closer to being eighteenth century in its thinking. So I saw that it wasn't just that you couldn't solve any race problems, but you couldn't get any money appropriated for cities, because these men had no sense of what was going on in the urban environment. And they were all so overwhelmingly militaristic, they were the military establishment. So, I saw political reform of the Southeast as being the prerequisite for realizing constitutional democracy in the whole United States. Practically everything that was wrong could be traced back to this part of the country.

"Also, the Nixon Administration is really acting to encourage the worst elements in the South. I decided that we couldn't let the so-called Southern Strategy push the South back into the Dark Ages and that the only way to stop this was to develop some leadership that would speak out against it, to give people an alternative. And not only don't I have anything to lose, but I've really had experience in the South, talking to people who were our enemies, helping them to realize that there can be reasonable solutions to social problems, solutions that don't hurt people. I decided that I'd like to try to run a campaign—even though I come out of the civil-rights movement—in a district that's only a third black, and where I would have to get some votes from white people who traditionally were segregationists. I think people are tired of voting for the lesser-of-the-evil kind of candidates, and there's a growing involvement with blacks on the part of whites in the South. I don't want to write off any segment of the community. My idea has been that if you talked to people, and listened, you could find a way to represent them."

The Fifth District included much of Atlanta and suburban

Fulton County. The current representative was Fletcher Thompson, whom Young described as a "sort of Agnew-Goldwater Republican, with a touch of Lester Maddox." Thompson had become part of the growing Republican effort to "take the South from George Wallace," another way of saying that he had moved steadily to the right, and Young therefore saw the campaign as "a real test of issues and the whole racial maturity of the South." How his strategists figured that he had a chance of beating Thompson in a district that was 70 percent white was a bit of a mystery, although he surely had a better chance against the odds than Julian Bond would have had. While Bond was despised and hated by most of white Georgia, Andy could make a realistic try for maybe 25 percent of the white vote. He was campaigning hard in both the white-liberal and black sections of Atlanta, attempting to build a coalition that crossed both racial and economic lines. Young saw what he called a "radical middle" emerging in the South—a coming together of not only white and black liberals but working-class whites as well, the latter supposedly willing to support a black candidate out of frustration with Republican economic policies. "Whenever prejudice costs money, folk give it up," he would say, but it was difficult to have his kind of faith.

Many young volunteers had joined the campaign. In addition, a good deal of money had come in from across the nation. The challenge against Congressman Thompson would come in November, but meanwhile there was still a September primary to get through in order to win the Democratic nomination. Two white candidates were in the running, and as if that weren't enough, Young had a black opponent as well. Not just any black opponent but a young man who had been in the forefront of the civil-rights movement in Atlanta. And just for a bit of an ironic twist, his name was King.

3.

"Julian Bond double-crossed me. He and his other friends. They screwed me. Sure, I'm bitter. It was like finding your best friend in bed with your wife."

Lonnie King figured that Andy Young had spent about sixty

thousand dollars so far in the primary campaign, and he was also bitter about that. On this day, in fact, Andy was taping TV commercials in a studio just across town. Lonnie considered this fact and then discovered that it was already three in the afternoon and he hadn't eaten lunch. It was extremely hot in Atlanta on this day in late July, so Lonnie wasn't wearing his suit jacket. He was a big, handsome, good-natured fellow with a kind of polished look about him. He was thinking about Julian Bond and about all that money Andy Young was spending and about how he, Lonnie, was going to fool everybody by winning the primary contest anyway. Grinning, he said, "There'll be a lot of people who'll say, 'I knew you could do it all the time, Lonnie.' But now they're sitting back, on the sidelines, because they wanna make sure to be on the side of the winner."

Lonnie took a last look around his headquarters, a large sidewalk-level hall with small rooms adjoining the main one. A few helpers were there, but otherwise the place seemed deserted and lifeless. While Andy Young had set up a series of offices on Exchange Place, Lonnie was down here on Auburn Avenue, away from the Establishment part of Atlanta, in a grubby black neighborhood, and in Lonnie's opinion that, too, was appropriate. Lonnie considered himself the "man of the people" in this race, and therefore it was fitting that his campaign headquarters had little glamour and that in fact it was located just a few blocks from the old YMCA where he had spent so much time as a boy.

He walked out of his office and into the hot, thick air on this afternoon. He crossed the street, stopping to chat with two black men, and then he continued on up the sidewalk to a small, dusty café. There were five wooden tables inside and a jukebox. The only patron was an elderly black woman who sat alone in a corner, hunched over a plate of hot food. Lonnie took a table near the window and ordered the fried-chicken special with a glass of iced tea. He was bitter about a lot of things, true, but by God he was happy as well. The problem was, he explained, that Andy Young just didn't have any grass-roots background among the black folk here in Atlanta. Young was a carpetbagger, you see; he was riding along under the shadow of Martin Luther King and getting help from all those SCLC friends of his. That's the way Lonnie felt, and if you wanted to know the truth, the odds really gave him a kind of secret pleasure, because Lonnie King was nothing if not a fighter.

The thing about Julian Bond was very messy. "I was laid up in the hospital for a while," Lonnie said as he plunged into his fried chicken. "I was in the hospital, so I decided against any involvement in politics. But then I got out, and I thought that someone ought to make the race in the Fifth District. I called Julian and said that I'd be a candidate but not if he was gonna run. He said he figured he probably would, so I told him, well, in that case I'd run for county commissioner. A month later he still hadn't made an announcement, so I called him again and asked why not. He said he just hadn't gotten around to it yet—and the next thing I know he comes out and says he supporting *Andy Young* for Congress. So, I was double-crossed."

What made all this so unfortunate was the history of the two young men, for in a real sense it was Lonnie King who had gotten Julian Bond involved in the civil-rights movement in the first place. Bond had led a sort of middle-class Southern Negro childhood, a rather sheltered existence, as the son of a respected Negro educator. From the time he was five until he was seventeen he had lived in Pennsylvania, where his father was president of Lincoln University, and Julian had attended the George School in Bucks County, a Quaker boarding school, where he was the only black kid on the campus. By the time he graduated, his father had gone to Atlanta University, and so Julian matriculated at Morehouse College ("the Harvard of the South") where he and Lonnie first met. A husky, football-playing Navy veteran, Lonnie approached Julian Bond in February of 1960 and showed him a news clipping about the student sit-ins taking place in Greensboro, North Carolina. As the story goes, Lonnie asked, "Do you think it ought to happen here?" Bond replied, "Well, maybe," and Lonnie persisted, "I mean, don't you think we ought to *make* it happen?" "Well, maybe." "Okay then," said Lonnie. "You take one side of the drugstore, and I'll take the other. Let's call a meeting of some of the other students."

The wave of student protest that swept the South and eventually the nation had just begun, and Lonnie King had been responsible for Julian's initial involvement. The two young men became leaders of Atlanta's student sit-in movement for desegregation of public facilities, helping to organize the Committee on Appeal for Human Rights, which soon coalesced with other groups to form the Student Nonviolent Coordinating Committee, the brave new band of young people known affectionately as Snick. Now, ten years later, Lonnie was president of the Atlanta NAACP, he was running for Congress, and Julian Bond, his friend, had turned away from him to support Andrew Young.

Everyone knew that Bond himself had wanted to run for Congress and that he was waiting until after the census was taken this year. After that, the district would be reapportioned. A new district, one more heavily black, would be ready for Julian Bond to capture in 1972. Why should he run now and lose both the Congressional race *and* his seat in the Georgia House? In Lonnie's view, Julian had decided that Andy Young should make the race because (1) he'd probably lose, and (2) he wouldn't try for the seat again in 1972, leaving Bond a clear field. "I've upset Julian's plans a little bit," said Lonnie, a grin spreading over his large face. "Because he didn't figure that I'd challenge Andy. And he knows that even if I lose this time, I'll become the favorite, in the black community, to run again in 1972."

"Would you run against Julian at that time?" I asked.

"Sure."

One way or another, black politics in Atlanta, while on the upswing, was not, as they say, together. On the plane to Atlanta I had met Bayard Rustin, who had expressed dismay at the prospect of two good black candidates "killing each other off." Young was obviously the stronger of the two, but the black community was sure to be split, depriving Andy of 50 percent of the votes and thereby forcing him into a runoff election with one of the two white candidates in the Democratic primary. "What I can't understand," Rustin said, "is why one of those guys didn't get out of the race." He commented that in many cases, personal ambition "superseded the color thing" and that when it came down to the nitty-gritty, so to speak, blacks, just as easily as whites, could be "political animals."

All of which made Lonnie not a little defensive. In his opinion it was Young, not himself, who had disrupted the natural flow of events; and moreover, what was so terrible about a little competition among blacks? "At the last count there were *eight* white people running for governor of Georgia," he pointed out. "And I haven't heard anybody talking about how any of those candidates are splitting the *white* vote. Some people say this race between Andy and me is hurting the black community, but let me say to you that there probably hasn't been this much interest among blacks in Atlanta concerning any race prior to this time. I believe that it's spurring voter registration, and so I'm not going after white votes like Andy is, not now. But I'm also doing this despite the *black* establishment, which is just sitting back, waiting. And I'm fighting that whole clique—Julian and Coretta King, the SCLC crowd. It's overkill, you know? They're bringing in all that money and all those national names just to beat a poor man. Well, they're scared."

We walked up Auburn Avenue toward Lonnie's storefront office, past an eating place with a jukebox blaring and beneath a movie-theater marquee whose red-orange lettering simply announced, "Always A Good Show." And that's just what Lonine King was gonna give 'em, all of 'em, whether they liked it or not. "With all of Andy's money," Lonnie said as we stopped outside his headquarters, "Andy *should* win by about nine to one. But an awful lot of people are gonna be surprised."

We went inside, to the rear of the office, where a blackboard indicated his strategy for "mobilization" on primary day, September the ninth. Listed were committees for telephoning, providing transportation, watching the polls, and so forth. "I'll tell you something," Lonnie said, now almost whispering. "I wouldn't miss this race for the world."

Five

1.

Julian Bond sat in the half-filled first-class section of a jetliner on the runway of the airport in Atlanta, waiting for the 11:20 A.M. takeoff. Although he was constantly flying somewhere around the country, on an average of twice a day for five months out of the year, usually to make a speech of one kind or another, he harbored in the back of his mind a general nervousness about air travel. "The more I fly, the worse I get," he said, smiling. One wouldn't have guessed his apprehension from outward appearance, however, for Julian Bond was above all relaxed and casual about his life. "He isn't looking ahead," his friend John Lewis had told me. "He's just living for a moment." And at this moment, Bond was thinking about how terrifically Billy Eckstine had performed at the Bird Cage over on Atlanta's heavily black west side the night before. Thirty-year-old Bond had gone backstage to see the fifty-nine-year-old singer, and Eckstine had told him, "Your uncle was director of the YMCA in Pittsburgh when I was coming up as a boy. I was a boy of the streets at the time. I might have ended up a gangster or a thug, but your uncle helped straighten me out. He put me on the straight and narrow."

Now the plane was taking off, and Julian leaned back in his seat, thinking about that conversation, and he began to imitate the way Eckstine had sung at the Bird Cage. He was hoping to get a return flight back to Atlanta that same day, later in the afternoon, so he could go back to hear the great black singer perform again.

We had met only the day before, a Friday, in Paschal's Restaurant on Hunter Street, which is near the Bird Cage and near the Bonds' new home. Paschal's is a sort of meeting ground for a lot of black leaders in Atlanta, the kind of place where Julian Bond could feel at home while being interviewed by a white reporter. And I was more than a little reluctant to subject Bond to still another list of the same old questions: "Tell me, Julian Bond, which way is black America heading? Do you hate white people? How come you haven't yet given up on the System, Mr. Bond? And just how *do* Negroes feel these days?" No, I hated the thought of conducting such an interview, for I suspected that Bond himself was tired and bored and irritated with white newsmen, probably most of all because they seldom directed their questions within the framework of the black man's viewpoint of America, and too often, I imagined, Bond was placed in the position of calming white fears rather than articulating black needs and goals.

Our appointment was for 12:30 in the afternoon, and doubtless Bond was used to this kind of thing: a reporter from out of town calls his office, which is listed in the Atlanta phone directory, and requests an interview. "Well," replies the secretary, whose low-keyed, pleasant tone seems to fit the image one has of the urbane Mr. Bond, "he's due back in town tonight and scheduled to fly out again sometime on Friday, so if you'd please leave your name and where you can be reached, I'll mention it to him when he calls in, and we'll see. . . ." Later on: "You're in luck. He's not leaving town until Saturday, so he can see you at Paschal's for lunch." The secretary, a white woman, has been most pleasant and helpful, and one soon learns from his friends that Julian himself is basically a "nice guy," even in the face of all this tremendous and persistent attention that he gets, and despite the fact that some of the articles written about him don't always turn out so well. For example, Douglas Kiker had done a piece on Bond for *Playboy* magazine, and Julian's friends were quite unhappy about it. Not that Kiker had been inaccurate, but he gave the impression that Julian Bond was a fellow who had sort of drifted through the crosscurrents of recent history and that events had thrust him into the forefront of black leadership almost despite himself. "It is not so much that Bond has made things happen as that things have happened—and continue to happen—to him." Kiker went on to picture Bond as "the most conservative, cautious radical in the nation," if indeed he could be called a radical, and noted that he had "only a misty idea" of where the future would lead him.

"Sometimes," a friend of Bond told me, "I feel like punching some writer in the nose after he's written an unflattering piece. But Julian probably wouldn't even *say* anything about it to the writer. He's just too nice a guy, that's all."

Like most people, when I thought of Bond I remembered two singular events in which he had played a leading role. In January, 1966, he had been barred from membership in the Georgia legislature because of his criticism of American military action in Vietnam. Bond had been one of eight blacks elected to the House in 1965—they were the first to sit in its chambers in fifty-eight years—and already his white colleagues were saying he was "guilty of treason." That January, when the House of Representatives was to begin its session, the Student Nonviolent Coordinating Committee issued a statement condemning the war and urging young men to work in the civil-rights movement rather than join the military. A few hours after Snick issued the statement, a local radio station called Representative-elect Julian Bond and asked him whether he endorsed it. Although he hadn't participated in drafting the statement, Bond had picked up a pacifist outlook back at the George School, and he simply told the truth.

> Why, I endorse it, first, because I like to think of myself as a pacifist and one who opposes that war and any other war and eager and anxious to encourage people not to participate in it for any reason that they choose; and secondly, I agree with this statement because of the reason set forth in it—because I think it is sorta hypocritical for us to maintain that we are fighting for liberty in other places and we are not guaranteeing liberty to citizens inside the continental United States. . . .
> I think that the fact that the United States government

fights a war in Vietnam, I don't think that I as a second-class citizen of the United States have a requirement to support that war. I think my responsibility is to oppose things that I think are wrong, if they are in Vietnam or New York or Chicago or Atlanta, or wherever. . . .

I'm against that war in particular, and I don't think people ought to participate in it. Because I'm against war, I'm against the draft. I think that other countries in the world get along without a draft—England is one—and I don't see why we couldn't, too.

When asked whether he would maintain this view if war were declared on North Vietnam and if his statements might become treasonous, Bond replied, "I don't know if I'm strong enough to place myself in a position where I'd be guilty of treason."

On the first day that the legislature was to meet, Bond broke out in a rash of hives as the moment approached, for he already knew that petitions challenging his right to be seated had been filed by seventy-five House members. All he had to do, really, to avoid the whole controversy, was to show a little old-fashioned humility—*beg* a little—and say he was sorry for being such an uppity young black boy. Four years earlier, in 1962, he and some other black college students had been evicted from the House gallery for refusing to leave the white section. Now, sitting downstairs as an elected member, Bond remained poised and calm in the face of still another eviction. He sat there very politely, an extremely cultivated and clean-cut young man, in a conservative gray suit and vest, twenty-five years of age, as unlikely a radical-traitor as one could imagine—and the storm grew around him.

At a special hearing on the matter, after the clerk refused to swear him in, Bond said he concurred with the Snick statement "without reservation" and said he admired people who had the courage to burn their draft cards. "I admire people who take an action, and I admire people who feel strongly enough about their convictions to take an action like that knowing the consequences that they will face." He said he had never *advocated* that anyone burn his draft card. "In fact, I have mine in my pocket and will produce it if you wish."

The House then voted by 184 to 12 not to seat him. After the

Supreme Court ruled unanimously that his freedom of speech had been violated, he took the oath of office in January, 1967, having lost a year of service; and through it all, he had not once retracted or altered his original statements. He was now a national figure and undoubtedly the most hated black man in Georgia. His constituency, mostly poor blacks, could take a real pride in his victory, for they had helped him with their votes. Now they had a local hero, a young militant from their own midst who had looked those white racists squarely and defiantly in the eyes with such cool, such *presence,* that they nearly went blind with rage. Victories of any kind were hard to come by for blacks, especially in the South, and now the name of Julian Bond had become a symbol of victory, evocative of courageous thoughts and of victories still to be won.

The other event had occurred at the Democratic National Convention of August, 1968, in Chicago, when Bond led a biracial delegation of liberal Georgians in competition with another one led by Governor Lester Maddox. Bond's delegation unexpectedly wound up with half the Georgia votes at the convention, and in the process, Julian found himself acting as floor leader of the Georgia Democratic Party. Then a national television audience watched as this polite, handsome black boy was nominated for Vice-President of the United States, although at age twenty-eight he was seven years too young for the office. Bond gracefully withdrew, but suddenly he had become the "wave of the future."

2.

I parked my rented car in the rear of Paschal's motel and restaurant and walked up the back steps, aware of being perhaps the only white man in sight, wondering where and in what disposition I would find Julian Bond.

He was sitting at an obscure table in the dimly lighted restaurant with some friends. One immediately recognized the bushy hair and the chiseled, boyish features of his face, although he looked a little puffy around the eyes as if he hadn't gotten enough sleep. He was wearing a short-sleeved, light-yellow shirt, with no tie, and checkered pants. I noted that Bond's arms and legs were very slight, but when he stood up it was clear he had gained some weight around the middle. "It's mainly because of all those meals while traveling," he remarked to someone as he patted his stomach. "You eat in the plane, and then eat again when you land." But he didn't seem too worried over the weight problem, and in fact when we went to a table in the corner he ordered a big lunch.

I remembered reading that Bond was the sort of person who would never speak first to strangers, that by nature he was reserved, if not shy, and therefore, in the absence of the Big Interview, we sat there for a while without saying anything. At some point in his life, I thought, or maybe from the beginning, Julian Bond must have learned the art of being—well, Julian Bond. Few men have the ability to be themselves. Fame, ambition, nervousness, self-consciousness, pride—any number of psychic energies can, and usually do, turn a man into someone other than himself. Few men can remain in the public eye without undergoing some distortion, however slight, of their personalities, their physical behavior, their speech. Yet Bond, who might as well have been on stage most of the time, so much of a star personality had he become, was somehow able to absorb the forces around him and to respond to them in a natural, unaffected, undistorted manner. It occurred to me that this was perhaps his greatest asset, this natural ability to be himself, and I noticed that he was in no hurry to make any kind of impression except to be polite and, strangely, almost downright obedient.

"I'm sure you must hate being interviewed like this."

"No," he replied, smiling. "No, not at all."

While we sat there eating, waitresses and customers kept either coming over to say hello or to catch his eye. A group of black fellows stopped to chat with him for a few minutes, all of them somehow much more animated than Bond, as if he were infusing them with energy, making them behave a little more flamboyantly than usual. And some folks came to ask him if he'd mind being photographed with them at their table for a moment, and he complied. The manager of the restaurant-motel greeted him and said he could use the swimming pool, free of charge. "For you, *any* time, Mr. Bond." And Julian smiled, lighted a cigarette, poked at his food, acknowledged still others who came over from time to time just to say, "Hi, Brother," shake his hand, and then move away. If you're Julian Bond sitting in a restaurant, especially in Paschal's, you can't help but notice that everyone is aware of your presence, and the feeling must be somewhat eerie.

One of the black fellows who had stopped by to chat was Ivanhoe Donaldson, a friend from Snick who had run Bond's first campaign and who was now the key man behind Andy Young's strategy in the Congressional race. Donaldson had been involved in nearly a hundred campaigns over the decade, preferring to remain in the background in order to maintain his effectiveness. After he left our table, Bond remarked to me that sometimes he wished he could become "less of a politician" and more like Donaldson, who was able to work behind the scenes. "In my campaign," he said, "Ivanhoe was the detail man. But me, I'm not really cut out for that. I'm a pretty good *idea* man—I'm maybe the best idea man in the world—but I'm not the type that can follow through on ideas and make them work."

He was full of ideas for making money, ideas for starting his own business, and in fact he had been involved in several things —a record company which had yet to cut a record, a consulting firm that he was pulling out of, a fast-food chain which had backfired on him. The latter had been a kind of noble experiment, intended as a training school for young black managers who were to share in the profits of the business and eventually buy out the original owners. Mismanagement and other troubles ran the business into debt, and then, ironically, five former black employees began picketing the chain, accusing Bond of being a tool of white business interests. The white man was Dr. Gerald Reed of Atlanta, a long-time liberal who had signed $100,000 worth of notes to finance the operation. The New York *Times* played up the story on its front page, quoting Dr. Reed as saying, "No one could accept the fact that Julian or I did this for noble purposes."

"My latest project," Bond told me, "involves a grocery store down the street from where I live—an elderly Jewish couple who want to sell out and move out of the neighborhood. And at first I just thought I'd get a black guy to take it over and run it the

same way they've run it, which is the way all small stores are run
—higher prices, and so on. But then it struck me that there's no
need for another grocery in that black neighborhood. There are
fifteen of them within a mile radius, I'm sure. What would be an
asset to the neighborhood is a co-op grocery store, one that could
be owned in effect by the people in the community and one that
could bring prices down to a more than reasonable level. Now,
that's become a sort of project of mine. I don't want to just replace one set of white capitalists with a set of black capitalists,
although if I couldn't do anything else, I'd *rather* that black
people ran that store."

Bond then went into some detail about another idea of his,
this one involving a nighttime cleaning service for rumpled
businessmen who fly into cities at night and leave again in the
morning. He became quite excited over this idea, pointing out
that the cleaning service could be installed at airport motels
and such places, so that the businessmen could drop off their
clothes, hop into bed, and wake up the following morning with
an entirely cleaned and laundered wardrobe. "Now, that's a pretty
original idea," said Bond, but at this point his mind began to
wander, and it became clear that he was much more enthused
over the idea itself than with the prospect of actually putting it
into effect.

Still another of his ideas was to establish a "journal of black
political affairs" which would reach about ten thousand people every six weeks. Again, Bond's biggest contribution was to
have the idea in the first place; whether it would ever get off
the ground was another story. He showed me a nine-page proposal he had drawn up himself and which he had been sending
to people around the country in order to drum up support. The
proposal began this way:

> There are over 1,500 black elected officials in the United
> States today, and their number is constantly increasing. There
> are countless thousands of other elected officials whose elec-
> tions depend on black votes, and more thousands who re-
> present constituencies where black voters comprise a large
> minority.
>
> As the re-newed 1965 Voting Rights Act spreads its effect
> throughout the South, and as more American cities lose their

white citizens to the suburbs, the phenomenon of the black elected official will become more commonplace.

The possibility exists presently that black voters can control 150 Southern black-belt counties, and that 50 major American cities will have majority black populations within the next two decades.

Additionally, it is not unlikely that the general electorate may become increasingly politically color-blind, and that blacks will be elected from white constituencies in the future. . . .

Despite the history, present surge and future promise of black political activity in the United States, there presently exists no regularly published source of factual and interpretive material on this subject available to scholars, politicians, and the general public.

The proposal went on to discuss the mechanics of putting out such a publication, with a notation to "please address all inquiries" to Julian Bond. Up to this point, the response had been disappointing.

"One time," Bond said, "I thought about taking a tape recorder and interviewing some black college students. I figured that since I was speaking on so many campuses, I had an opportunity to get their views from all over the country. In public, it seems that they always have the same opinions on every subject, but when you get them alone, they become individuals. I thought I'd take my tape recorder up to the dormitory, you know, at night, and interview some of them. But I found I was too tired from the traveling."

In the summer of 1968, Bond had carried out a similar idea, one involving tape recordings of black candidates, for the Southern Regional Council. He had done all the interviews by phone, and they were later printed in a booklet called "Black Candidates —Southern Campaign Experiences." One of Bond's favorite interviews in the booklet was the one with Charles Evers, who in February of that year had taken a leave of absence as field director of the Mississippi NAACP in order to run for Congress in the state's Third District. Evers had lost, but he told Bond:

I don't know of anything I'd really do differently. . . . All I discussed was what we gotta have and what we are gonna do and how we are going to change the system and what we

are going to do for the poor people. . . . I think the campaign was one of the greatest things that you could mention.
It gave Negroes hope, because for a while Negroes believed
that the vote didn't count. It inspired Negroes to become
more involved in politics. And it is gonna help to elect Negroes and change that rotten system.

"Don't become a racist," Evers had told Bond during the interview. "Talk about the issues and the problems of the Negroes and
what you are gonna do to change them. Once you are elected,
don't turn white and forget the Negro. If Negroes can get together, they can *control* and *rule* something. My advice is to control something. Control the economics of the county, control the
ballot of the county, the politics of the county—in other words,
control the entire county where we are predominant. In Mississippi, we have twenty-nine counties predominantly Negro. We
are going for broke."

The last line from the interview was what Bond liked best.
"We don't holler black power," Evers told him, "but *watch it!*"

Over three or four cups of coffee after lunch in Paschal's, we
discussed several more of Bond's ideas and interests. He was very
much excited about the possibilities of filmmaking and mentioned
that at one time he had thought about starting his own newspaper. At Morehouse College he had studied comparative literature and had written for the literary magazine. He left college
in the middle of his senior year, in 1960, to work full time for
the Atlanta *Inquirer,* a black weekly, eventually becoming its
managing editor. In 1962 he became "communications officer"
for Snick, a post he held for four years, working out of the Atlanta office while the movement spread across the South. And
really, Bond was a combination poet and writer as well as a politician, composing all his speeches by himself, using two fingers of
each hand on the typewriter, sprinkling his copy with generous
helpings of historical matter and quotations, and with original
turns of phrase, anecdotes, insights. Mainly what he did with his
speeches was to come right out and say things very directly, things
that people have maybe thought about but haven't formulated
quite so openly or forcefully. And Julian gave the truth a
kind of perspective that made you sit up and take notice, and

this, basically, was the poet inside him. It all seemed to go very well with his cool, detached, sometimes impish approach. The words leapt out and spoke for themselves, allowing Bond to remain intact as an essentially mysterious kind of person.

In his speeches on college campuses, Bond was usually quite pessimistic, telling students that black Americans have entered a period of "gloom and despair" similar to the one they experienced in the Reconstruction period a century ago. "The similarity between that period and this one is very frightening," he told them, pointing out that Reconstruction ended with repressive laws requiring racial segregation in all aspects of life. Progress in both periods, he said, was marked by a belief that racial equality could be won through the courts, with the help of liberals, but now, just as a century ago, the belief has proved false, and the liberals have grown tired of the fight.

He told his audiences that the explosions of the ghetto were "part of a process that believes that when life becomes intolerable and government unresponsive and unrepresentative, then men have not just got the right, but the duty, to rise up against it and strike it down." He predicted more clashes in the 1970's between blacks and police, and more violence against symbols of the white Establishment. He was anything but violent by nature, but he would be less than honest if he did not warn against a growing discontent. And he turned around the question of violence, placing it in another context:

> When violence is referred to in America, the people always talk about *blacks* being violent. But the real violent people are those who send a black child through 12 years of school and he comes out with only a sixth-grade education. The real violent people are those who yell about black mothers on welfare and then pay a farmer $25,000 not to grow food.

Now, in the summer of 1970, Bond was running for reelection, unopposed, to his seat in the Georgia House of Representatives. On his mind was the nature of power, specifically his own political power, and he commented, "I don't really have any power as a politician. You take State Senator Leroy Johnson, a kind of black-establishment politician—he's played the ropes, and therefore he has a great deal of power, more than I do." And it was true; Julian Bond was far more of a national figure than a local power. But on the other hand, he was far more comfortable with an almost all-black constituency, for it freed him from the necessity of, as he put it, "pandering to the white community." In other words, he didn't have to stretch and maybe distort himself as do many other black politicians, those who must depend upon white support for election. He didn't have to "care about what white folks think" so much.

The legislature is in session only forty days out of the year, Bond explained, and when it does go into operation, he is usually unable to influence the large issues of the state. Instead, he works hard to accomplish some "little things" on a year-round basis. Black folks in his district are nearly all poor (an average yearly income of $2,500 per family), and the unemployment runs between 30 and 40 percent. They are poorly educated (on the average they have completed only the sixth grade), and most of the men are forced to watch their womenfolk go off to work as domestics or kitchen helpers, taking care of other people's children. The people call Bond for his help in getting their sidewalks repaired or a streetlight replaced, a sewer system installed—and these things, he knows, are often more important to people than most of the big issues that the legislature confronts. When Julian Bond first got into the General Assembly, he didn't vote on many matters, those which he felt didn't concern the people of his district, but later he discovered that the newspapers had been listing him as "absent" whenever he failed to cast a vote. "After that," he said, "I voted on everything, no matter what it was. They had me down as having just about the worst attendance record of anyone in the House, yet I had been there the whole time. Now, I vote on everything."

As he spoke, it seemed to me that Bond had two personalities or functions. On the one hand he was down here in Atlanta, Georgia, living a stable, happy existence with his wife and five children, working out of an office set up in the basement of a small apartment building, with the secretary and a couple of desks —and on the other hand he was this terribly important, complex, elusive public figure who created crowds and ripples of excitement wherever he went. He was a radical militant in Georgia, but the same man, with the same outlook, was pretty much an ordinary liberal up in New York or on the campus of any large urban university.

"Maybe I *should* have run for Congress this time," he said near the end of our conversation. "At least I would have avoided the thing with Andy and Lonnie running against each other. And the worst thing is that after it's all over, Lonnie'll never forget about it as long as he lives. He'll always carry a grudge. I swear, I really didn't think he was planning to run. He *should* have run for county commissioner. That's a position of great power. That's *real* power."

3.

The next day, Saturday, the plane took off from Atlanta. Bond lighted up a cigarette and ordered two Bloody Mary mixes, with bourbon instead of vodka, pocketing the little liquor bottles for a later occasion. The ride lasted only about forty minutes. The plane arrived in Montgomery, Alabama, shortly after 11 A.M., and Bond stepped off the ramp in the hot sunshine. Meeting him at the gate were five people—a white man and woman, her two young children, and an attractive black woman. The latter was Joan Cashin, the wife of Dr. John Cashin, who on this first day of August, 1970, would become the first black candidate in nearly a century to run for governor of Alabama.

Six

1.

In his campaign headquarters, a storefront office in a shopping center surrounded by new high-rise apartment buildings, Richard Austin sat reading the latest Detroit newspapers. His office was almost barren; the light-gray tile floor was clean, the atmosphere cheerful but subdued, like the candidate himself. Yellow-and-black chairs had been placed neatly along the walls, and one of the few posters on display showed Austin's oval-shaped face and the words "Ability, That's the Difference."

He spread out the newspapers on the desk in front of him, adjusted his black-rimmed glasses, and read a quote from someone supporting Sheriff Gribbs:

> Look, Gribbs has got this thing locked. Any reasonable white man is going to be the next mayor of Detroit. And that's Gribbs. All we've got to do is keep him breathing.

Dick Austin read the quotation again, shaking his head slowly as if in disbelief. *Any reasonable white man. . . . All we've got to do is keep him breathing. . . .*

For the third time, now, he looked down at the words in quotation marks, perhaps hoping they would just go away. Then he removed the glasses and folded them into his breast pocket. He leaned his elbows on the desk top, resting his chin on his hands.

A great weariness seemed to come over him, as if all of his fifty-six years as a black man in America, having been totaled up and evaluated, were now resting on the thin walk wire of what he had just read.

"What that means," he whispered, "is that Gribbs, after all, is *white*, he's a *man*, and he's *reasonable*, and that that's all it's gonna take for him to win this election."

Austin stood up, still shaking his head. "I just can't believe it," he said to no one in particular. His voice, in its natural tone, came out high-pitched and weak, perhaps the result of years of having to filter all anguish and anger through a strainer of patience and restraint. "I can't believe that the people of this city," he went on, "will vote for just *any reasonable white person* over the most qualified man, who happens to be black."

His words seemed to have conviction behind them, but you could tell by the involuntary wavering of his voice that he was trying too hard. He had spent a lifetime working with white people, trying to please them, trying to prove himself to them so they would accept him on the basis of his ability and character, not on the color of his skin. When he had come to Detroit from the Alabama and Pennsylvania coal fields at the age of twelve, a white man had given him his first job. He worked as a bootblack at a discount shoe store owned by Julius Parker, a Jewish immigrant who had fled Poland to escape persecution. Then he studied accounting and took over Parker's bookkeeping, and all his life since then he found it necessary to work with white people, to make his way through the channels of white society, to try to break through the color barrier and be judged as an equal man. Every time he attempted something, people told him it couldn't be done because he was black. When he became the first Negro auditor of Wayne County, he had to prove himself to the white men who were already there. "I think the other two auditors were a little wary of me when I came into the office," Austin told me. "But after I'd been with them for a few months, they recognized my value to them as a member of a team." Eventually, Austin was instrumental in developing a program to pay off a $20-million county debt, and later he became chairman of a blue-ribbon committee to find more money for the public schools.

"The fact that people on that committee, people from all walks of life, responded to my leadership—well, it didn't surprise me, but I was just *pleased,* you know? It gave me more confidence that I had some leadership ability to work in the broad community. I mean, this wasn't just a 'black' thing, it was the *total* community. It was a matter of whites responding to my leadership."

And now he had to prove himself again, not just as a man with certain credentials but also as a black man. "I haven't lost hope in the system," he told me. "I think it can be done. But it takes faith, and you have to know how to work with people. And ya know, it could be that *because* I'm a Negro, I've worked *harder* at working with people, understand what I'm saying? I take nothing for granted when I'm working with people; I assume everything's gotta be won. You gotta win respect, gotta win everything, to make them see your point of view. You take *nothing* for granted. And I think this is the way to work with people, the only way to be assured that they'll go along with you. Do you understand?"

2.

At times during the primary campaign, Austin timidly suggested that the color of his skin might be a factor, might have some influence, in the election. And then Gribbs would call a news conference or issue a press release to announce to the good citizens of Detroit that, no, Austin was wrong, race was not an issue in this campaign, and then it began to look as though Austin himself was injecting racism into the whole thing, so he'd back off and make Gribbs look like an offended saint. Each man had a real problem in this regard: While race was *the* issue in Detroit, neither man could afford to let the other bring it up, and the result was that the two of them circled around it, never getting down to the real issue, that racism was the primary cause of the city's slums, poor education system, and high crime rate. The confusion came when the issue of race was mentioned as a factor in how people would vote, for this very real aspect of the campaign tended to obscure race as a factor in the condition of the city itself. What Gribbs was saying was this: If a white person says he is going to vote for me, don't immediately assume he's a racist; that is reverse racism. What Austin was trying to do was point out that many people in Detroit, in fact, were going to vote against him precisely because of his race. In my opinion, Austin should have gone beyond the question; he should have pointed out that his blackness was not just a skin color but an attitude, a concern, a philosophy. He should have allowed his blackness to become a positive force instead of merely indicating that it was a political liability, which of course it was. As a matter of fact, he should have listed his blackness as one of his qualifications! This advice goes against every moderate and even liberal outlook, for it tends to divide candidates along racial lines and, some would say, polarize the community. Or does it? For one thing, the candidates *already* were divided along racial lines, the community *already* was polarized. By worrying about becoming a "black racist," Austin was being forced to go to the other extreme, to play the white man's game, and Gribbs's subtle approach was working—we were supposed to forget entirely that Austin was black, even though at least 25 percent of the voters would vote against him precisely for that reason.

It is just possible, though, that people will come to realize that blackness is more than a skin color, that it is an *experience,* and therefore, because of that experience, a point of view. True, Austin was the better man on the basis of sheer professional and civic background, and no doubt he felt that to run as a "black" candidate would diminish him as a man. After all, he might have argued, Gribbs didn't have to run as a *white* candidate. But despite Austin's many other qualifications, his blackness still further set him apart from the others. In asking voters to be "color blind," he was in effect joining Gribbs in asking them to overlook the single overriding fact of his life's experience.

Yet his concern now, as it had been throughout his life, was to be accepted by white people *despite* his color. Both Detroit newspapers had endorsed Austin *and* Gribbs for the primary election, and this disturbed him. We were in his campaign car one night, being driven to one in a blur of appearances, and he leaned back in the front seat, lighting a small cigar. "There's a simple answer," he said in a soft voice, "why both the *News* and the *Free Press* refused to come out for just one man in the primary. See,

Gribbs is the white alternative. He's the white alternative to the most qualified man who happens to be black. The newspapers aren't *attempting* to arrive at a decision at this point. What they're trying to say is this: 'We're inclined to go along with Austin, but just in case you're not *ready* for a black mayor, we got a white one, too. And so this is our *white* choice. We got a black choice, and we got a white choice.' "

It was distasteful for him to say these things; he would never have done so in public. "Gribbs *is* the white-supremacist candidate," he exclaimed. "He is! See, we haven't made an issue of it, but it's racism. There's a whispering campaign that white people aren't ready to elect a black mayor, so even though Austin is the best candidate, he can't win. This is a racist-type campaign!" Austin turned around in the seat, facing me with an expression full of emotion. "But I don't *buy* that," he said. "I have more faith in the people of this city! And I'm gonna be the most disappointed guy in the world if the results of this election bear that out, that whites aren't fair-minded enough to consider me on merit."

We stopped at a home in a black neighborhood, and Austin gave a short talk on the need for the federal government to stop the war and reorder its priorities. In the car again, after a few moments of silence, he returned to his former train of thought.

"Listen," he said, "in a speech before the *NAACP*, Gribbs's *wife* made a statement that this community wasn't ready for a black candidate for mayor. This was before the NAACP! Can you imagine? I don't think she *meant* any harm by it—and *that's* a tragedy. She was being very sincere when she said it. What in effect she said was 'Look, uh, it isn't *time* yet, so why get all steamed up over this? It's just not time. See, we whites still have supremacy. Sure, you have 40 percent of the population, but just because you have that, don't even *think* about having one of your own people as *mayor* of this city.' "

Austin was silent for a while, as the car pulled into a parking lot. "Let me assure you," he whispered to me, "that if this community were 40 percent *Jewish*, we'd have a Jewish mayor. Or Polish or Irish or German. But no, when the dominant minority is black, and when the candidate is black, then there's some serious question about whether we even ought to *think* about him.

This is nothing but white supremacy! I mean, call it anything else, but it's nothing but pure evidence of white supremacy and the notion of black inferiority. I believe the people should have the right to express themselves at the polls, and I'm determined that they should have that right. And if they vote that way, substantially, then I'll admit that I've had the wrong impression. But I'm not going to despair at *this* point. I mean, just at the meeting we went to this afternoon, where it was all whites, there wasn't any reference to race at all! Those people are supporting me because they think I'll make the best mayor! And they're working hard, too. This is *white* people. And it's *bound* to have some results. I just *can't* believe that all of this work is going to fall on deaf ears."

3.

So far, Austin was concentrating his exposure in the black community and among white liberals. The first step in the campaign was to bring about unity among all segments of the black community and then, in the general election, to widen his audience in the white community, even including those who were hostile. In Austin's view, black unity was the first credential that he or any candidate had to have. "If we can unify that one large segment of Detroit," he told me, "then we can bring together the people of *all* segments of the city. The big question for Detroit is whether we can all work together. And I am the *only* candidate who can bring in the black segment."

How successful he had been in gaining black unity—or, perhaps more accurately, in arousing black enthusiasm—was open to question. One of Mayor Cavanaugh's aides had told me, "Of course, everything isn't all peace and tranquillity among the black brothers, either. *They* fight among themselves, too. There's a number of blacks who *aren't* for Austin, you know. Some don't think he's militant enough. He doesn't talk *tough* enough for them. Of course, you're not gonna get rough talk out of a CPA, whether he's black *or* white. He's an *accountant,* for Chrissake. He's a superior man, a high-class guy, but he's the way he is *re-*

gardless of being black. He's an accountant, and he wouldn't be a hell raiser whether he was a Chinaman or a Greek."

I spoke to L. M. Quinn, the editor and general manager of the Michigan *Chronicle,* a large black weekly. Quinn, a slight, short man dressed in a white short-sleeved shirt, was sitting behind his desk in a small building overlooking a park in downtown Detroit. He adjusted his glasses, puffed on a pipe, and spoke slowly, carefully, admitting that while blacks were now more sophisticated —or *because* they were more sophisticated—there had been some divisiveness among them in the beginning. At least three different factions had wanted other candidates, all of whom were more militant than Dick Austin. But, said Quinn, "the social climate will of necessity make Dick just what he is—a black candidate, one with wide experience and who represents more or less the liberal thinking in the community, both black and white." Austin had contributed heavily to the Democratic Party and to labor, Quinn pointed out—"and therefore it put both the party and organized labor in a bind, so to speak, and they *had* to come out and support him, even though he was black." In fact, it occurred to me, if the primary had been partisan, if Austin had been the official candidate of the Democratic Party, he probably would have had a much better chance of winning the whole election. Quinn went on to say that Austin was probably the only candidate, and possibly the only *black* candidate as well, who could unite both sides of the city. "He has broad support from white liberals," Quinn added, "and many of the black militants are now on his bandwagon. Most of them are. Not all, but most of them."

One particular black leader, State Senator Coleman Young, who was certainly militant in outlook if not by definition, told me that he was unenthusiastic about Austin so far. I met Young at a television studio some dozen miles away from the center of town, and together we drove back to the city on the freeway.

"The black leadership couldn't decide on a candidate," said Young as he drove the car. "Austin wasn't the first choice, not by *any* means. But he *forced* the issue by coming out. His initial support came from a splinter coalition, a black-intellectual group, so to speak. It did *not* include the people loyal to our two black Congressmen, John Conyers and Charles Diggs. And it definitely didn't include the militants. Austin was a self-starter, with no broad base of support in the black community. He didn't have any enthusiasm going for him. There's a *respect* for Dick but a doubt on where he stands on many isues. He's an *Establishment* person, a black cat who's made it, and he hasn't felt the need to communicate with the people down below. He lacks fire, drive, militancy. For example, he's hedged all over the map on the issue of a civilian trial board for police. That's a big issue for blacks, but Austin won't campaign on it because he doesn't want to alienate white people.

"See, Austin, like many Establishment blacks, and like many white liberals, too, probably assumes that black voters have no-where else to go but to him. But if he keeps hedging all over the map, the blacks won't be fired up! And they won't register, and they won't go to the polls to vote! Right now, we got a black population of more than 40 percent, but our *registered* black vote is very low. It's only about 22 percent of the total population. Now, that's one out of every two black voters who isn't regis-tered! See, they're *alienated, estranged,* from the political system. They're in *despair* over the system, because it hasn't ever *worked* for them. But they *will* register, and they *will* vote, if they're fired up! So you need an *inspiring* candidate, black *or* white, to bring that 22 percent up to, say, 35 percent. Right now, if you held the election today, Austin would need a hell of a lot of white votes, because the black registration just isn't enough. He needs that white vote, sure, but he has to direct himself in a fiery manner. Not a racist manner but a fiery one."

Young conceded that a more militant black candidate would, in turn, "bring all the bigots out of the woodwork to vote *against* him," but at the same time, he argued, such a candidate would also bring out more of the black vote. "And I don't believe that fiery talk will alienate the white liberals," he said. "And that's the whole point! The liberal whites should understand that we've got to play to our strength, mobilize our *own* troops, in order to win. But Dick isn't campaigning in this way. See, he's trying to woo the whites, to keep those whites who would be on his side. But that isn't necessary! He's a naïve guy, a good guy, and he can be bullshitted by the white liberals. He's indecisive, and he's communicating that to the black people. He's honest, though. You'd see a whole new direction in city government if he were elected."

One evening I had dinner with Austin in the delicatessen near his headquarters, and he admitted having had a "terrible time" in gaining acceptance from the black community. "There were many people, even blacks," he said, "who wondered whether this was the year that a qualified black man ought to even make a try." He paused, sipped his tea, and wondered at his own statement. "The young militants weren't enthusiastic about me, either. The hardest time I've had was with a *black* audience, believe it or not. An audience that didn't think I was black enough!"

He lighted one of his small cigars and frowned; then, becoming enthusiastic, he went on. "The way the young people are thinking now, it makes us all realize that this country *has* a future, you know? They aren't bound by our prejudices or biases. And believe me, many of the older *black* people have even been affected by white prejudice and racism. I mean, many older blacks can't be trusted. And that's why the young militants question *me*. They question even me! With good cause, too! I'm of an older generation, and they wonder whether the scars run so deep that I can be trusted with leadership in this new society. Will I relate to the young people? Will I be able to represent their point of view?"

Dick Austin puffed on his cigar and stared up at the ceiling as if to ponder his own question. It occurred to me that Austin's age was not a true index of his outlook. Given the realities for blacks in our society, of necessity it had taken him a long time to arrive at this point in his political career. At fifty-six, when most white men have reached or passed the peak of their promise, Austin was, in a real sense, just beginning. The sad irony of it all was that now, when he had arrived at the starting gate, after so much struggle and perseverance, he was being judged as already too old.

"See," he went on, "the reason the young militants didn't warm up too well to me was because they hadn't *seen* enough of me, in some of their own activities, at least. I admit it, I haven't been active in the issues and projects of the young, black militants. Most of my work in recent years has been in organizations like United Community Services. But the work I've been doing is just as important as what they're doing. I've tried to get these community groups to reorder their priorities, and I'm trying to carry the message to the Establishment, while the black militant couldn't even get his foot in the door. I *have* to carry the ball, because they haven't arrived at that point, yet. And because *they* haven't, they don't trust *me!* They wonder whether I've sold out, see? So, I've had to try to convince them that we *aren't* so far apart, after all. We're just working in different circles. But we're all working toward the same objectives. Can I be trusted? I think . . . I hope they've come around to thinking that, yes, I can be trusted."

Another evening, shortly before midnight, Austin drove me back to my hotel after a long series of campaign appearances. Outside my hotel, as I was about to leave the car, Austin said, "I'll tell you when I first felt that the black community was really beginning to respond to my candidacy. This is a very strange way to measure it, but I attended a *funeral* in the black community. The little church was just packed, and all the people who had shown up couldn't get inside. I knew the deceased and thought I'd pay my respects. And when I got there, I realized it was almost impossible to get in. So I was just going to pay my respects and leave—no point in trying to inch my way through the crowd and all. Well, the funeral director saw me standing there, and he took me by the arm and carried me right through that crowd, right up to the front of the church. And one of the *ministers,* who was sitting up there, saw me coming and got up! He got up and gave me *his chair!*"

Dick Austin was smiling—giggling, to be exact—in a boyish, carefree manner that I had not seen in public. "So I sat up there in front of the church," he continued, still giggling, "because this is where they *wanted* me to sit! When that minister got up and gave me his seat, oh, man, I *knew* I'd arrived." He was now laughing so hard that he banged the dashboard with his hand. After I got out of the car, he waved, still chuckling, and then drove off through the dark and empty streets of Detroit.

Seven

I was still circling over the identity of Richard Hatcher, having dutifully recorded that the mayor of Gary, Indiana, lived in an all-black residential neighborhood just south of Midtown, that he neither smoked nor drank, seldom used profanity, and did not, according to friends, lose his temper. "Well, he does," commented an associate, "but internally, in strange and Oriental ways." His roots, I found, went back to a strong religious and puritanical family atmosphere. His mother used to take him to church often, and after she died, his father brought the children—there were fourteen, but only seven survived to adulthood—into the Baptist Church.

At times I had the impression that Hatcher looked at things in the simple terms of Good and Evil, not naïvely but by general instinct, and it was apparent that he had brought some such outlook to bear on both his personal life and public career. At one point in school, he told me, he had toyed with the idea of joining the F.B.I., dropping the notion only after the recruiters "didn't seem to be very interested in black guys for agents." Then he came out of graduate school with honors in criminal law and went on the staff of the Lake County prosecuting attorney. Later he became a deputy prosecutor, and he sometimes sounds like one in his speeches as mayor: "We wage a never-ending campaign to destroy the hydra of graft and corruption." Within his first year of office he had driven much of the organized crime from Gary, one of his early accomplishments having been to hit the bookies and prostitutes and after-hours liquor joints. He picked an honest white cop to clean up the force, later hiring a black career officer as chief, doubled the police strength to nearly 425 men, and was now the first to admit that Gary's cops were more aggressive than they had been, especially in the black Midtown section. In the past, blacks could commit crimes against *other* blacks and obtain light punishments or none at all, if indeed they were pursued and caught, while the same crimes, if committed against white people, brought swift police action and heavy punishments. It was one of the ironies of the new black political movement that most blacks, once in office, became tougher in regard to law and order than their white predecessors had been—simply because blacks have been the chief victims of crime. On the other hand, police brutality had virtually disappeared from Gary.

> We have declined the invitation of law-and-order devotees to crack the skulls of gang kids for the dastardly crime of assembling and associating with each other. Simultaneously, we are endeavoring to get at the root cause of that which is destructive in gang activity by creating social programs to ameliorate the problem.

During one of my visits to Gary, I accompanied Hatcher to a local radio station, where every Friday morning for an hour he takes telephoned complaints—or praise—from local citizens. At one point he reached in his jacket pocket and took out a list of five people who had been convicted for littering in the city, and proceeded to read their names, addresses, and fines over the air—as further punishment. And later, if I wasn't mistaken, he quoted the Bible while explaining the importance of his antilitter program.

After the radio show, while riding through the streets of town in the back seat of his air-conditioned black Cadillac limousine, Hatcher stretched his legs and remarked, "My father sort of indoctrinated me with the basic notion that, well, it's good to be good. You know, that it's a very good thing, the highest achievement, to do what is right. To be honest, to have integrity, and that sort of thing. And that that, in and of itself, gives you a certain degree of satisfaction. To know that you did not do something that was wrong. To know that what you did was right, even if you lost in the process of doing it."

Some local and state primary elections had taken place during this time, and Hatcher was suffering from private misgivings over whether he had "done the right thing" by supporting the candidates that he had. In one case he had supported an incumbent Congressman, a white man, over a young black candidate who had had little chance of winning. Hatcher told me, "I would say that for the first time, without regard to who won and who lost" —the incumbent Congressman had won easily—"for the first time, I feel that I really compromised a lot of things, in terms of whom I supported. I told my staff this morning, 'We've sort of forgotten *who we're supposed to be,* in this last election, and we really better get back.'

"I think what happens," he went on in a soft voice, "is that after you *lose* a lot of times, you say, 'My gosh, it sure would be nice to *win,* just once.' So, in response to that kind of feeling, you do things that may very well *assure* that you're going to win, but at the same time you *give up* something, you pay a price, for that. And I feel bad at not having made the effort. Maybe it's not completely fatal, because I think I realize at this point what a price was paid for just having a few winners."

I had the feeling, as Hatcher spoke, that he was undergoing a painful kind of self-analysis and that he was being particularly severe with himself. "The approach that we originally took to the whole idea of political power in Gary," he was saying, "was that while in the short term we were gonna lose, ultimately we'd win. Because initially we ran some candidates, and they lost pretty badly, and everybody laughed about it. But we could sorta see a trend that was developing, you know, and we stuck with it, and things worked out. And I think that that's what you have to do. You can't really—can't really compromise."

2.

After the primary election, Hatcher held one of his regular Wednesday-morning press conferences in the gray, four-story building which embodies City Hall. The reporters had decided that although some of the candidates Hatcher had supported *did* win, not *enough* of them did, and therefore they concluded that Hatcher's personal support was crumbling. He had been more right about the effects of compromise than perhaps he knew at the time, because even after backing a few winners he was put down as a loser overall.

He had told me beforehand that the local news media had been the source of his "greatest frustration" in Gary. There were two major radio stations, and the *Post-Tribune* had a complete corner on locally printed daily news. It was (and is) an entirely white-controlled press with much opinion on, but little insight into, the black community. Most blacks I talked to felt they received inadequate representation, despite their majority of the population and new political power, and Hatcher himself had charged that some of the reporters and radio men were racist in attitude. In fact, he wouldn't even deal with a few of them. "We have truly failed to communicate the host of positive things that have happened," he told me. "The local paper will emphasize some minor thing, like that I arrived ten minutes late to a press conference. Maybe *during* the press conference I announced a new multimillion-dollar program for Gary—but they'll start off with the fact I was late." It is true, though, that previous mayors had never been late to regular press conferences, but that was because, as Hatcher liked to point out, they had never held any in the first place.

In his Washington, D.C., speech he had given this picture of the Gary news media:

> They are more than a random collection of individuals. They are business institutions operated to make money from people who have money. They are not about to bite the hand that feeds them. More importantly, their responses, their social values, their world outlook naturally coincide with their class position in the economic structure of this society. Their influence is pervasive, and they are aware of it. They are giddy and reckless in wielding their power because they are free from counterinstitutional assault. It is not so much that they rally the opposition, but they confuse and neutralize potential allies. To that extent, the news media in Gary are a constant abrasive. It is only natural then that they attack a

black mayor attempting reform, rather than a corrupt county machine.

Another thing—George Wallace was quite popular among the mill hands and their wives, and this showed up in some of the radio talk shows. I listened to one in particular during which most of the conversation between callers and host was devoted to lecturing blacks on everything from patriotism to education to welfare. "I am a taxpaying American," the caller invariably announced, and at one point the host, referring to black mothers on welfare, commented, "They don't do that for the rest of us, do they?"

Hatcher complained that one local radio station made a practice of "harping on each and every crime that occurs in the city, and somehow, no matter where it occurs or who does it, I wind up being blamed for it." He had a pet story about the time an announcer said that a little old lady had been robbed and beaten in Portland, Oregon, "and Mayor Hatcher had no comment."

On this particular morning the reporters gathered as usual in the dull, beige-curtained conference room on the second floor of City Hall, and they sat on swivel chairs on either side of a long, wooden table—a grubby, cynical group of eight men, some with notebooks and pens, a few with portable tape recorders, and three of them manning the lone TV camera poised at the far end. While waiting for Hatcher to appear, the reporters debated with themselves on how to approach him, and one man, still wearing his tattered tan raincoat, finally summed it all up in a raspy voice right out of one of those old movies about grubby police reporters: "Let's face it, the Machine is still king around here. We should try to establish that the Machine is back in control and that Hatcher is dead."

Just then he came into the room with that bouncing stride of his, very much alive, a dapper, schoolboyish figure in a dark-blue, double-breasted suit with a blue-and-white tie, and he approached the podium at one end of the table, a rather guileless look on his face as he adjusted the black-rimmed glasses under the TV light.

"Okay, gentlemen," he said casually, the hint of a sardonic smile appearing. "Free-for-all this morning."

At first the reporters hesitated, but then one man asked, "Doesn't the primary election show that the Machine is still intact?"

"Well, I don't know. . . ."

They circled around him, pecking at him, and he kept glibly sidestepping their thrusts, occasionally flashing a hand or a forefinger up for emphasis, but mostly he leaned calmly on the podium and kept the edge out of his voice, giving no sign of whatever inner reactions he was having. The reporters lighted up cigarettes and pipes, filling the room with smoke. One man with earphones on his head kept picking his teeth while Hatcher's voice was being piped into his skull. If nothing else, the press conference dramatized the difference between Hatcher's image outside the city and the kind of nitpicking he endured on his own turf. He had taken over City Hall and had turned the whole political order upside down, but they were still asking the same old questions within the tired old context, as if, subconsciously if not deliberately, they were trying to forget that black people in Gary had risen out of their former position as the tool for white political dominance.

"What about the Nigra vote?"

"Well, the *black* vote . . ."

"Is this a case where for once the Nigra community didn't vote black?"

"Well, not for *once*," said Hatcher, somewhat visibly annoyed for the first time. "They've supported white candidates for years."

"Wasn't it a rather light vote in the Nigra community?"

"Well, it was a light vote all around," he replied, rubbing his eyes. (It was impossible to tell that his left eye was artificial; indeed, I had not learned for many months after first having met Hatcher that he had lost that eye in his early youth, after another youngster had hurled a stone at him.) "In fact," he went on, "the *heaviest* vote was in a black district."

"Apparently, sir, the Midtown precincts haven't united in a concerted effort to support black candidates."

"Well, not along racial lines, as in some white areas."

"Sir, do you really have an organization?"

"Well," Hatcher returned, smiling despite himself, "I don't have a *machine*, if that's what you mean."

"Sir, you campaign for Nigras across the country, and—"

"Not so much, really. Besides, they weren't all Negroes—blacks, I mean. They were black and white."

"Sir, didn't you sponsor a recent spaghetti dinner at which only four hundred out of nine hundred people showed up?"

"Well, I think there were supposed to be nine hundred *meatballs* at that affair, not people."

Throughout the whole thing, they kept picking his brains on petty, minor matters, trying to drag him down into the swamp of Gary politics, and he kept turning their questions around. He was the only man in the room with any class, and perhaps he was merely condescending, playing along out of some grudging respect for tradition. Watching the conference, I was reminded repeatedly of how traumatic it must have been for whites to lose the top elective office to a black man; it would take a long time for the press conferences to evolve into something more than these weekly rounds of standoff dialogues between Hatcher and the local press corps.

At any rate, a silence now filled the room and Hatcher waited for them to think of a single question of substance. Almost as an irrelevant afterthought, one reporter ventured, "How was the crime situation last month?"

Hatcher answered quickly and in some depth. The crime rate in Gary had risen 46 percent in the first three months of the year, according to the F.B.I., but violent crime was now on the decrease. Burglaries, car thefts, and the like still needed to be fought back. After supplying his answer, Hatcher looked about for another question, perhaps one dealing with his new programs for the city, but the reporters had finished. When he left the room, the newsmen were disgruntled because they hadn't tripped him up. "Very frustrating," said one. "The mayor can tell a lie so convincingly it isn't even funny. If you can outwit him at a press conference, you can pin a medal on yourself."

"Hey," another man said as they all got up to leave. "Do you know how to give an elephant an enema?"

"No, how?"

"Very slowly," he replied, and much laughter filled the room.

3.

Down in the basement of City Hall, some of the reporters gathered over coffee at the lone table there, to relax a bit before filing their stories about how Hatcher was on his way out.

"What gets me," complained one, "is the way he distrusts us. He actually thinks we're all racists!"

"Well, see, he just didn't like our line of questioning. He thinks politics is dirty and filthy. He's attempting to be a statesman. He's a politician who doesn't like politics!"

"Hell, he's not *even* a politician! He doesn't know how to play the game!"

"I'll say one thing about him, though—he's a brilliant man. He should be running the Southern Christian Leadership Conference or something like that, where there's no politics involved, just image and charisma and leadership. Every time he makes a trip out of town, he makes us look better. Yet people here, they criticize him for it. The local people aren't looking at him from the right viewpoint. If he's done anything for this city, it's to give us a better image."

"Yeah, but see, he's a lousy administrator. He's intelligent and a decent guy, but on the local level he's failed. Things like garbage collection, routine stuff, and especially his down-to-earth politics. For example, he's let his precinct organization go to hell. He hasn't built a *machine* for himself! He admits it! He's just relying on the force of his personality, and that ain't enough."

"Well, Hatcher should learn to compromise, to *give* a little. He went his own way, and he's rubbed a lot of people the wrong way, and he's also got a knack for saying the wrong thing at the wrong time, and too loud."

"And it didn't help any when those blacks came in and scared the shit out of the City Council, either."

"Robert Kennedy, *he* knew how to play the game, all right. When he came through here in '68, he laid the money out to the Nigra precinct workers, he sure did. Now, there was a *real* politician."

Later, I joined Hatcher in the restaurant of the Gary Hotel, where he was munching on a bacon-lettuce-tomato sandwich. He smiled when I told him of the reporters' assessment of him as a politician. "They're talking about politics *Gary*-style," he said. "If I became the politician they imply I ought to be, I'd be doing a lot of things, I'm sure, that they'd be very unhappy about. They'd be calling me every name in the book. First of all, to build an organization takes a whole lot of money, much more than I happen to have. But where do you *get* that kind of money, to put people on private payrolls and so on? From *underworld* operators, that's where. Gambling, vice, prostitution—if they want me to take *that* money, well, I suppose I *could* really build a machine for myself. But, man, we'd be so corrupt! We'd be the very thing they say they're against! They just don't realize what they're saying to me."

4.

One Friday morning Hatcher was leaving town to speak to a college audience in Texas, and then he was flying East, one important stop being Newark, New Jersey, where another black man, Kenneth Gibson, was running for mayor of a large city. In the limousine on the way to Chicago's O'Hare Airport, I asked him whether he carried with him some overall vision that served to tie all the pieces together, whatever I meant by that, and without hesitation he turned to the past and his personal memories of growing up. "You have to realize," he said, "or look in terms of where I come from, and I think that has almost everything to do with whatever I am at this point. Not in a good or bad sense, but just what I am." He told me how he had grown up in the "worst slum" in nearby Michigan City, in a section called the Patch, "where there were no paved streets, and our front door opened onto an alley." He reminisced about how as a boy he used to go over to the railroad track to steal coal from the hoppers when they stopped on the sidings overnight. "I really thought we were going *up* in the world," he said, "when my father bought a coal stove with a kind of covering that made it look like it was brown metal. I felt, you know, we had really *made* it at that point, having a stove like that." As Hatcher spoke of those days as a young boy in the slums—how the "big day of the week" was when his father went down to the relief office to bring home grapefruit and sugar and potatoes, and how the children ate syrup and bread as a steady diet—I kept remembering that I hadn't really asked him for this personal background, that rather, this was Hatcher's way of responding to a question about his vision of himself and his work. It was as if there were some things he *dared* not forget, as if in fact he was afraid that with all of his recent notoriety he might forget what had driven him to get there in the first place, and that if he ever did forget, he would lose something fundamental and unique about himself, would lose direction and become just one more politician, a *Negro* politician, one more black cat who has made it in this white man's country.

". . . and to see my mother work very hard all of her life," he was saying, "until she got sick, got cancer, and couldn't work anymore . . . and I think, out of all that, first of all, you come out of that with a feeling of unworthiness, you know what I mean? Well, maybe you don't. . . . You come out of there with a feeling that, not that you don't count, but that you're just not as good as other people."

Hatcher explained that his father's influence had been "the only thing that sort of gave me any kind of real drive or anything like that." His father, once a sharecropper in Macon, Georgia, had worked for thirty-six years molding railroad-car wheels in Michigan City; now seventy-eight years old and a deacon in the Baptist Church, he was still working, this time as a custodian in the Michigan City courthouse. It was an odd, even poignant juxtaposition—a father who could neither read nor white, working as a courthouse custodian, and an intellectual son, able to speak almost fluent French after just two years of study, presiding as mayor of a nearby city.

"He kept pounding away at us," Hatcher said of his father. "He kept saying, 'You children, you have to be better than me. That's all I care about. And I'll be satisfied if your life is a better life, and if *you* do more, and *you* achieve more, than I did.' And he just kept pounding away at, you know, how I should study hard and work and so on. . . ."

Again without my prompting Hatcher began to speak of his growing up, not only as a member of a poor family but in terms of what it meant to be black. He recalled the white teachers in his school with some bitterness. An art teacher used to "just routinely kick me out of the class and send me to the principal's office to be expelled, because I didn't just bow down to everything she said, and because I had the audacity to answer her when she would say something." Another teacher would insult the black girls by saying things like, "You girls, if you're real nice, I'll let you come over to my house this weekend and clean it up."

"I look back at it now," said Hatcher, "and I see how I never realized things. I knew it was wrong then, but looking back now, I see how really unjust so many things were. It involved almost everything—the track team, the football team. . . ."

He told me how he had gone down to the YMCA to learn how to swim but was told that he didn't *need* to learn. "They said, 'Oh, you can swim,' but I couldn't swim at all! They just weren't gonna have any black kids swimming in the pool. The school had a contract with the Y, so they had to let us go down there, but when we arrived, they'd say, 'Oh, you can swim' and then send us right back to the school. And I haven't learned how to swim to this day."

But the point, he went on, is that "you come out of it all with just an overwhelming sense of sympathy and empathy and concern for everybody else that's in that kind of situation. You know what they're going through, and you want to make a difference, that's all. And I think that that's the basis for most of my concern. That life in America, for poor people, especially for a poor black person, is so unjust, and that everything's stacked against him. Really, it is. And they don't have any spokesman. They're too busy, they don't even have time to speak for themselves. They're too busy trying to survive. When you look at government and at the economic structure of a community, you realize that people in key positions are looking out for *other* people in key positions. They looking out for the other haves—they really are. But there's really no one, in a key position, for the most part, that's looking out for the have-nots. There's no one really trying to represent them. Now, that, for me, that's like the basis for wanting to do certain things. Even though I guess I'd be lucky to say that 50 percent of my time is spent trying to do things like that. That's probably a very liberal guesstimate. The thing that sorta keeps you going is that you know there *are* certain things that *can* be done for them."

Eight

1.

Newark. I went there with mixed feelings. I had always thought of Newark, New Jersey, as an unreal place, a shadowy urban pit hidden somewhere beyond the stench of all those oil refineries and freight yards in the swamps along the turnpike, and ever since the Newark riot of 1967 I had thought of that city's ghetto as somehow more dangerous, primitive, rage-filled, wild, violent than others. Yes, the city had become a national symbol of corruption and urban misery and racial hatred, a crumbling concrete cavern of black fury, and in my thoughts of Newark I once again envisioned the nightmare of the roped-off, all-black city at nighttime, the ultimate example of how the technological giant can be destroyed from within by the inhuman, immoral workings of its own source of energy and power. And I thought of the people, trapped within the giant but with no control over the madmen who worked its hidden levers. One could read of the "accelerating downward slide" of Newark and how the city was "overwhelmed" by problems and "divided" beyond the measure of sanity and "about to explode" again at any moment. To meditate on Newark was to contemplate the breakdown of what was once a dream of high human collective endeavor: the city. The city was supposed to be the marketplace for intellectual ferment, the crossroads for great themes and ideas and new forms of expression, the cultural center for the civilization. Instead, we had Newark, the model of the legacy

of urban problems that the new black mayors would inherit, with
its staggering welfare load, unemployment, bad housing, street
crime, pollution, corruption, soaring tax rate, failing health care,
deteriorating schools, racial hatred. Newark had the highest percentage of substandard housing among large American cities, its
older sections marked by wholesale blight and parts still boarded
up and abandoned; the most crime per thousand citizens; the sec-
ond-highest population density; and while it had the heaviest per-
capita tax burden of major cities, its schools were still among the
worst in the country, with a 32 percent dropout rate. Newark could
claim the highest rates of venereal disease, of new cases of tubercu-
losis, and of mothers who die in childbirth. It had the second-
highest rate of infant mortality. It was an old city, with not enough
jobs or industry, the black unemployment rate running twice that
of whites, a city in which outsiders profited from the powerlessness
of the people who lived there. As the *Village Voice* put it, "In
July, 1967, 3,500 New Jersey National Guardsmen and state troopers, most of them from the white suburbs, invaded the black Central Ward, destroying black-owned stores, brutalizing the residents,
and killing a score of them. . . . For blacks, that experience is
repeated on a smaller scale every working day when 500,000 com-
muters from the suburbs invade the city, strangle its services,
launch superhighways through its guts, sell it heroin, leave their
garbage hanging in the air, use the police force to keep things
quiet, and take their salaries home to the suburbs to be taxed." The
city was a patchwork of decaying ethnic neighborhoods, with poor
whites and even poorer blacks fighting each other for whatever
crumbs were being left at the bottom of the pit, each side mistak-
ing the other for the enemy. The downtown prospered by day but
became a ghost town after 7 P.M., the population of the core-city
dwindling from 800,000 by day to less than 250,000 by night, and
the overall city was already well over half black, somewhere around
65 percent, and becoming blacker and poorer every day. The uprising which had left twenty-six dead and $10 million in damage
was traced in part to a "pervasive feeling of corruption in the city
government." Now, Mayor Hugh J. Addonizio, head of the reign-
ing white political establishment, was involved with ten other members of his administration in sixty-six Federal indictments dealing
with corruption and organized crime—and yet the man was running

again for election! Yes, I went to Newark with no small sense of foreboding and doom, for the situation had become so intolerable that it was frightening to contemplate the mood of the city's black citizens if they could not elect a mayor to represent them and give them some small dignity and control over their lives.

2.

The campaign was a circus. Arriving on the periphery of the action, I considered that I was gazing down at an array of clowns who were frantically calling attention to themselves amid the chaos. In the center ring was a short, squat, pudgy, round-faced, low-keyed, good-natured, methodical, pragmatic little man with a slight moustache, Kenneth Gibson by name, a civil engineer, a *structural* engineer, suggesting that he was going to become the first black mayor of a major Northeastern city by virtue of sheer logic, by the riveting of one steel girder to another to the top, a man who wore undapper sports jackets and somewhat baggy pants, a thirty-eight-year-old candidate who seemed to be swept up in something much larger than himself—he was making history, after all—and yet whose personality, perhaps more than any other single factor, was preventing the campaign from enveloping Newark in a catastrophe even more bloody and ruinous than the one three years before. If elected he was going to (1) pick up the garbage, (2) get rid of the police director, who himself had become a major clown figure in the circus, and (3) be an honest person. And beyond those three firm resolutions there was "no magic formula" for Newark, no promise other than a sense of decency, possibly harmony, a strong business sense, a stand against the Mafia, a spirit of renewed determination to accomplish what might, in the end, prove impossible—for it had occurred to many onlookers, including me, that we would *never* be able to undo what we had done, that we already had lost too much ground, that the whole circus tent was going to collapse and smother us all no matter what happened down there in the ring.

Gibson's was the act to watch, for although he was making less noise than the others he possessed an uncommon amount of inner strength and conviction and stolid optimism. He seemed the antithesis of black rage, speaking as he did about wanting "all the people in the city working together" and referring to the mayor's job as a kind of corporate presidency. He had come out of the Deep South, from Enterprise, Alabama, arriving in Newark with his family at the age of eight, the son of a butcher and a seamstress, growing up with them and his brother Harold in a one-room flat in the center of the black slums, graduating from Central High School near the top of his class in 1950, working in factories, going off to the military with the Army's 65th Engineering Battalion in Hawaii, taking courses at night while holding a job with the state Highway Department during the day, and emerging finally with his degree from Newark College in 1963. He began work for the Newark Housing Authority that year and was later put in charge of basic engineering in urban renewal, still later becoming the authority's chief engineer. In the sixties he was involved in community and civil-rights activities—antipoverty, YMCA, Urban League, NAACP, CORE—and ran for mayor in 1966, polling 20 percent of the votes and suddenly becoming a strong political force in the city. And naturally none of this history explained why, or how, Kenneth Gibson was able to leap into the forefront of the mayor's race in 1970.

3.

Heading into Newark, I had a vision of the man called Imamu Amiri Baraka, clad in a black dashiki, lying in wait on the edge of the city, his slight, agile, crouched form casting a Batmanlike shadow over the light-gray sky, perhaps across the face of the Prudential Insurance building itself. Imamu Amiri Baraka! Also known as LeRoi Jones, the "militant poet-playwright." I envisioned this thin, bearded black man, his head still bandaged from the gashes he had received "in the process of arrest" during that hot summer outbreak of 1967, emerging from jail two days after the end of the shooting and resolving to do everything in his power to transform the political life of the city's ghetto, to build a Black Nation in America, beginning in Newark. There was an irony in the suicidal black rebellions which have come to be known as riots, for despite the destruction and spilled blood there was also a liberation, an unleashing of spirit, an awakening of self-recognition, a new black unity, a determination that black destiny must be placed in the hands of blacks: "We will govern Newark, or no one will govern it."

I had read some of Imamu's statements, observing that unlike a good deal of the black-power rhetoric I had heard, these utterances were direct, confident, clear, and swift in purpose:

> Newark is in the control of an Italian nationalist army called the police department. We are constantly harassed by a city government that has already been indicted, by criminals who are trying to make us convicts.

> What we are interested in now is communication and understanding. Is the white community dedicated to a new Newark or will they let it become a ghost town?

> We want to get control of the space where 300,000 black people live, not only for us to live in, to work and to play in, but for our ideas and the development of concepts that are of benefit to us as a people with a peculiar ethos.

> What's happening in Newark is a preview of what will happen in the cities of America. We want to set an example in Newark because the cities will be black, and whites will have to come to the mature understanding that no matter how they'd like to see it happen, blacks will determine the way it will happen.

> Our revolution is a revolution for black liberation. The Black Nation is the only thing that will guarantee our survival. We are moving in Newark to gain our political control, not because we are interested in American democracy, but because we are interested in black survival. We are trying to control the police.

> We're not interested in just getting one man access into the political establishment. Real control of this space, this land we live on, is realizable this year, 1970. We can win back control of this land through the political process.

> I think people are beginning to believe in their own political power, and you're gonna see an enormous creative input

suddenly from the black community if we can elect a black mayor.

If Gibson is elected, he won't have to answer to the kind of pressure Stokes gets. The people who really control Newark don't live and don't vote here, and there's no No-Man's Land, no liberals in the middle ground in Newark. It's very polarized, with less token symbols to trap you in the middle ground.

We've come to the conclusion that the city is ours anyway, that we can take it with ballots.

In the wake of the riot, Imamu Baraka–LeRoi Jones went about his task with a single-mindedness that was rare in the history of black political involvement. Voter-registration efforts were concentrated in the black ghettos, and a genuine grass-roots education drive was carried out along with Imamu's movement toward African identity. The culmination of all of this was a remarkable community-wide Black and Puerto Rican Convention held in November, 1969. This was an ingenious development, yet so simple and obvious that one could wonder if a true stroke of genius were not in fact merely a pure strain of the most common sense. The goal, quite simply, was to unify the black and Puerto Rican communities behind a single slate of candidates and, equally important, to arouse nonwhites sufficiently for success, to set a fire under their souls until they regarded ballots as important and powerful tools. In order to do this, they held a convention—not that any such mechanism was needed in order to put up a black candidate for mayor, for all one had to do was sign up, as Austin had done in Detroit, but they went ahead anyway and held a meeting, a gathering of blacks and Puerto Ricans exclusively but including virtually every segment of those communities, and they *called* it a convention, which lent an air of authority to the whole thing—a simple idea that turned out to have incredible impact. Some three thousand blacks and Puerto Ricans met for three days in a junior high school in a black section of Newark, and out of this "convention" came Kenneth Gibson, the "people's choice" for mayor, and a slate of seven nonwhite candidates for the City Council. For once, black people were going through the front door of the political process—or rather, having been denied access, they created a front door all their own—instead of having to step inside through the proverbial side entrance. Gibson made the statement that "the poor and disenfranchised can no longer tolerate being controlled by machine politicians, and politics must become synonymous with social and civil rights." Later, in a rare moment of slightly militant-sounding public comment, he stated, "Today, black people select their *own* leaders and their *own* political candidates. They won't be happy about other groups trying to put up puppets and Uncle Toms."

What Gibson was referring to, in part, was an informal "time-table" that the white business Establishment had set up for Newark's political future. If such arrogance can be believed, the "script" called for an honest, or "clean," Italian for mayor in 1970 and then a nice, "cooperative" Negro to complete the transition in 1974.

I arrived in Newark in June of 1970, almost seven months after the Black and Puerto Rican Convention and just a week before the final election. Much had happened up to this point, involving the full cast of clowns in the circus. In December, Mayor Addonizio had been indicted for taking part in a huge kickback scheme that extracted hundreds of thousands of dollars from firms doing construction work for the city, confirming the "widespread feeling of corruption in City Hall" on the part of Newark residents, ghetto folk in particular. The powerful insurance executives, the men who represented the downtown financial centers and suburban political interests, those who held sway over such vital things as land use and planning and money, had been forced to turn away from Addonizio, who was simply bad public relations, and, lacking a "clean" Italian with enough strength to replace him, were now openly supporting Ken Gibson, who was looking more and more like a winner. In fact, that was probably the *only* consideration which had motivated both the business leaders and the two major newspapers to help Gibson—the fact that they couldn't afford to be on the losing side of city politics. Having a vested interest in the future of Newark, the Establishment was forced to lend its support to the man chosen by those in the ghetto, the man who was, in a real sense, running *against* the so-called Establishment. And the image of Imamu Amiri Baraka, clad in his black dashiki, a briefcase held at his side, striding into a conference room in the Prudential building, was an irony worth savoring.

Gibson had become the front-runner in the campaign by virtue of an election in May in which he had polled nearly twice as many votes as Addonizio but not enough for a majority, thereby requiring him to face the incumbent mayor in a runoff on June 16. There had been four white candidates and three blacks in the May election, the whites getting a total of 48,874 to the blacks' total of 40,043, meaning that, although Gibson had led the pack, he faced almost certain defeat if the runoff were to split strictly along racial lines. With victory almost in their grasp, the blacks had every right to fear that it would be taken from them in the runoff, and meanwhile, whites were afraid that a black madman would take over City Hall and carry out some unimaginable reign of terror and revenge.

Which brought my mind around to an image of Anthony Imperiale, who in the world of caricature could serve as the white man's counterpart for LeRoi Jones. The riot had polarized the city, giving rise to both black *and* white militancy, the latter embodied in the figure of Imperiale—I now had visions of the Imperial Grand Wizard of the Ku Klux Klan—who had come to prominence as head of a white vigilante group that patrolled the streets in order to "preserve law and order," which in clearer language meant they were almost a citizen army preparing to wage war with the blacks. Imperiale was a construction worker with a large following in Newark's heavily populated poor-Italian community, which had elected him councilman at large. He had run for mayor against Addonizio and Gibson in the May contest, receiving nearly 14,000 votes and coming in third. After losing, he eventually threw his support to the embattled Mayor Addonizio, saying, "I don't have to tell you where my heart lies. We have fought the raping and the insurrection, and that's what we will continue to fight." And later, referring to Addonizio, he told his followers, "I will break my fat belly and my back for this man, and you'd better do the same." Imperiale, a karate expert, was remembered in the black community for his references to "Martin Luther Coon."

Despite all the solid issues at stake in Newark it was inevitable that the campaign would degenerate into a racial one, and at times it seemed that Newark might become the battleground for America's first urban civil war. There were charges that some of Gibson's "extremist" supporters had used "terrorist tactics" in trying to drive the other two black candidates out of the first election. Reports of threats, physical assaults, tire slashings, and smoke bombings were continuing to circulate in both political camps. Apparently the rise of black power at the polls was a process of uprooting too traumatic for ordinary mud-slinging politics to contain. Sound trucks went through the streets blaring, "Don't turn Newark over to the Communists and Outsiders," and Addonizio, who said that he had "never used the issue of race in my twenty-two years of public life," went on repeatedly to inflame his supporters by warning that "Gibson is part of a raw and violent conspiracy to turn this city over to LeRoi Jones and his extremist followers." At times the mild and methodical Gibson was almost lost amid the flurry of anti-Jones rhetoric and a stranger might have received the impression that the fiery poet-playwright was in fact Addonizio's political opponent. Jones stayed clear of the campaign, but the mayor unrelentingly used him, as part of a strategy of desperation, to generate fear and hatred among whites. "I want to make it clear," he said, "that I haven't brought race into this campaign. My opponent has, though. I wasn't selected by a *white* convention, but he was selected by a *black* convention. *I'm* not identified with extremists, but *he* is." Night after night, Addonizio called upon Gibson to "repudiate the Black Convention as un-American"—the irony being that down through the years, it was fine for Italian-Americans to gather together to select their own candidates; it became un-American when blacks merely sought to do the same thing. Wherever Addonizio went, the mere mention of LeRoi Jones produced a chorus of boos and shouts: "LeRoi Jones says, 'If you want to rape women, go out and rape white women; if you want to steal, steal from whitey.' I tell you, friends, everything we have invested in our city, everything we have invested in our jobs, in our children, and in our homes, is at stake in this election."

At some white gatherings, the women would be sent out of the room so tape recordings of Jones could be played. "We'll never let a nigger get elected," came the predictable response. Not to be outdone by anyone, Imperiale called the campaign "a war between Americanism and Communism" and pounded his followers with talk of "raping and insurrection," adding, "If you don't get out and vote, you're gonna have the most radical black mayor you've ever seen!" The fear and hate literature was spread around like confetti, some with pictures of Jones, calling him "Gibson's chief aide" and adding such captions as "Gibson has a place for Jones in his cabinet" and "LeRoi Jones says, 'Kill whites right now.' " Even the mayor's police director, Dominick Spina, who was campaigning almost nightly for him, described the election as a "black-versus-white situation" and declared, "For the white man in Newark, this is a matter of survival." "Whether we survive or cease to exist," he told throngs of fearful, angry whites, "depends on what you do on June 16." One white councilman running for reelection was moved to announce, "With a Gibson victory, blood will flow in the street."

Meanwhile, Gibson tried to aim his efforts at holding the city together, at one point suggesting that, even if he did win, it would be impossible to govern in such a polarized atmosphere. He continually warned his aides to walk away from all provocations and was required to do so himself several times when he was spat at and threatened and insulted with racial obscenities and even challenged to a fight by some young white hoods. "Baboon! Nigger!" they yelled from a distance.

A key figure in the midst of all this turmoil was a man named John Caufield, the former fire director who had been appointed by Addonizio. After the mayor was indicted, Caufield decided to run for mayor, winning some 12,000 votes and coming in fourth behind Gibson, Addonizio, and Imperiale. A week later, he announced that he was throwing his support to Gibson in the runoff election, which was not only an act of some courage but a tremendous boost for Gibson. Blacks may have comprised 65 percent of the population, but only some 40 percent of the electorate, and therefore Gibson needed a sizable slice of the white vote. The question was, how many of Caufield's "moderate" white supporters would join him in voting for the black candidate?

The price that Caufield had to pay was higher than that which most men would have tolerated. Like Gibson, he was spat upon and jeered at, and he was even manhandled by a group of white youngsters while out campaigning for Gibson. At one rally he was repeatedly caller a "nigger lover" and, with his wife and children, just barely got away unharmed; whites hurled insults and rocks and pounded on Caufield's car as it rolled away. Midnight callers threatened to burn down his house and to run his children over in the streets.

Off-duty black policemen began voluntarily to accompany Gibson on his rounds, to provide him with some physical security, and near the end of the campaign there was a rumor that Addonizio's people had hired a "black goon squad" to break up his own appearances so he could blame black militants who supported Gibson. One night, a shotgun blast ripped through the living-room window of a Negro minister who was supporting Addonizio, and Gibson called the shooting a "hoax" perpetrated by Addonizio's camp in order to discredit the Gibson campaign. Saying that he had received bomb threats at his home and headquarters, Gibson requested official police guards in addition to his volunteers, and he also asked Federal and state agencies to investigate a plot to assassinate him. A car owned by one of his white women supporters was reportedly torn apart one night, and a black woman on his staff was roughed up by some white policemen.

4.

On Broad Street, across from Military Park, down a block or so from a movie theater and between rows of shops and restaurants on this busy downtown avenue, was a storefront, and as I approached from a distance along the wide sidewalk, I could tell the place by the vague outline of an immobile crowd out front in the midst of the hurried pedestrian traffic. The crowd was not large at all—maybe a dozen people were kind of spilled out of the storefront into the sidewalk, standing in clusters of two or several, and some leaned against or sat on parked cars along the curb. Two cars, with posters on their sides and loudspeakers on the tops, were double-parked, one with its motor idling. Black men with walkie-talkies ran back and forth from the cars to the storefront; white hippie-looking youngsters passed out leaflets to those walking by. The crowd itself was not even a crowd but the appearance of one, because the passersby tended to slow down at this point, to glance quickly in the windows or through the doorway, and on many of the faces of these curious pedestrians I noticed a hesitation, then a sudden recognition, and then something like the expression of an outcast. This was especially so on the faces of the white on-lookers because, for just a moment, they had stumbled right into the nerve center of something very . . . well . . . *black,* and therefore, to them, something alien and strange and even intimidating. It was as if a single patch of sidewalk and one storefront in the ghetto had been transplanted mysteriously to the busy downtown commercial district, and those who lingered long enough to notice the posters came to recognize what it was all about.

I recognized and welcomed the mood of Gibson's headquarters, for it reminded me of other storefronts and moods in my recent past; and because I myself was white, I initially shared the sensation of being on the outside. But this experience was soon counterbalanced by the feeling of the place itself, which carried an undercurrent of excitement, of animated goodwill bordering on danger, of people coming together for some purpose beyond the scope of their individual lives, an unspoken combination of nervousness and anticipation that produced a quality of behavior not unlike that of a crowd going through the turnstiles and into the stadium for the final game of the World Series. I sensed an unreality at the Gibson headquarters—no, a reality that was too sweet, too good, to be an accurate reflection of the tempo of the great bulk of the rest of the city. Were there not black militants now gathering to celebrate an outpouring of hatred, and were there not similar gatherings of whites? No, it was unreal, for here prevailed an atmosphere of friendliness, the energy of amateurs, a belief in something better than the reality beyond. There were young black girls at the desk in the far corner of the office on the first floor, and white and black college students roaming about with leaflets and buttons, the ring of loud conversation and laughter, a periodic surging of chaotic comings and goings—and, no, this was not the place where the tension showed, and so I stayed inside a long time, from early afternoon until after dark, putting off the time when I would have to venture out again. For having come to Newark, I knew that inside the shelter of this storefront I was not really in the city yet, still on the outside of whatever it was that made Newark what it was.

Nine

1.

In the parking lot of the airport in Montgomery, the small welcoming group ushered Julian Bond into the back seat of a beat-up station wagon, and he sat there rather uncomfortably, his coat off and tie loose, as the car lurched forward and headed southward and deep into Alabama's black belt.

"Julian, do you have a *written* speech?"

"Uh, no."

"Well, that's okay. We have a tape recorder."

Once out on the highway, Bond said he was hungry, so the car pulled into the lot of a roadside diner. The group went inside and sat at a round table in the rear. Bond devoured a cheeseburger and french fries. He paid the tip for everyone at the table, recalling that at one time he had been a bus boy in an eating place on a highway in Pennsylvania; since then, he said, he had always been a pretty big tipper.

For the next thirty minutes, the car sped through rural farm country, past tall green grass with occasional grazing cattle, taking narrow country roads where for long stretches of time there were few signs of civilization. The windows of the car were rolled up for an air-conditioning system that refused to work, and the heat became almost unbearable. Strings of sweat were pouring down the sides of Bond's face as the car swerved onto a bumpy dirt road, creating great swirls of dust in the air outside. "I think we're lost," someone said, but Julian Bond didn't pay much attention because now, for diversion, he was deep in the middle of comic book which he had found on the seat of the car.

The station wagon wandered over a narrow road through some woods and came alongside a green muddy lake. "We're here," came a voice from the front seat. Around another bend, up a slight incline overlooking the lake, stood a cluster of tall pines; and beneath the cool shadow of the trees were nearly three hundred people, mostly black, who sat on fold-up chairs facing a wooden platform. Even in the shade the air was thick and hot, so the men and women on the chairs made good use of the specially created fans on which was printed, "Vote For *Yourself* For A Change" and "Vote The Eagle To Freedom."

A stranger might have guessed that these black folks were merely holding a picnic of some sort out here in the wilderness at the edge of Flowers Lake, so unlikely a setting for a political convention did it seem. Most of the people here were poor, many were old (or aged before their time), and although they were gentle and religious people, they had received threats that their meeting would be disrupted if it were held in a city, which was the main reason they had chosen this secluded spot under the pine trees overlooking the lake.

They were members of a new and dramatic political force in the South, an independent, predominantly black group known as the National Democratic Party of Alabama. The year before, NDPA candidates had won control of the Greene County Commission and Board of Education, an impressive victory that signaled the probable end of white political domination in Alabama's black belt. The NDPA was a splinter group, an alternative to the regular state Democrats who had supported George Wallace for President in 1968. The Greene County election the following year was the NDPA's first chance to prove itself as a viable political force in Alabama, and for the first time in its 153-year history, the county passed from white to black control. The transition had been long overdue, since blacks outnumber whites in Greene County, ten thousand to three thousand. All through Alabama's black belt, the Negro majority has traditionally been dominated by the white minority, the political life of rural counties across the state having been in the hands of the landowners, almost all of them white. The number of blacks who could vote had been kept under control by a requirement that no one could even register unless he was "vouched for" by a voter who was already qualified—and since 1950, white voters had simply stopped vouching for blacks altogether.

All that had begun to change in early 1965, when Stokely Carmichael arrived in Lowndes County with his loyal band of Snick workers. That was the year of the Voting Rights Act and the formation by Carmichael of a new political party which would become the model for the NDPA:

> The county courthouse has always been the symbol of oppression for the rural Negro. But we are going to make it the symbol of liberation. . . . We're going to emancipate the black belt counties, courthouse by courthouse, starting with Lowndes. We're gonna build political parties run by poor people that will run candidates for everything that runs. We're going to elect sheriffs, school boards, tax assessors, everything in Lowndes County with our party. We're gonna call it the Black Panther.

As he walked through the woods toward the gathering of blacks in the clearing, Julian Bond had a full and personal awareness of this history. Here in this secluded spot, nearly five years after that speech by Stokely Carmichael, the NDPA was going to nominate a list of 169 candidates for office in the State of Alabama, ranging from Dr. John Cashin's nomination for governor down to the smallest county positions, for the election in November, 1970. The delegates were facing the wooden speakers' platform, listening to one of their candidates for probate judge. As Bond walked up the hill over the dry leaves and pine needles, holding his jacket in one hand, the black candidate's voice drifted up through the hot, still air in the tall trees: "People are afraid to come to meetings! People are taught to think they're incompetent! But there's nothing wrong with 'em that a good NDPA election can't cure!"

"Yeah, that's right!" returned some of the audience.

"We want people who gonna serve with a *depth of feeling!* The time for tokenism is past! We got to free our minds! The white man has unchained our legs but not our minds!"

The appearance of the young Georgia legislator caused an immediate stir. Several people came over to him at the edge of the clearing and crowded around him, shaking his hand and whispering greetings. For a moment it appeared as if a prophet had come into their midst, and the man on the platform, sensing this new development, pointed in Bond's direction and shouted, "We have with us this afternoon, I see, a young man from Georgia!" Now, as all heads turned to see, the man's voice took on the tone of a preacher at the height of his sermon: "We've brought this young man here today to help tell us *where we're going,* and *how we'll get there!*"

Bond set down his coat, loosened his tie, and climbed to the platform. He began to speak immediately, without notes but with a cutting edge on his voice that lent an authority to his words. He congratulated them for "getting down to the business of taking over the government of Alabama." Probably none of them had ever put it in such direct terms, and so their response was almost one of surprise as well as agreement. Bond continued, referring to "poor black people who've had no relationship with the power that runs us. . . . We were told that politics was *white* folks' business. Then, when we got into it anyway, we were told that politics was the art of *compromise* and that therefore we shouldn't speak out on things. Then, when we started speaking out anyway, we were told that politics was only the art of the *possible*—they said we could go *half* a mile but not all the way. We could only go *part* of the way. Well, we've learned by now that politics is *not* the art of the possible or even the art of compromise but simply the art of seeing *who gets how much of what from whom.* And you know that we haven't gotten any of the what from you-know-whom."

Bond spoke all this in rapid, underplayed delivery. Occasionally a tiny breeze trickled through the woods from the green lake, but otherwise the delegates had to keep fanning themselves to cool the sweat that was coming all the way through their clothes. Bond wiped his forehead and quoted a bit from black leaders of history, and here again he seemed to be able to put things in their ultimate context, to get to the heart of the matter without effort.

"If your streets are paved," he said, "then your politics are together. If the police treat you with respect and say, 'Yes, sir' and

'Yes, ma'am,' then your politics are together. If your schools tell your children about themselves, about their identity and history, then your politics are together. But if our streets are still muddy, if the police still call us 'Boy' or 'Girl'—then we haven't gotten our politics together yet."

Julian Bond spoke about "making power concede" and illustrated this theme with an example: "If a man has his foot on your neck and you say, 'Please, sir, won't you get your foot off my neck,' chances are he *won't* move it. But if you grab his foot, twist it, and make it hurt *him* like he's hurting you, *then* he'll lift it."

He told them that he makes three hundred speeches a year, mostly in front of college audiences, who are mostly white, and that being down here in rural Alabama was something special for him, something different and good. "It's a great pleasure to speak to people who look like me," he said. "What you do here at Flowers Lake is like"—and here his mind formed a quick analogy—"a stone in a lake. The ripples flow out to every part of this state and then to every part of America. People look at you, and they see what you do, and it gives them courage to go on. You have a grave responsibility. You are engaged in a politics as small as whether the garbage gets picked up, and a politics as large as whether the world gets blown up. You set the standards for the rest of us. It's very embarrassing for me to come here from Georgia, because, unlike you, we don't have our politics together yet. We also have a man running for governor. His name is C. B. King, and I'm about the only black elected leader in the state who's supporting him! People become afraid. You've heard only too often what they say to us, that we might make some of our white friends angry."

"Yeah! That's right!" came some voices from the audience, and Bond wound up by telling them that they certainly didn't need someone like himself to zip in from out of the state to lead them. "You need the leadership that has come out of yourselves," he said. "To find your real leader, just look in the mirror."

Later the delegates broke for lunch. They lined up outside a small, concrete, one-room building, and they filed inside to get some spareribs and cans of cold soda. They came outside again and ate in groups at benches and tables set up under the trees.

Bond wandered about, holding court with various little clusters of people that collected around him, and again he felt a strong sense of history in this place, in these people, many of whom were old-timers in the struggle for civil rights, having come out of the movement with Martin Luther King from nearby Montgomery (just twelve miles to the north) and from over in Selma or Birmingham.

"You have to take an historical approach," he told me as we picked at the spareribs. "First, because people need to be reminded of their victories. And this state, Alabama, has had a lot of them. Particularly now it's important to see things in perspective, at a time when Northern activists are denigrating the *whole* past of the civil-rights movement, and saying that *nothing* has been accomplished, that *no* victories were ever won. And you need to have a sense of *movement,* as well. To see that you've moved from place X to place Y to place Z, and that you want to go to place A. And I think it helps people if you remind them of where they *have* been, where they've *gone* from there, and where they *may* go, in the future."

Dr. Cashin, who would be nominated to run for governor against Wallace later in the day, stopped over to chat with Bond. The two were good friends, Dr. Cashin, a dentist, having put caps on Bond's teeth a while back, for which the younger man was extremely grateful. On the plane, Bond had said of Dr. Cashin, "He's an unusual guy, in that he's personally, financially pretty well off. Both from his dental practice and I understand he has business investments, too. And he's not the kind of guy who, in the black community, is usually associated with grass-roots politics. That's *one* thing that makes him unique. The second thing is that he uses his own income, his own wealth, his own affluence to further the cause that he's interested in, which again makes him different from most politicians, black or white, who are reluctant to use their own money for anything. A great many politicians are well-financed, but they'll use other people's money, they won't use their own—on the theory that if you have to use your own money, then nobody else is interested in what you're doing. But Cashin is not afraid to do that, and he's not afraid to make alliances, of any sort, that will help bolster his position, without at all compromising. For instance, he's worked out some kind of arrangement with Elijah Muhammad and the Nation of Islam. He and Mr. Muhammad own a plane, jointly, and Mr. Muhammad and the Nation own property, farmlands, in Greene County, which immediately begins to provide farming employment for people that Cashin is helping to give political employment or representation to as well. Yet he also, despite all this, has a fine relationship with a very, very few white liberals in Alabama. And with liberals in the Democratic Party all over the country. He's a member of the New Democratic Coalition, and he works very hard at maintaining all those relationships that he's established. He's just really an unusual guy."

Dr. Cashin's home was in Huntsville, Alabama. For a long time his father had been the *only* dentist, black or white, in Huntsville, and therefore had developed an interracial clientele. Dr. Cashin himself still had both black and white clients, although for now he had just about given up the practice of dentistry in order to give himself to the political activity. The NDPA, of which he was chairman, had a more moderate tone than its predecessor, the Lowndes County Freedom Organization, or Black Panther Party, as it was popularly known. At the head of the statewide ticket, Dr. Cashin had virtually no hope of beating Wallace, but he could seriously weaken him by drawing away the nearly 300,000 black voters in Alabama who comprised 30 percent of the electorate. As Bond had put it, "Cashin can say, 'Vote for the Eagle' and get many more black voters coming out to vote for him, at the top, and to vote the straight ticket all the way down." The campaign for governor was a symbol of new black political strength, and also a mechanism for winning local offices in black-belt counties all over the state.

The Alabama dentist and the young man from Georgia talked about the lack of jobs and good schools, and about the desperate need for better medical care in rural areas like this one, and Julian Bond mentioned that he was scheduled to speak at the upcoming convention for black dentists to be held in a plush hotel in Miami Beach. Dr. Cashin put his arm around Julian, and as they walked, he said, "You tell 'em they ought to be down here in the woods, instead of in Miami."

2.

We had about thirty minutes to make the three o'clock plane back to Atlanta that afternoon. While at the convention at Flowers Lake, Bond had kept looking at his watch as if he didn't dare trust anyone else to worry about his schedule, and indeed they were all asking him to stay on through the proceedings until evening. "Or why don't you stay overnight?" someone asked, causing Bond to look at his watch with even more agitation. When it was suggested that we should leave right away if we wanted to make the plane, Bond was the first one to stride off down the hill toward the car. When we got there, the station wagon was jammed in between several other cars along the narrow dirt roads. "Looks like we're stuck," said the driver, and Bond, exasperated but calm on the surface, hopped from the car and began clearing away some large fallen tree branches and logs in order to provide an escape route. "I hate to cut things this close," he remarked as we heaved one of the long logs out of the way. "Somehow, I feel a deep hunger to get back to Atlanta, back to my district. I'd like to see Billy Eckstine again—but beyond that, I just want to *be* there. You'd be surprised how people think I'm never there. They see me in Atlanta and say, 'What are you doing *here?*' and I say, 'What do you mean, I *live* here.' They think I'm never home! So at least I'll be there, tonight, if we make the plane. Not that I expect any of my constituents to call for assistance from me to-night—it's just that I'll be able to *say* I was there."

Back in the car and on the highway at last, drenched in new sweat because of the exertion with the branches, Bond leaned back, lighted a cigarette, and checked his watch again. He was gazing out at the backwoods Alabama countryside that was going by when someone in the front seat broke the silence abruptly: "What's going on in the colleges?"

It was one of those sweeping questions that almost beg for a sarcastic reply. And yet Bond was a Method actor, because even though he knew his lines he seemed to be saying them for the first time and without a trace of annoyance: "Well, the students seem to be hungering for either a definite program or a leader. I get question after question about Ted Kennedy and Gene McCarthy, as though I were their confidant. But the students are confused.

I could stand up in front of a college audience and spell out, say, a five-point program, but they'd refute it point by point, no matter what it was. They're confused, and they're also a changing group. Some kids are just learning what others have already learned. . . ."

A short while later, in response to a shift in the conversation to black studies, Bond remarked, "I think it's a very fine exercise for us to be able, in an academic surrounding, to be able to study our own history and so on, but what bothers me about a lot of the black students I see in black-studies courses is that they don't seem to be able to make a connection between the history they study and the present in which they live. They make no application of the ideologies they may pick up, the lessons they may learn. It's a phenomenon that I've seen on a great many college campuses— where the black students are caught up in what you might call the Malcolm X Syndrome. That is, they will listen to Malcolm X's tapes or records, or read his autobiography, but they won't apply the lesson that they've learned, the lesson he was espousing—which was, I think, that you need organization, and you need to be in-volved with people. And too many students, I find, can quote from Malcolm X extensively, on every subject, but don't put his quotations or his ideology into any kind of action. It's an intellec-tual exercise only, and as such I think it's a failure. It has no living application."

The car swerved into the airport grounds and pulled up along-side the main door of the terminal. "Wonder which gate we're at," Bond said, nearly running through the corridor. Sixty seconds after he stepped on board the plane, the door closing behind him immediately, it rolled down the runway and lifted into the air.

3.

He went home that night as planned, to his wife Alice and the five children in his new house in Atlanta, a brick house painted yellow with black iron gates on all the doors and windows, set back from an unprepossessing street, Sunset Avenue, N.W. In ad-dition to his separate office, he often went downstairs to the base-ment of the new house, where he was surrounded by bookshelves, honorary diplomas, a Vietnam Moratorium poster, a few portrait sketches of himself in shorter hair but with the familiar brooding, intense look about him, the eyes squinted and lips pursed, and where he had installed a stereo set, a small black-leather sofa, and a round table encircling the white post in the center of the room. The basement had a white-tile floor and dark-wood paneling, with dozens of books on black history lining the shelves, a light-green electric typewriter poised on the desk, and on the wall above a Ben Shahn print with the words: "You have not converted a man because you have silenced him."

"I'd like to be an intellectual," he commented, now shuffling about in sandals, his blue short-sleeved shirt hanging loose. Not long ago he had appeared in the racially torn city of Cairo, Illinois, for a Black Solidarity Day rally and had read some of his own offhand poetry along with Imamu Baraka–LeRoi Jones, who had delivered his poem "Nationtime." "There's a tremendous intellectual difference between us," said Julian Bond. "He is, I consider, an intellectual. And I consider myself *wanting* to be an intellectual. He has a *razor* mind, just unbelievably sharp, and in addition to that, he has talent, as a writer, poet, playwright. And the third difference is that he is probably less compromising than I am. He just has a singlemindedness that I don't have, in pursuing his vision."

Intellectual or not, Bond was much in demand for precisely that quality he admired in LeRoi Jones. What people, black people most of all, want from Julian Bond is a kind of leadership which he is not fully capable of giving them. They ask him, if not in words then with a collective anticipation that you can feel when he gets up to speak, to tell them, as the man on the platform at Flowers Lake had said, "where we're going and how we'll get there." You can hear it in their mood: *Lead us, Julian Bond.* And he seems to be trying to tell them: *There is no single leader, that time is past; now, we must all lead ourselves, together.*

He was scheduled to leave around noon the next day, from Atlanta by plane to Chicago, then from Chicago at 9 P.M. to Miami Beach, the following day on to Memphis, Tennessee, and back to Atlanta.

I met him in the plane just before takeoff the next day, Sunday, and he was sitting near the aisle, wearing a bright pink short-sleeved shirt, his shoes off, and reading the Sunday New York

Times. Alice was sitting beside him next to the window. We arrived at 12:30 P.M. at the airport in Chicago, nearly an hour earlier than the time he was supposed to be met, so it became a matter of stalling around, waiting. He and Alice went downstairs to get their bags, then back up to the main lobby, and decided to get some ice cream at a counter. Then Bond had to stand in line for a while in order to get Alice's plane ticket straightened out. A young black couple came up and greeted him, then moved away, and later some small black girls in party dresses stopped for his autograph. In fact, many of the black people in the terminal recognized him, by the Afro, the face, the slim slouching form of him, but almost none of the whites even looked, much less made the identification.

We went back to the entrance of the main corridor of O'Hare, the point you have to pass in order to get to or from most of the gates, and we sat down like kids on the low black radiator that extended along the wall beneath the huge glass windows. "Maybe we'll see some famous people," said Bond, meaning it. "I'll bet just about *everybody* comes by here, at one time or another." Including Julian Bond, I thought but didn't say, as we sat there watching the huge procession of humanity, back and forth, in front of us. A black serviceman came over and shook Bond's hand.

"Just getting home?"

"No, man. Just going."

"Vietnam?"

"Yep."

They chatted a while, and it occurred to me that Julian Bond wasn't acting like your ordinary well-known person, he was talking to this guy as if they were old friends, buddies, no big laughs or slaps on the back, just one guy rapping to another guy; and while Bond might forget about it five minutes later, the black serviceman would carry this moment around with him during his whole tour of duty and even after, assuming there was going to be an after for him.

"Stick with it," he told Julian, who nodded, seeming to know what he meant. "Is this *Mrs.* Bond, by the way?"

Alice, who is at once shy-acting and playfully sharp, replied, "No."

"Oh," the serviceman returned, embarrassed.

After he had left, Julian Bond turned to his wife and said,

"What'd you say that for? You probably gave him the wrong idea."

"He didn't look very surprised," she answered, smiling at her ability to keep him on his toes.

"Well, looks like they're not here to meet us," said Bond after a while. "Where's that letter they sent?"

Alice opened her purse to get the letter and two small vodka bottles from the plane trip fell out and rolled across the floor of the airport terminal, causing her to blush and turn away as if she might disappear. Bond retrieved the bottles and then took the letter, which was addressed to "Brother Bond." He read it over and folded it up, muttering, "We probably missed them."

"Typical," Alice said almost to herself.

We wound up lugging the bags downstairs, down the escalator and outside, where we boarded an airport bus which eventually took us to the Conrad Hilton Hotel.

"They're supposed to have rented a 'hospitality' suite for us in the hotel," Bond said, but when he asked about it at the desk, he drew blank stares from everyone. "They don't have any 'hospitality' suite," he reported. "Well, let's get some lunch."

After leaving the bags with a porter, we ordered some steaks in the hotel restaurant. The waiter, who was white, made a big fuss over Bond, who in turn was recalling some of the wild scenes from the 1968 Democratic National Convention. He showed Alice where the plate-glass window had caved in when the police had rushed into the crowd. Midway through lunch he became certain beyond all doubt that the man sitting alone at a table against the wall was none other than Glen Campbell, the singer. "I'm positive that that's him," said Bond, barely able to restrain himself from going over to ask for an autograph. It took the rest of the lunch, and much furtive scrutiny of the man, to determine that, no, it wasn't Glen Campbell after all.

From the Hilton we went by taxi to a building in the southwest section of Chicago, arriving shortly after four o'clock. We were ushered through a hallway to a small back room, where we sat and waited, with drinks, for something to happen. A young black woman asked Julian Bond if he'd like to hold a press conference for the reporters, wherever they were, and he shook his head, adding, "Let them buy a ticket."

The scheduled event, to take place upstairs in a large dining hall, was the second annual benefit for the Helen Robinson Library and Study Center, a one-room storefront on South Wentworth Avenue run by volunteers whose purpose was to further black culture and educational opportunity, and according to a brochure, "to reaffirm history in our everyday life, to practice self-control and to live together in peace." The evening's session was billed as "Raps and More Raps," and the rapping was going to be about "Today's Youth, Tomorrow's Leaders." Bond and Nathan Hare, publisher of *Black Scholar* magazine, were the guest speakers.

Nathan Hare arrived, seating himself opposite Julian and Alice, and soon a young female reporter from *Muhammad Speaks*, the Black Muslim newspaper, came in and requested an interview. In the process of asking the questions she wound up answering them as well, leaving little for them to say, and only once, briefly, did she take any notes. "In other words, Mr. Bond," she said, answering another of her own questions, "you still believe that working within the system is worthwhile?"

Bond said yes, started to clarify, and was asked, "Are you a pessimist?" He replied yes, but— "Would you characterize Nixon as antiblack?"

"Oh, yes. Definitely."

"Which is the larger issue—race or class?"

"Well, I think you could make a case that race is the bigger issue. We have to worry about how we're treated, not only because we're poor, but because we're black people. Because that's the major reason why so many of us are poor."

"What is your view of the gang situation in Chicago, Mr. Bond?"

"Well, I think the gang kids have to feel the disapproval of their own community. . . ."

After the interview and more waiting, we went outside, where a televison camera was set up, and Bond was trapped by a white interviewer who pumped him with questions. Then he was surrounded by an assortment of black people, many in colorful robes, a few snapping pictures or holding tape-recorder microphones near to him, and he signed a batch of autographs. Near six o'clock we went upstairs to the dining hall, where people who had purchased tickets were sitting at large round tables facing a low-level stage at one side of the room. There was an invocation, then the singing of James Weldon Johnson's poem:

> Lift every voice and sing
> Till earth and heaven ring. . . .
> We have come over a way
> That with tears has been watered,
> We have come, treading our path
> Through the blood of the slaughtered.
> Out of a gloomy past,
> Till now we stand at last
> Where the white gleam of our
> Bright star is cast.

And after more singing, some poetry and other readings, "the Most Honorable Julian Bond" was introduced. He went to the microphone, to a standing ovation, and spoke of the young blacks, of oppressed people in Vietnam and Cuba and Alabama, and referred to blacks in the United States as "America's own domestic colony." He said we were likely to see more violence in the future and told them that effective movements could only be built by many people, not by the few. He said a movement must be built to "take control of institutions" affecting black lives and that such a movement "must consume all our waking hours."

After Nathan Hare spoke, the "rap session" began. People stood up and asked questions, at times with much emotion and confusion, one black man exclaiming, "I'm so balled up I just don't know who to follow anymore." After a discussion that rambled over a dozen subjects, resolving none, there was an African dance put on by some young girls, and then some socializing and, for Bond, more photographs and autographs. A black girl cornered him and said, "You like dope?"

"No."

"You should."

"Well, what kind?"

"Speed."

"Well, speed kills, doesn't it?"

"No, it's nice. You should try it."

We were driven back to the airport in time for a couple of quick hot dogs and then the nine o'clock plane, and Julian and Alice fell asleep for most of the ride, arriving somewhat dazed in Miami Beach near one in the morning. In their hotel room in the Plaza, Julian discovered that someone back in Chicago had broken into his small suitcase. A leather case had been ripped open, and the cuff links that matched one of his shirts had been stolen, along with a pearl-handled switchblade knife he had brought for protection.

4.

Bond was scheduled to speak to more than a thousand black dentists and their wives in the large Elegante Room in the Plaza Hotel at around 9:30 the next morning. The theme of the convention was "The Black Dentist Biting into Real Issues," which made Bond chuckle out loud. He hated Miami Beach and everything it stood for, and beyond that he didn't think much of the dental association, either. He was also going to speak to the black *doctors'* convention later in the week, "in the plushest hotel in Atlanta."

"They're similar," he said. "The black doctors, who are the most affluent class of people in the black community, allow their professional association to be controlled by outside interests, the drug companies. The same used to be true with the black disk jockeys—their professional association was controlled by the record companies. And the dentists, I'm sure it's true about them, too. It's just horrendous to me that the people that you do business with will finance you in convention, where you're supposed to be sort of discussing things independently. It's just the worst kind of buy-off. Every professional group in the world does it, I suppose, but I don't like to see it done. The dentists—meeting in Miami in the midst of all this affluence, and spending a lot of money, which I'm sure they've worked very hard for, pulling many teeth and filling many cavities—it just rubs me the wrong way, that's all."

But few of the dentists could have known these feelings of his, and after all, he had come all the way down here to be their keynote speaker. He was up there at the head table with seventeen other people, all much older than he—and then I realized they wanted Bond here *because* of that kind of viewpoint, because he was young and militant and therefore functional. He would shake them up a bit, give them a little reminder of what was really going on in the black struggle while they spent the remainder of their time and money in the Florida sun.

He received a big introduction: "A young man who has battered down the bastions of hate and bigotry. . . . His peers, mesmerized by his charisma, captivated by his charm, forgot his tender age and nominated him for Vice-President of the United States."

He began with a joke about Spiro Agnew, praised the dentists for their good works, acknowledging the importance of health care —and then he pulled out some statistics relating to poor people ("Death comes much easier to them"), noting that there are 30 million people who are unable to afford proper medical care, that "private practitioners have a responsibility to the poor," that there are 116 counties in the nation with neither a doctor nor a dentist and many more with only one, that there is a lot of exploitation in rural areas especially—in all, a grim picture. "You people should be different," he said. "You have a different responsibility. You must continue, as you have done, to make sure the interests of the consumer are overriding." Then he covered a wide spectrum of issues—education, military spending, the urban crisis—and wound up reminding them of the struggle, of the emotions they had invited him to remind them of. The dentists stood up and roared.

We had lunch in the hotel with a young black dentist from South Carolina who had gone to college with Bond, and they reminisced about their school days—getting drunk once at a football game, the good old times. "I just can't get over that *Honorable* Julian Bond stuff," said the young dentist.

In the hotel lobby, looking out at the swimming pool, the ocean, the palm trees, Bond posed for pictures, signed more autographs, all with that attractive civility and courtesy and grace he is so famous for, the gentleman militant from Georgia, with Alice tagging along but trying to avoid the photographers.

On the two o'clock plane to Memphis, Bond read part of a *Life* magazine, noting a picture of Julie and David Eisenhower, the latter looking "like Mortimer Snerd." For some reason I asked him what he would say to the young Eisenhower couple if, by wild perchance, he were to find himself locked in a room with them for an hour. "We'd exchange pleasantries, then say nothing. I'd have nothing to say." A moment later he added, "They'd probably talk about school."

For the final hour of the plane ride, Bond was certain, again beyond all reasonable doubt, that sitting behind us was none other than Jean-Claude Killy, the skier. The man behind us was with a young woman. "They both have French accents," said Bond. "Maybe they're using assumed names, traveling clandestinely. They were probably *water*-skiing, off Miami Beach." Right on, Julian, but again it turned out not to be a Famous Person after all.

The plane descended through the thick clouds and circled over the sprawling green hills of Tennessee, and as soon as we came off the ramp in Memphis, we were swept up by a delegation of blacks holding placards. I noted with interest the emergence of one face from the crowd, coming toward Bond with a big grin and a huge hand on the shoulder, and, now playing Bond's Famous People game, had the notion that it was Charles Evers, the mayor of Fayette, Mississippi.

Ten

1.

"How are ya, Julian?" said Evers, a big bear of a man with bloodshot eyes and a brooding, sorrowful look that failed to vanish from his face even when he smiled. He was wearing a pale-yellow short-sleeved shirt and a tie with no jacket, and next to him Bond seemed like a sleek young deer, an Ivy League, intellectual cat with a bushy Afro, reserved in manner and somewhat sleepy, maybe bored. The Memphis crowd had no idea where he had come from or where he was going. All the fifty or so black people on hand at the airport knew was that he was here, he and Charles Evers, two of the biggest black political wheels in the country, come all the way to help them, and somehow they had to make every moment of it count. They were in the final week of an election campaign, and like all other people involved in politics, but really more so than most, they were filled with hope to the point where it virtually blinded them to the possibility—no, probability—of losing. Although blacks comprised 40 percent of Shelby County, they still had no representation in its government, none at all, and by God, this was the hour of change, a whole history might be reversed in its tracks. This was the high peak of their campaign—Julian Bond and Charles Evers!—so they jostled around, almost beside themselves with excitement and yet with strangely grim expressions, some walking backward up ahead, others frontward from behind, still others moving sideways, forming a circle around the two celebrities, like a swarm of bees, and heading swiftly along the corridors of the airport, up a ramp and into a tiny conference room specially reserved for a meeting with the press.

Bond was ushered into a seat at the head of the long, marble-topped conference table. Evers, who had been interviewed earlier by the handful of reporters, took a chair in an obscure part of the narrow, rectangular room, which was now filled to overflowing. Along one wall was a group of very young black girls in yellow dresses and straw campaign hats, holding election posters. They were not from Memphis, it turned out, but from Fayette, Mississippi, brought up by Evers in a bus. "My own delegation," he said with pride. "Ain't they something, though?"

Flanking Bond at the far end of the table were two of the black candidates in the local election—Melvin Robinson, an insurance salesman running for sheriff of Shelby County, and Harrel C. Moore, candidate for county commissioner. "Mr. Bond," said one of the three white newsmen present, "what is your purpose in coming here to Memphis?" The inference in his tone was clear: What do you, an *outsider*, mean by coming in here and stirring things up?

"Well," said Bond, coming to life suddenly for the television camera, "I'm here to support the black candidates who, in the judgment of people I know in this city, will be good for the people of Memphis."

The reporters then informed him that a local Negro political figure, O. Z. Evers by name, was supporting the white candidate for sheriff, Roy Nixon. According to the reporters, O. Z. Evers had urged Melvin Robinson, the black candidate, to get out of the race because he hadn't any chance of winning.

"You go ahead and say what'cha feel," said Charles Evers to Julian. " 'Cause that O. Z. Evers, he ain't no kin to me!"

Hardly needing any such prompting, Bond replied, "It's a shame that black people do that way."

"It has been suggested, Mr. Bond, that blacks shouldn't *waste* their votes on black candidates who can't win."

"Well, black people aren't fooled by that trick any more," Bond returned. "We have to get away from our *own* myths about ourselves. We have to get away from that old self-hate. We have to point out the truth, that the white sheriffs just haven't done a good job. We can't keep letting other people set the standards for us. We just got to stop fooling ourselves with the myth that the white man's ice is colder, that his sugar is sweeter, that his medicine is stronger. There's nothing wrong with people voting as a bloc. White people have always done it. They voted for George Wallace and Richard Nixon as a bloc, but no one called it that. As soon as we vote black, it's called a bloc vote, and people say it's wrong. But when whites do the same thing, it's called something else, and people say it's something good and beneficial. Every other ethnic group has gotten together, every white group, and now it's time for the black bloc vote to rise up."

Nothing could have pleased the audience more. This tremendously important person named Julian Bond, one of the few national black heroes, had come all the way to Memphis, personally, for *them,* and he wasn't afraid of anything. If *he* wasn't afraid to say these things, then *they* would have the courage to stand up to the white people after he was gone. But while he was here, they roared their approval of what he was daring to say.

What impressed me in Bond's remarks was that he was defining a viewpoint which had been evolving over the past few years in towns and cities all across the country where blacks were a sizable portion of the population but with no representation. In the first place, no longer were black people content merely to throw their support to the lesser of two evils, either to a white man *or* to a black candidate who failed to articulate their needs forthrightly. It was no wonder that in the past there had been so much apathy in the black community when it came to politics, given the lack of alternatives offered, but now they were getting behind their *own* candidates, whether they could win or not, and to hell with those who would use them as pawns. Moreover, Bond was saying that the old standards for deciding who was qualified or not were no longer relevant or even accurate. First of all, there was no way that blacks could be qualified for leadership, in the usual sense, since they had been deliberately and systematically denied the opportunity to gain experience in the political process, not to mention experience in government itself. And as far as the black community should be concerned, the candidate they wanted didn't need to have a college degree, didn't need to be a lawyer, didn't need to be a professional politician. He needed only a concern for the poor and oppressed; his *attitude* was what counted most, and the experience would come later. Melvin Robinson, the insurance man, was sitting there looking like a farmer, not even a *potential* sheriff. By all standards of white American culture he was absolutely unfit to become the chief law-enforcement officer of Shelby or any other county. Yet by the black community's standards, he was the only candidate they could count on to represent their interests. Knowing their viewpoint, and unchained to the white political structure, he would become *their* sheriff as well as the sheriff of the whites; he would assume office with a concern for fairness and justice and equal treatment; and in so doing, he would also benefit the white community by reducing tension and hostility, although it was too much to expect most whites to believe, or understand, that irony.

2.

When the press conference was over, Evers' girls lined up for a few rousing chants, and then everyone charged out of the room through the airport terminal to the front of the building, where a motorcade, of sorts, was waiting. Melvin Robinson's campaign manager, an energetic black man with a voice half-gone from shouting at rallies and meetings, told me that this moment was "the turning point" in the campaign for county sheriff. "I went down to Fayette to see Mayor Evers," he said, out of breath from excitement. "I went down there, and I *begged* him to come up to Memphis and help us out, to give us a boost. I even got down on my knees and *prayed* with him, and that convinced him to come. He said, 'How can I refuse?' So he promised to come, and he called Julian Bond and got him to come, too. It'll make the black people realize the *importance* of this election. They'll start to believe that they have a chance! I tell you, this is the turning point!"

Bond and Evers got into one of the cars near the front of the motorcade, which was actually just a line of cars with a few posters on them. (There was no great crush of people lining the roadsides for it anyway, since the white-controlled media apparently had avoided giving any advance publicity to the arrival of the two black celebrities.) Julian Bond was signing autographs, as usual, and

Alice was going along in her quiet way, seeming to blush whenever singled out for attention.

I got into a car with Evers' security man, Alphonso Deal. He had come up to Memphis from Fayette a few days earlier in order to inject some degree of order and logic into the local planning for the mayor's appearances. Deal was a professional cop from Philadelphia, Pennsylvania, winding up a year's leave of absence from that city's police force. He had spent much of his time trying to professionalize, train, educate, and supervise Fayette's seven-man department, although his main job, as it was at the moment, had been to protect Charles Evers from meeting with the same fate as that of his slain brother, Medgar. The driver of our car swerved into the motorcade behind the car carrying Bond and Evers, and Deal noted that he had had a difficult time trying to make plans for security because there was such a lack of planning to begin with. As he said this, a white woman drove up, saw the carloads of black folks, and leaned on her horn, yelling something from behind her rolled-up windows and locked doors. We moved off, through the outskirts of Memphis, and at an intersection two white men in a blue pickup truck jeered at us before driving away. "Hostility," muttered Deal, and at that point the driver of our car informed us that we were nearly out of gas. "You're kidding," said Deal as we pulled out of the motorcade and into a gas station. From then on, we never did catch up with the other cars again. Deal, now completely frustrated, looked ready to hop out and walk in disgust all the way back to Philadelphia.

As we drove around looking for the lost motorcade, the local news came on the car radio. There was a report of the first airport press conference, the one Evers had presided over. In response to a statement by O. Z. Evers, the local Negro politician, that a black man couldn't win the sheriff's contest, we heard Charles Evers reply, "Any black man who says that is sicker than a white racist." And now that the man he was trying to protect had become the most controversial figure in a place that was already hostile, Officer Deal slumped down in his seat, hoping for the best.

About a half hour later, we drove into a black neighborhood to Mel Robinson's house, where the motorcade had either ended or dissolved. Evers and Bond had already arrived. They were sitting in the enclosed patio in the rear of the house, talking quietly and occasionally watching television. Later, over a terrific dinner of ham, baked beans, biscuits, iced tea, and several other choices of food, Evers entertained Julian and Alice and everyone within earshot with an outporing of anecdotes and opinions ranging in subject matter from the late Robert Kennedy to watermelon. The man was so animated and full of energy that he could barely sit still. Several times, during lulls in the conversation, he would abruptly say things like "We got to get out to the people" or "I wanna see some folks!" Sometimes he spoke so fast that it was almost impossible to follow his train of thought, and he seemed to mix everything together—politics, social comment, comedy, tragedy —as if he could not contain within himself all the conflicting and entangling thoughts that came to him. Next to Evers, Julian Bond began to look several years younger than he was, almost like a pupil in a classroom.

When Bond asked if he had been paid for his work in Kennedy's 1968 Presidential campaign, Evers said, "Hell, no, I never take money for that. You don't take money from politicians, 'cause if you do, they'll think they don't owe you anything." It was obvious that Evers enjoyed talking about Kennedy, with whom he had come to feel a strong kinship. "Bobby was always cussing," he reminisced. "Always cussing. I really loved that Bobby. He started out as ignorant about us black folks as anyone could be, but he learned. He wasn't afraid to learn."

Somewhere along in the dinner conversation, Evers mentioned that he was thinking of running for governor of Mississippi. "I'm gonna run a *poor* man's campaign," he said. "I'm *always* gonna run a poor man's campaign." He elaborated at length, explaining that instead of buying a lot of television commercials he'd go around the state with sound trucks in order to "go to the people."

"You got to speak to the people!" he went on. "We got to remind our folks of the past! Not just history, but what they just gone through. If you're in Detroit, you gotta bring up the riot. Got to remind folks of the beatings, the jailings, the chains, got to talk about these things. . . . I could be the best governor we ever had in Mississippi, 'cause I'd be concerned about the welfare of the people. But first I gotta do a good job in Fayette. If I was governor, my first order of business would be to get the people together."

"Julian," he said later, "you and Alice should take off a few days and come down to Fayette for a visit. Just come on down and relax. Maybe we should have 'days' for people every now and then. Just come down and visit, any time, and we'll hold a 'day' for you."

Bond nodded, answering that he might do that.

"We're building new roads for our people," Evers said. "We don't take bids for our road work, though. No, sir."

"You don't?" asked Bond, nearly choking on his food.

"Hell, no. I don't want no white racist to come in and underbid our local people. No white racist is gonna come in and build *our* roads and sewers—no, sir."

Bond stared at him with an expression of both awe and amusement.

"Look," Evers explained, "they can't put me in jail for building roads, can they? We hired a local man—a white fella, by the way—with local labor, to build streets. Sure, I didn't follow the law! What's the law ever done for us? Our folks never had paved streets. Never!"

Evers went on to say that he had introduced other things to Fayette, and he ticked off a list of them. "We got a law against cussing, too," he added. "No cussing in Fayette, that's right. And no hitting women, either. Now, I'm tellin' ya." And he told a story of how he was driving out of town one day when he saw a white man selling watermelon on the roadside. "I turned the car around and went back to the Town Hall, got my aldermen together, and we passed a law against selling watermelon on the road, that's right. I'm just *sensitive* about that kind of thing, you know? It's that whole image of black folk dancing, singing, clowning like fools, eating watermelon—we got to get away from that old image. It's degrading."

The first scheduled event after dinner was a rally. Rising from his chair, Evers reminded everyone in the living room, especially those who were going to speak to the crowd, to call him Mr. Mayor and to refer to Julian as Representative Bond. "Give us those *titles*," he said. "We got to teach our people what it's like for black folks to have respect. Now, let's go see those folks. I hope there's a lot of 'em, because I'm in the mood to talk to 'em. Come on, let's go see the folks!"

3.

On the way to the rally I rode in the car with Mel Robinson, the black candidate for sheriff, in whose house we had just eaten. On the car radio, a local station was giving the news, and while the Evers–Bond press conferences were only several hours old, the station was already broadcasting the reactions of local politicians. We heard O. Z. Evers of Memphis challenge Charles Evers to a debate. "Negroes in Memphis have been voting for seventy-five years," said O. Z., "and we don't need anybody, white or black, coming in from out of state—and that goes for Julian Bond, too— to tell us how to vote. For Charles Evers to tell us how to vote is ridiculous. Negroes have only been voting in Mississippi for a few years. For him to advocate voting for a man just because he is black is racism."

In the front seat of the car, Mel Robinson angrily denounced what he called the "biased press" in Memphis, but his mood was really more one of despair than of anger. "The whites control the media," he said, "and they stop communication! They're trying to stop people from coming to this rally!" He said the "power structure" had avoided any advance notice of Evers' and Bond's arrival—and in fact, the media were now publicizing *reaction* to their statements and neglecting to report the statements themselves. "Think of it!" Robinson exclaimed. "We have Charles Evers and Julian Bond! We should have had *coverage* about their coming here! But they blocked it out! Evers—there's a guy, well, he oughtta be in the United Nations! But the white press blocks it out, and we can't afford to buy any television time. Now, after Evers gets here, they cover him only as a *wedge to divide* the black people."

From what I could gather, the black voters of Shelby County, although a third of the electorate, were still convinced in great numbers that politics was, as Bond had said elsewhere, white man's business. They were distrustful and afraid and confused and frag- mented. Middle-class blacks like O. Z. Evers were still supporting white candidates, which alone was not a fault, but in so doing they were turning their backs on the vast majority of blacks who were still poor and still unrepresented by their government. Local black ministers had even denied the grass-roots campaigners access to their churches until it became clear that the community was becoming aroused.

"We had to start our campaign at the bottom," said Lee Branch, Robinson's campaign manager. "We had to go underground, so to speak, and work among the poor blacks first. Then, we go to the middle-class blacks, and later the whole community." There were six white candidates for sheriff, and Branch was hoping that they would split the white vote among themselves, allowing Robinson, with united black support, to come out ahead.

But all of this strategy was only on paper. The fact was, they simply hadn't the money or the media or the time or the experience to make it work. They had done the job on the grass-roots level, but it was only the necessary beginning.

"If this race is lost," Robinson said as we pulled up near the location of the rally, "black people are gonna lose a whole lot of hope."

4.

The turnout was disappointing. We were out in a semirural section of the county, in a poor neighborhood, on a vacant lot full of pebbles and weeds next to Ware's Grocery and Market, surrounded by tall grass and standing under a hot blistering sun that made it seem like noon rather than six o'clock in the evening. There were maybe two hundred black folks here altogether, maybe half of them too young to vote. Evers' girls were singing, "Julian Bond's got so-o-o-ul!" Older black folks stood watching them, as if trying to comprehend. Lee Branch jumped onto the back of a green pickup truck and tested the microphone. When he saw that it worked, he screamed, "Everyone come on up here, so we can get the *thing* going!"

Bond climbed aboard the truck, his coat off, and he stood there while one of the girls led the chorus in some vibrant soul singing. Evers mingled in the crowd, shaking hands and sending out the vibrations of his apparently inexhaustible energy. Alice remained near the edge of the vacant lot, chatting with some of the women, one of whom carried a baby on her back.

Lee Branch was speaking now, his voice croaking: "O. Z. Evers came from the old school! They sold us out! For Cadillac cars, for big government contracts, for big houses! Black folks got to learn to *help* black folks! Do you realize that Charles Evers is *mayor* of Fayette? And Julian Bond, that he was *elected* by his folks? These two men have given their time to come help black folk in Memphis, but black folk *from* Memphis say they can't come—that's a disgrace! The only thing Roy Nixon is promising you is a bigger jail! And that's why we need Mel Robinson in there as sheriff of Shelby County! And now I'm gonna introduce Representative Julian Bond. All the way from Atlanta, Georgia! They said he wouldn't be here, but here he is!"

Bond took the microphone and gave a short speech, rapidly delivered, urging everyone to go out and tell their neighbors, friends, and parents to vote. He told them that the election was important "for black people everywhere," and added, "You tell the doubters to just look at Mayor Evers. People said he wouldn't know how to run the government, but he's the best mayor they ever had."

By the time Evers got up on the truck he was ready to become the Big Daddy of them all. "Until you get men in office who care about *all* of us," he said, "there ain't gonna be any peace." He said that in Fayette he and his aldermen had told the white folks, "Now, you been in charge all these years, doing your thing. And now we're gonna do *our* thing. You may not *like* our thing, but we're gonna *do* it." True to his own previous advice, he reminded them of the terrible conditions that existed, giving a vivid picture of "young black men sleeping on cold steel beds in the jails. . . ."

"Elect our folk," he urged, "so we're free enough to walk up to the sheriff and tell him when he's right and when he's wrong. Don't be afraid to vote bloc! Don't get hung up on the fact that we're not qualified! I ain't seen a white man yet who was *born* a sheriff." And then he sort of leaned forward, as if to tell them a secret. "We're gonna end all this hate, all these rundown streets and shacks and shanties. We got to end the hatred and suppression that's still with us from over the years. Not by throwing bombs but by throwing votes!"

After the rally, which had been too small to make any real impact on the outcome of the election, we drove into Memphis to an apartment, where we sat around for about an hour, waiting for some liquor that never arrived (it turned out that the fellow bringing it had gotten trapped between floors in an elevator, but we didn't know that at the time). Bond mentioned to me that he felt the campaign was "incredibly poorly managed," and Alice added that the rally would have been much larger if it had been held near some housing projects, perhaps with a band and some entertainment.

Meanwhile, Evers was annoyed because one of the speakers had used the word "honkies" in referring to the white folks. "He shouldn't have used that word," Evers complained. "That's the kind of thing they called *us,* like 'nigger.' We can't start in with that. We got to be better than that. Somebody should tell these folks to loosen up on that kind of talk."

Evers was a little more subdued by this time, and he went to the window and stared gloomily at the skyline of Memphis. "Bad memories of this place," he said. "My wife didn't like me to come here, no sir." He had taken a room at the Lorraine Motel, on whose balcony Dr. Martin Luther King had been killed.

It was dark outside when we headed across town and through a black neighborhood—passing by Hustler's Discount Store and Afro Cleaners—to the small St. Paul Baptist Church. Bond and Evers were led through a side door and down a dark corridor, but that entrance was locked. We made an about-face and trooped up some stairs, down another dark corridor, someone leading the way with his cigarette lighter aflame, and finally into the church, which was only one fourth filled. Julian, looking tired and hot and rumpled and somewhat harried, began checking his watch again. "We should be on our way to the airport right now," he said in a low, worried tone.

We sat through some singing that made it seem as if the church was overflowing with people, and Bond was then introduced as "one of the most outstanding men in the United States, probably the first black man who'll be the President of the United States— he was too young, but he's growing older every day."

And Bond gave his grass-roots speech again, urging the audience to "make up your own minds" instead of "letting others tell you what to do." He told them not to be swayed by politicians, black or white, who pass out a few dollars or a bottle of wine at election time. "The issue is whether you're going to be represented, whether you're gonna get someone who'll *do for us*. Never mind the college degree—politics means that your garbage is collected, it means that the policeman doesn't call you 'Sally' or 'Joe.' To get your politics straight, I advise you to listen only to your own conscience."

As soon as he finished his speech, Bond checked his watch and said that we had to rush to the airport for the plane back to Atlanta. We left Evers at that point and just made it to the airport in time for boarding. As he was showing his ticket to the man at the gate, a young white fellow with long hair and a beard rushed up to him, out of breath. Bond, startled, looked at the man cautiously, as if wondering what to expect now.

"I recognized you!" said the bearded fellow to Bond. "And I just want you to know—I think you're a good ass."

Bond thought about that for a moment, rubbed his eyes, and answered, "Thank you."

5.

A few days later, all the black candidates that Bond and Evers had tried to help were defeated. Roy Nixon became the new Shelby County sheriff, with more than 61,000 votes. Another white man came in second, with 31,000, and Mel Robinson was third. He had gotten over 21,000 votes, which was a good beginning, but as expected the black community had split its votes in about four directions. And O. Z. Evers filed a $1-million suit against Charles Evers, charging that he had been slandered.

Eleven

1.

When Charles Evers was sworn in as the first black mayor of Fayette, Mississippi, on July 7, 1969, he reversed nearly a century of history in a single day. Although blacks are the majority both in Fayette and in Jefferson County, they had been kept down by white supremacy in every aspect of their lives. Few went past grade school; most were out of work and dependent on welfare; their health care was almost nonexistent; most lived in tin-roof shacks in unbearable heat and poverty. And while none of this can be reversed in a single day, black people now have the political power necessary to begin to change their lives. No longer do they live in the grip of terror. "We took the whole town away from white people," Evers declared, "and not a single Negro was beaten up. A few years ago, we'd have all been killed. Maybe that ain't much progress, but it's something."

And when he took that oath of office, Mayor Evers set forth a theme that he still repeats over and over:

> My white brothers, you don't have to fear as blacks once did when you drive through Fayette, because there's a black mayor there. We're not going to do to you what you did to us. But we're gonna make damn sure you're not going to do it to us again. . . . There will be no more hatred in Fayette, there will be no more guns carried around this town, there will be no more clowning and cursing in the streets and being

disrespectful to people. We are going to have a clean and decent town.

Everything comes together in Fayette, a dirt-poor, rural town in the heart of the Deep South, some fifty miles south of Vicksburg and twenty-three miles northeast of Natchez, crossroads of the old slave trade and center for the not-so-old activity of the Ku Klux Klan. It all comes together, because years and years of slow, painful black progress in America have been compressed into one small period of time. In microcosm, Charles Evers is setting out to prove in Fayette what may be the ultimate irony of America— that the people we brought to this country in chains are the ones who have the chance to set it free. If America's moral dilemmas have been created by its own racism, militarism, economic greed, and violent nature, then it is just possible that black folks, if given the chance, will be able to turn us around before it is too late. That is precisely what is going on in Fayette, whose history of racism, economic exploitation, and violence is as American as the proverbial apple pie.

2.

"We were in about as much hell as anyone could be," said Will T. Turner, one of the five black aldermen serving with Mayor Evers. We were sitting on the front steps of a little white church on the outskirts of town, watching the sun go down over a distant field that seemed to extend to the edge of the world. At age forty, Turner was the youngest of the aldermen, a tall, thin fellow, a man without formal education but whose simple, direct words went further in making the point than any narrative I could muster up:

"I grew up in Fayette. Nowadays, our young peoples is going farther. In our time, coming up, we had to work, and so we couldn't go to school. At one time, all the money we could earn was back in the cotton fields. We'd have to go out and chop cotton and gather corn. I went up to the eighth grade. The rest of my schooling is just mother wit. Most of it is a gift from God. After I got up and grown, and seeing that I didn't have a chance to go to school, I cultivated what I had. We used to walk six miles to school—rain, shine, or whatnot—and sometimes my shoes didn't have no bottoms in 'em. And as we were going to school, the whites would pass us on the bus, and spit at us, and throw spitballs and rocks and all, and jump us in the bushes.

"We couldn't walk the streets in peace up to a short while ago. You couldn't walk the streets on a Monday morning with a white shirt on, 'cause you were supposed to be out picking cotton. You couldn't be on that street unless you were a preacher or something, or they'd want to know what funeral you were going to. Like I'm dressed now, with a shirt and tie, I couldn't walk the streets this way, no. 'Get off this street,' they'd say. If a crowd of us got too numerous on a Saturday, they'd come put ashes all down our backs. The policeman would kick us or blackjack us on the street or spit tobacco juice on us. They'd put us in jail, kill us right up on the street in town, lynch us, mob us, and nothing was ever done about it. In '65, a black man was shot three times on the icehouse steps. He used to walk on cans and cups, and he shined shoes for a living. The white man who killed him, for nothing, shot him in the head three times. The sheriff never even put the man in jail. He was a stranger, and he was just escorted out of town, that's all. Never even a hearing on it. They shot us all the time, and never any punishment. But if you were black, you just didn't have a chance. They'd put us in jail, and once they put you there, they had you in a slaughterhouse.

"There was a time when we didn't know there *was* a City Hall or nothing. We didn't even know they had meetings. Only thing we knew, we'd go and pay our light bills, telephone bills. And on election day, we'd see all the peoples gathering in town, and we'd know they was voting, but we go *around* town, never through the crowd. Some black folks *claimed* they voted, but I don't know if they did or not.

"A lot of us were afraid, and we didn't have courage enough to step up. See, the whites always had done something to our minds. They always thought they were superior, and a lot of us thought so, too. So we never did get grown. The NAACP started here in '64, '65. When we said, 'NAACP,' we'd say it *low*, you see. And so actually it was sort of like a *secret* organization. See, we were living in fear. We wasn't *too* scared, but we knew we didn't have a chance.

You speak up, and they'd be ready to mob you till you get out of town, and if you didn't, they'd come for you and kill you. So that's why we was scared.

"When I got my NAACP card in '65, I had it wrapped in a piece of paper inside my wallet for a whole year. And one day I was in the City Hall, pulling out my Social Security card, and the first thing I pulled out was my NAACP card. Man, I started shaking. They'd mob you right away!

"When we started meeting, the Klan would ride in all around, and the sheriff was *with* 'em. We could just make a false statement that we was having a march, and all the highway patrolmen would be right here in town. The highways would be empty.

"During the making of our NAACP branch, they were bombing our churches, beating us, cutting people in two with a power saw, and throwing 'em down here in the river, burning our homes, threatening our lives, pulling us off our jobs, and all that. One man was bombed in his car. The Lord let him pull through, but he was crippled for life. And that's what started the ball rolling. We said, 'They're killing us for nothing, so at least let's die for *something*.' You know the story of the rabbits—the hounds, the horses, the cows, the mules, and the foxes were all after the rabbits, which was us. So the rabbits said, 'Let's go down to the river and drown ourselves.' So the rabbits all went down to the river, they got together, and suddenly all the hounds and foxes got scared and started running. Once the rabbits got together, once they got their minds together, they got strong.

"So when we had a march, we'd have a big one, all of us together. The first march, that's the only time my stomach ever went back onto by backbone. Mayor Evers was up there, and we knowed we was going to jail that night. We marched up there, and we seen the sheriff up there, the patrolmen, and whatnot, and we walked on up toward them. Mayor Evers was the NAACP field secretary then, so he was up there in front. He always wanted to lead the march, and we all wanted to be around him. And they had all those guns and billy clubs and auxiliary po-leece—they'd made policemen out of *everybody* that night, all rabbit hunters that night—and we walked on up there, and I just knew some guy was gonna get killed. My stomach went into my backbone. And what gave me courage was they said, 'Which way you want to go

—this way or that way?' And Mayor Evers replied, 'This way.' They said, 'Okay, go.' From then on, man, we were marching. There was so many of us, we scared 'em.

"See, we here strictly followed leadership. We all went to jail. If one went to jail, we all went. By the hundreds. We got beat by the hundreds. We got gassed by the hundreds. We formed marches from the churches. We'd come to mass meetings, and they'd shoot at us on the way. Shoot at us out of their cars as we were walking along the road.

"The important thing was we believe in God. They can't understand why we sing and pray. Somehow or other, God has answered our prayers. See, we *believe* in Him. That's all we ever had. If we didn't believe in God, we wouldn't be anywhere.

"We didn't intend to run an all-black slate. Only thing we asked for was three aldermen to represent us, even though we're 76 percent of the population. They could take the mayor and the other two aldermen. But they said, 'No, if we run with blacks on our slate, we don't know what the other whites'll say about us.' So they said they'd run an all-white slate. And therefore, we didn't have no choice. We ran an all-black slate, and we won everything from dog catcher on up to the mayor himself.

"What makes the white people afraid, now, is that they think we'll use the same old hate and prejudice toward them as what they used toward us. But we not gonna do that. We're gonna love 'em, treat 'em right, because we all are human beings."

3.

"Hear ye, hear ye! Po-leece Court, Town of Fayette, now in session. By order of Mayor Charles Evers."

He was not only the mayor, but the town judge and prosecuting attorney as well, and each Friday at 5 P.M., in a back room of his little red-brick City Hall, the court session gave him a chance to assume all of his varied roles at once. Sitting there behind the table in a white short-sleeved shirt, a gavel in his hand, Evers was mayor, judge, prosecutor, teacher, father, moral leader, and several other things, putting on a grand show for the folks in traditional small-town fashion. Here was justice in its most primitive, per-

sonal form—and God help you, black or white, if you've broken
the law. He had often told his folks that Fayette could become
"our Israel," meaning that here, if nowhere else in America, they
had the chance to build a new society from the ground up, to
start from the beginning, almost as if civilization itself were being
reborn in tiny Fayette, pop. 1,700.

Gathered in the courtroom on fold-up chairs, facing Judge
Evers, were mostly young blacks, boys and girls, but a few older
folks as well. Evers turned the whole thing into a kind of extra-
curricular schoolroom. It was a chance for him to educate the
youngsters, and the two dozen or so in the room clearly respected
his authority.

"I wish we didn't have to have this kind of session," he began,
using that fatherly tone of his. "But as long as persons break the
law, we have to have court. We make no exception. Anybody accused of any wrong has a right to come here and get a fair trial. It
makes no difference—black, white, blue, green, yellow, gold, cousin,
wife, husband, whatnot—it makes no difference. If you break the
law in this town, you gonna be tried, not for the color of your skin
or the texture of your hair, but for what you been charged. You're
gonna get justice, and *nobody* is an exception, from the mayor on
down. First case."

Some whispering followed at the judge's table, and then Evers
announced, "There'll be a slight delay until the accused gets some
counsel. That shows we mean to be fair in this court. There isn't
no other judge in this state that would allow this. Just want to
make sure everybody gets a fair shake. If you don't have a lawyer,
at any time, you're welcome to have one. We have a lawyer that's
paid for by the city, to take cases. Not somebody I handpicked,
but a man that will do a good job as public defender. To *defend*
you. Don't worry about a thing, 'cause he just does a good job.
Some of you here have been represented by him and said he's very
conscientious. Our public defender's out right now, getting a few
facts, delaying us a little while, so we'll wait."

Which gave Evers an opportunity to add a few more words of
wisdom to those on hand: "As I said before, I hope the day will
come when we won't have these kinda things. We black folks ought
to have had a lesson enough. We been mistreated, thrown in jail,
fined, abused by bigots and other folks in this country here, and

now that we have our *own* government, the least we should do is *respect* it."

"Yes, suh. Yes, suh," said an elderly black man in the audience.

"You may not always *agree* with it, but at least respect it. That's all we're asking. In many cases, we get more trouble from our own. But if anybody thinks for one moment that we're gonna do anything different than what's right, they can get up and move to another town. Ready, now?"

"Yes, Your Honor."

What followed was somewhat incredible, considering that this was the decade of the 1970's, that it was a time in which the nation was suffering from all manner of crime and bogged down hopelessly in its urban court system. While the nation's big cities were plagued with drug addiction, murder, assault, robbery, organized crime, down the line, the town of Fayette on this afternoon was concerned with the fact that a young black man, perhaps twenty years old, had used "vulgar terms" within the city limits. While the rest of the nation was worried about ROTC buildings being bombed and women being raped in alleys, Fayette was concerned that people call each other "Mr." and "Mrs." and otherwise refrain from any form of impoliteness. No question about it, they were starting at the beginning, and Evers cast a gloomy, mournful eye at the young man dressed in an old Army shirt who was standing before him now, pleading not guilty.

With a crack of the judge's gavel, the trial began. It lasted a good forty-five minutes, with several witnesses taking the stand (they came up and sat on a chair next to Evers' table), each examined and cross-examined by the town attorney and defense lawyer, two young black men who treated this case as if it were a matter of electric chair versus life imprisonment. The defense lawyer first asked, "Can we have a jury?" and Evers, giving it only a moment's thought, replied, "No, that's not necessary."

That bit of impromptu justice (or nonjustice) accomplished, a black Fayette police officer took the stand and related all the events leading up to the night of the vulgar language. Evers leaned back in his chair, arms folded, and listened to the testimony offered by all involved.

It seems that on the night in question, the defendant was sitting in a car with another young man, parked on the asphalt pavement outside the Evers Motel, Restaurant, and Lounge on Route 61, a place of business owned by none other than the mayor-judge himself. They were alone in the car, minding their own business, when a guard approached and asked them to move on. They refused. Minutes later, a police officer came over and displayed his billy club, threatening to whip the defendant's "a-s-s" if he didn't either go inside the restaurant or drive away. The defendant replied by using the terms "m-f" and "b-s" and then left the scene.

There was much debate concerning the circumstances and motivations surrounding the usage of all three vulgar expressions: "a-double-s" and "m-f" and "b-s." The defense lawyer argued quite strenuously that his client was provoked into his bad language by the police officer. The prosecuting attorney contended that the provocation was beside the point: "The question at hand is, did your client use the words 'm-f' and 'b-s' within the city limits of Fayette or did he not?"

Judge Evers considered all of this with the sad-eyed expression of a bloodhound. He rapped his gavel wearily, as if he wished the whole thing hadn't happened; but such were the problems involved in the creation of a new civilization.

"As one black man to the rest of the country," he said, "I have all my life watched black folks stand around like cattle, on the *out*side, hollering, cursing, drinking, clowning, and not on the *in*side. So I always did say, someday I'm gonna have a place where my folks can come in, with air-conditioning, carpeting, and sit down and be like anybody else. So I made a personal rule of mine, as the owner, that no one stand on the outside of my place of business and curse, sing, dance, or shout—period. You come *in*side. If you don't want to come in, all I asked my officers is to ask you to move on, that's all. Not curse 'em, not harass 'em, but tell 'em what the rules are. You come in and sit down, or you move on. And that's for aldermen or anybody.

"In this town, we're not gonna be out cursing, using profane language. We're not gonna run that kind of town, where a man can get up and disrespect the officers or the mayor of the town. This kind of thing will never be; let me make that clear. And as long as we sit in leadership positions, officers and the rest of us, regardless of the price it may cost us, we gotta stand for this. If I gotta stand alone, I'll stand alone. I'm not gonna tolerate in *this* town no more 's-f'-ing, no 's-b'-ing, and all that kinda stuff—or any 'a-s-ses' either. To nobody! Policemens, on down. Any person in this town, if an officer addresses you that way, he's gonna get the same fine you gonna get, plus a suspension. We just ain't gonna have it. This is my stand on the kinda town that everybody can live in, and those who don't want to do what's right, I'm sorry. I'm gonna stand up for what's right, regardless of *who* it is. I'm not gonna make *no* exceptions, for *nobody,* at *no* time. For that reason I'm gonna fine you twenty-five dollars for cursing in the city limits and ask you not to do it anymore."

In a town where the personal incomes average less than six hundred dollars per year, a fine of twenty-five dollars—for cursing! —was very stiff indeed. The young black defendant stood up and said, "Can I say something for my behalf?"

"You certainly can," said Evers almost sheepishly.

"I'd like to say that this only happened because I was in front of *your* place of business. I can't get a fair, impartial trial in here, with you being both the owner of the place *and* the judge. I just cannot get a fair trial."

"You have the right to appeal it. The case is closed."

From where I sat, it seemed that Evers was more interested in dispensing education than justice. When I told him afterward that I felt he had been too harsh, he replied, "You remember we were discussing the street gangs up North? Well, those street gangs started with profanity!"

Later, I was told that Evers had given a stern lecture to the black police officer for using the term "a-double-s" while enforcing the law against cursing.

4.

The next morning, Mayor Evers was hunched over a plateful of eggs and bacon in the dining room of his Motel, Restaurant, and Lounge, wearing an olive-green jump suit from the civil-rights movement but looking more as if he'd just parachuted down in the grassy field out back. "Morning, reporter," he said, motioning first to me to sit down and then to the waitress to bring some more coffee. He was staying in his small apartment in town while his wife and kids were home up in Jackson. Evers had been out doing some "chores" earlier in the morning and was full of plans for the rest of the week, all of them revolving around his struggle for the little town of Fayette, as if it were a kind of miniature community set up on a table like model trains, and his enthusiasm for the task was still as fresh as that of any hobbyist. "Still need jobs," he was saying, and to that end he was heading up to Jackson to straighten out negotiations for the new chemical plant. (He is the kind of man who will sit in at such stuffy meetings and cut through a mountain of bureaucratic crap by declaring, "Now, gentlemen, we need that plant, need those jobs, so just tell us what we gotta do to get it.") Then on to Atlanta to see about a grant for a new recreation center—and the list of things to do was endless. He had been in office a little over a year now, and had accomplished many things (a new health clinic, some paved roads in the black community, an ambulance, a police car, a few small industries where before there had been none, a new garbage truck, a ditch digger, etc.), but still it seemed as if he was racing against time.

"How long you gonna be around?" he asked, and when I replied about a week and a half, he added, "Well, you won't have nothing to fear in our little town. We'll take good care of you. Just look at the streets downtown, they're full of people all day long. No tension here no more."

One thing, he was sick and tired and bored with all the interviews. Reporters were always asking him the same old questions, and he seemed to be giving the same old answers all the time. "I've given ten thousand interviews, it seems," he said. "I just don't need any more publicity." And having gotten that off his chest, he proceeded to talk for half an hour about anything that happened to come into his head. At one point he looked up and said, "At the end of your stay here, come tell me what you think, okay?"

Two young black girls came in the restaurant, and he called them over. "How'd it go?" he asked them. They had come into Fayette from a nearby town, seeking work, and had been told by the white storeowner that there weren't any application forms around. "Well," he said, "did you leave your names and telephone numbers?"

"No, he said he'd call us."

"How's he gonna call you if he don't have your numbers?"

The girls were stumped on that one and then became embarrassed. He tried to instruct them, urging them to have confidence in themselves, adding, "You're not gonna get the runaround, not here in Fayette."

When they had left, Evers was fueled up for another outpouring about how he was working for a perfect kind of society in this little community in the rural wilderness of the Deep South, one where people obey all the laws and otherwise are free to do as they please "as long as you don't step on somebody else's toes." He said he had been asked hundreds of times why he doesn't hate white folks, replying always that hating simply can't solve anything. "Medgar and I wanted to win," he went on. "And haters have never won anything. The only thing I hate is hatred itself, and racism. I've killed more white folks by winning than if I'd shot five hundred of 'em with a gun. But we need more of my folks in the spotlight, not just me all alone down here. Need more guys with nooses around their necks. It's awful lonely hanging here all by yourself. We got to build, not destroy. Elected officials are supposed to serve, not boss people, and that's what I'm trying to do." On and on it comes, the Evers Philosophy, which at times seems almost maudlin but turns out to be the real thing, more real than any amount of showmanship can either convey or cover up. And no question about it, Evers is a showman. He had been the first black disk jockey, on radio, in the state of Mississippi, and I wished I could have heard the Evers radio style back then because it must have been something. Even in the restaurant he would put on a show for the lunchtime crowd whenever he was in town. During my stay in Fayette, Evers often stopped in around noon, appearing suddenly from the kitchen, and he'd go around to all the tables, talking with the patrons whether they were friends or just strangers passing through, and he'd kind of *perform* for them all, trying to make everyone feel at home in the place of business of which he was so proud. One time the white county sheriff came in, and Evers greeted him with all smiles and backslaps, telling everyone in the restaurant that here's a man "who locked me up three times in one day, and now he comes in here to eat. What do ya think of that?"

"Wal," said the sheriff, taking his cue, "I figure you spent some time with *me,* so now I might as well spend some time with *you.*"

All the patrons in the restaurant howled with laughter. I wondered how many times these two—the black mayor and the white sheriff—had gone through this vaudeville routine.

Outside the restaurant, across the street and down a few hundred yards, set back a ways in the middle of a large field, was a modern public school for the children of Jefferson County. It had just opened for the new year, and not a single white youngster had shown up. I stood there, watching the black kids file outside, with books under their arms, thinking how similar things were—the white middle-class moving out of the big cities, the white people keeping their kids out of new integrated schools in the South. . . .

Suddenly Evers appeared outside. "Look at that," he said, pointing across the street. "That school used to be all-white. Now, no white children come at all. We won the whole school without firing a single shot."

There was a touch of bravado in his tone but a knowing sadness as well. Evers shook his head and went off with his own thoughts, the vigor in his stride, for a moment at least, gone.

Twelve

1.

The Reverend Andrew Young had been carrying his campaign for Georgia's Fifth Congressional seat to teas with wealthy white matrons in the ornate mansions of the north side and also to revival meetings in the plain black churches of the southwest. He was one of the few black men anywhere in the South with broad enough appeal even to think about winning in a district that was 70 percent white.

Now he was visiting with some high-school students in a wealthy suburban section outside Atlanta. Sixteen boys and girls, white kids, were sitting in a circle around him in a little community room next to a modern church. Andy lounged in an easy chair, one leg draped over the side, and instead of making any big speech he sort of sat there waiting for the right mood to drift into the room. That was his style. One supposed he just might fall asleep rather than bore the kids to death with political rhetoric. If they had nothing on their minds, well, he'd wait. The kids seemed no different from most high-school students in the North; some wore jeans and hippie-style clothing, a few had long hair and sideburns, and on the whole they were bright and full of concern. Yet for a while the mood refused to appear, so they sat there in silence, watching Andy Young rub his eyes.

When the discussion did get rolling, it became clear to the kids that Young was no ordinary politician. For although they knew something of his personal history, and although they knew they could count on him to articulate many of their own rather idealistic views, they also began to realize that he wasn't trying to win them over. In some ways he was more conservative than they were, and that was puzzling to them. When they asked him questions, he would seem to search for the wisdom of his own experience, regardless of what answer might have been popular among young people, and they could feel the basic honesty in his replies. If almost any other politician had come here preaching, say, self-discipline, the kids probably would not have listened, but when Andy Young gave the same message, they sat there quietly and thought about it. The conduct and quality of his life had earned him their respect, and so he did not have to conform to whatever trends were in vogue.

"You've said some nice things," said one of the more activist-looking young men in the group, "but don't you think you're being a little naïve? For instance, what good was the Civil Rights Act? The South isn't integrated yet, and there's still bigotry all around. A lot of people have just given up."

A thin veil seemed to stretch across Andy Young's eyes, blurring them for a moment, and he shifted uneasily in the chair as if wrestling with the thought that somehow Dr. King's life and work could have been in vain.

"Well," he said at last, "the black community in Gary and in Cleveland, they didn't give up. Anyway, I've always kinda thought that despair comes out of idealism."

Then he added a bit of humorous self-mockery in his best preacher's tone: "But all men sin and fall short of the glory of God, ya know."

"Seriously," he went on, "I have some hope in things. Five years ago, here in Atlanta, you didn't see black and white folks downtown coming in and out of the same buildings together. But now you do. I still feel that nonviolence is the only way to bring about creative social change."

"Look at Watts," a student injected.

"Well, look at it! What did it get them? There's a feeling in America that, you know, violence works—but it doesn't."

They asked him about the Black Panthers, and he said he felt the Panthers were basically "some intelligent black kids that got crushed in the ghetto. . . . They're bitter, 'cause they don't see much of a future. But it's like throwing a brick at a fellow with a machine gun—that's not militancy but stupidity."

The group fell into a discussion of the war and the draft, and Young told them that he was "against militarism" in general. "I'd like to see some sort of a 'maturation rights' bill," he said, "so a guy can go out and prove himself—but not necessarily in the military—and then relax about his manhood. One of the reasons I joined the civil-rights movement was because I had to know I was man enough to do it."

Young men should be able to give two years of service to the country in several possible areas, he said. "Like the Peace Corps or medicine or even the police in some city. We could have a peace offensive, an extension of the Peace Corps, that could make wars almost unnecessary. We could do lots more in the way of international peacemaking. . . . We've been backing some wrong governments around the world. . . . We should begin to think of ourselves as *world* citizens as well as national citizens."

When some of the kids mentioned how they were down on modern technology and "material goods," he agreed with them but, because of his own experience, felt compelled to remind them that poor people don't see their poverty in such romantic terms. "Most students can think of higher values because they know where their next meal is coming from," he said. "I happen to believe that we don't like Western technology 'cause we got so much of it. We have a new generation that has taken technology for granted and kind of outgrown it."

Then Andy Young told how he had gone down to southern Georgia to pastor two little churches down there in those rural, dirt-poor communities. "That's where I was gonna establish the Kingdom of God," he said with a smile. "I was gonna forget all material goods and concentrate on spiritual values for the folks. In the two churches I didn't have but about a hundred members. It was a very poor place, but the people wanted to be middle-class. They wanted to go to college *only* to get jobs so they could get rich, and they wanted automobiles, they wanted nice houses, Coca-Cola, television, refrigerators. And I was the only preacher in town that didn't have a big car. I had a little Nash Rambler, and folks used to say, 'Why don't you get a Cadillac?' And I fought that for a while, but I realized that it was a kind of lost cause. For example, I really don't like a shirt and tie, but you better not go into poor folks' communities in Georgia without one. No matter how hot it is, you better keep that tie up tight. The rich Americans going barefoot—the poor here and in other countries don't wanna see that."

Later, he added, "I really never saw myself with a career in politics. I thought that this race would be the one that would help turn the whole South around. If there'd been somebody else that had run, that could've won, I wouldn't have bothered. If I don't win, I don't know what I'll do after this."

Did he really think politics could be an effective force for change?

"Well, the whole purpose of life, as I see it, is solving problems. And the more you solve, the more you see. I think the best approach is to develop local programs and then build to national ones. One thing that Bobby Kennedy did—he knew that if you wanna know something, just invite all the experts in that field for dinner one night. And between eight and twelve o'clock you'll probably learn everything that it took them twenty years to learn. It's really not how much you know, but being able to know where to go to find out. Anyway, I see government being able to do those things that nobody else can do, that's all. . . . I have a concept of this campaign that goes beyond getting elected. I see it as a battle of ideas and points of view in a community. To get more people thinking about the issues, so that the community progresses politically. Things like medical care and housing and rapid transit —the process of running a campaign is a process of educating a community. I don't know—I'm getting a real education, getting around and meeting the folk. A lot of people got to know more about each other."

2.

There was a lot of optimistic talk about how Atlanta was the the most progressive city in the South and how therefore Andy Young, if elected, could set an example of new black-and-white "togetherness" that would pave the way for a revolution in politics. This was a "Southern strategy" just the opposite from that of the President of the United States. "Atlanta is ready to move beyond racism," Andy Young would say, and there was some evidence to back it up. Atlanta's business leaders had proclaimed that their city was "too busy to hate," which in translation meant that, if brotherhood wasn't yet permeating everyone's hearts, it was at least recognized as a practical necessity for progress. And besides, riots and demonstrations were simply poor public relations. Young would tell audiences that Atlanta had "put together a style of leadership that I think has great merit." He said there was room in this city for "people reasoning together to work out the problems of a complicated metropolitan area, and to make a meaningful life out of some terribly complex urban situations. . . . This is probably the city that has the least tension between rich and poor, between black and white, between old and young, of almost any other city I know anything about. Not that we've solved all of our problems, but we do have the capacity to solve them. . . . We don't want to be lured back into the past. . . . Atlanta can take the creative lead in just about every area of metropolitan life."

The South was full of contradictions, paradoxes, guilts, fears, ironies, and mysteries deriving from the tormented history of its people. There were some who believed that the South, despite its rural-dominated legislatures and its ultraconservatives in the Congress and its George Wallaces and Lester Maddoxes and its low-wage industries and poverty and hunger, was paradoxically the place where opportunity existed for the most progress. The optimists believed that the South could build up a society that avoided the mistakes of the North, and that the new black elected officials could help shape this progress as the South moves into an era of urbanization and technological growth. At least white people in the South were honest about their hatreds and prejudices, while in the North black people had been led on by the subtleties of liberalism, which had made them believe they were making progress when in fact they were not.

Blacks in Atlanta had greatly enhanced their political influence in the fall of 1969. In the first place, their voting strength had grown over the decade from about 29 percent to nearly 41 percent (the black population was now almost half that of the entire city).

In the October 21 runoff election, a liberal white man, Sam Massell, was put into the mayor's office almost entirely on the basis of black votes. Massell won with some 55 percent of the votes cast; of his 62,632 total, more than 45,000 had come from the black community. Two weeks before, a young black attorney named Maynard Jackson had been elected vice-mayor on the first ballot with almost total support from black voters. The number of blacks on the Board of Aldermen was increased from one to five, and the number on the Board of Education rose from two to three. No longer were blacks required to choose between a candidate of the white liberals and another white candidate whose racial views made him anathema. This time, the choices were greater, and blacks were able to desert their former "Northside allies" (white suburbanites) and elect candidates of their own preference. In an analysis of the 1969 elections for the Voter Education Project, Charles S. Rooks declared that a "turning point in the city's political history" may have taken place. A new "coalition" of voters, predominantly black, had emerged. Now, most whites had supported the losing mayoralty candidate, while almost all blacks, plus a minority of whites, had supported the winner.

The election campaign of 1970 was different, however. Andy Young was not running strictly in Atlanta, with a 41 percent black registration, but in the Fifth Congressional District, where the black vote was only 30 percent. He needed substantial white support to get elected, plus a large black turnout at the polls—and here was the basic problem, and more importantly, the point at which his strategy probably went wrong. In pursuit of white support, would he take the black voters for granted?

"He's too worried about the so-called white liberals," a young, militant black girl told me. "Andy isn't campaigning in the black community like he should," she went on, and I was reminded of Richard Austin's campaign in Detroit, where I had heard the same criticism. "He's too worried about losing the white liberals, and in the process he's not going to get the necessary enthusiasm from the black community. He's spending a lot of money, which is very evident from all the billboards and TV commercials, but he should be running a grass-roots campaign. To me," the black girl continued, "Andy seems to have lost a lot of the drive, the fight, that he once had. In a way, he seems to be running on the basis of his past, which is a very bad thing. Black people just won't turn out if they're not enthusiastic."

Another criticism of Young's campaign was that he should have been supporting C. B. King, the first black candidate for governor in Georgia's history. Instead, Andy was backing former Governor Carl Sanders, and this was even further proof that he was trying too hard to please the white liberals. What's more, the Congress of African People, with some 2,500 delegates, many of them dressed in colorful African garb, was meeting in Atlanta during the closing days of the primary campaign, and Andy Young had actually expressed worry over its effect upon his chances for victory. The total picture of Young that began to emerge, in the minds of many blacks, was that he had become too much of a politician after all, that he was somehow "embarrassed" by his own people, and that in an attempt to become a "mediator" between the races he had sold out. And of course, no one agreed with this assessment more wholeheartedly than his black Democratic opponent, Lonnie King.

3.

On Tuesday, September 8, the day before the primary election, Lonnie wore a blue shirt and a wide red tie, looking just as confident as he had appeared back in July. With less money and staff than Andy Young, he roamed restlessly around his Auburn Avenue campaign office, still convinced that his "poor people's campaign" was going to pay off. "I've taken myself to the people," he said, the inevitable wide grin spreading over his face. "I've been out there every day, and the question is whether my direct approach in going to the people will be able to overcome the gigantic amount of television and billboard advertising that Andy's been using."

During the campaign so far, the major white candidate in the Democratic primary, a lawyer named Wyman C. Lowe, had jumped on Andy Young by calling him a "revolutionary." (Which made one wonder, if that could happen to the mild, gentle-natured Young, what would have happened to the controversial Julian

Bond if *he* had been the leading black candidate. "I'd have been red-baited right out of the race," Bond commented later.) In an advertisement appearing in the Atlanta *Journal* on this day, Lowe had presented the following distortion to the voters:

> Andrew Young, one of the two black Democratic candidates for the office, in an interview by an ABC reporter with respect to Black Panther views that was broadcast on April 13, 1970, was asked, "Would you support the destruction of western civilization if you were convinced the rest of the world would thereby be liberated?" He replied, "I probably would."
>
> Would the security of this nation be harmed if a man having such revolutionary views became Congressman and then a Member of the Armed Services Committee, concerned with protection of this country? VOTERS OF 5TH DISTRICT AWAKE!!

Lonnie King, meanwhile, was having a good laugh over this development, because if anything *he* was the so-called "militant" candidate in the race. In fact, he had been trying to portray Andy in the exact opposite light. Not only was Andy Young something less than a revolutionary, King had told reporters, but the former aide to Martin Luther King had espoused a view that was similar to that of Lester Maddox! Apparently Young had made a statement that compulsory school bussing wasn't the ultimate social solution to the education problem. Lonnie held a news conference and exclaimed, "Whether he realizes it or not, Young's position on bussing only provides ammunition for those persons who are still fighting for segregation. I wonder if he realizes that his attitude toward bussing is the same as that of Lester Maddox."

With his white opponent linking him to the revolutionaries, and with his black opponent picturing him in league with the segregationists, Andrew Young had every right to wonder why he had decided to enter politics in the first place.

The night before the primary election, Lonnie and Andy debated each other for about twelve minutes on television, and the whole thing degenerated into something far less than an intelligent discussion of the issues. Only three hours before, Lonnie had told me that he was planning to sit there looking very dignified, that he wouldn't attack Andy Young because it would confuse a lot of blacks. "If I criticize Andy too much," he said, "folks'll think I'm attacking Martin Luther King." But something happened when he got into the television studio, because the debate almost immediately became little more than a squabble between two black politicians over who had done more for the cause of civil rights in Atlanta.

Andy began by trying to put the debate on a high level of dialogue, calling the election "one of the most important in the nation." He outlined such problems as the economy, the cities, education, health care, jobs, and the war. Lonnie came back and reminded everyone that he had led the "movement" in Atlanta during the early sixties for desegregation of movie theaters, lunch counters, and other public accommodations. They never did get beyond the question of who did more for integration, but even so it was instructive if one remembered that only ten years had elapsed since Lonnie King and Julian Bond had decided to begin the student sit-ins in Atlanta. They all had come a long way since that time, and one wondered what those whites who had fought against them were thinking now as they watched this debate between two black men running for Congress. Ten years hadn't solved all the problems—certainly not the problems of poverty and education—but times had changed.

Georgia voters went to the polls the next day, and later, in the evening, Andy Young's supporters gathered in a back room at Paschal's to watch the returns come in on television. It was a mixed bag of people—blacks and whites of all ages milling around, trying to glimpse the TV sets. John Lewis came in and sort of blended into the crowd in his quiet way, and at one point Julian Bond appeared, displaying the familiar regal presence that made it seem as if he might just float up to the ceiling and vanish at any moment. Andy Young came downstairs at 9:15 P.M. Only a few precincts had reported, so there was no speechmaking yet. The only real development was that the voter turnout had been very light, in both the black and white communities. Young desperately wanted to avoid a runoff situation, since it would tend to tarnish his image as a winner. He needed 50 percent of the total vote to gain the Democratic nomination without a runoff, and therefore a strong turnout, especially by blacks, was essential.

There was much speculation among the crowd about "black voter apathy." Had black people been so "conditioned to losing" over the years that not even the warm endorsements from the Reverend Ralph Abernathy and Coretta King could bring them to the polls? Was the disillusionment so deep? Was it also a practical matter, such as lack of transportation to the voting booths, especially in the poverty-ridden rural areas? Was it the depressing social climate abroad in the nation generally? In an interview a few weeks later, Bond would say, "The negative mood of black people and black voters is markedly deeper today than in past elections. . . . There is a deepening frustration among blacks with national politics and policies and the racist overtones of the campaign throughout the country."

The blotchy color television sets were inaudible because of the live rock music being provided in one section of the room at Paschal's. The waiting went on and on, until in the early morning hours the final count came through:

Young: 34,330
Lowe: 21,586
Gurley: 8,102
King: 7,997

Andy had won by a wide margin but had amassed only about 48 percent of the the total—just short of the halfway mark he needed to reach in order to avoid a runoff. Lonnie King had finished a disappointing fourth, making him the "spoiler" in the race as far as Young's people were concerned. With not even half of Lonnie's votes, Andy would have taken the nomination. Now, he would have to fight it out with Lowe in a special primary two weeks later.

4.

The next morning I went to see John Lewis at the Voter Education Project office on Forsyth Street in downtown Atlanta. Lewis was particularly pleased about the governor's race in which Jimmy Carter, a peanut farmer, had triumphed over Carl Sanders, the favorite. (Black attorney C. B. King had run a distant third in that race.) Not that Lewis had any great fondness for Carter. "If Carter wins the runoff," said Lewis, "it'll be a defeat for the established black leadership in Atlanta, and it'll give younger, more aggressive blacks a better chance in the system." Among those black leaders who had supported Sanders over C. B. King was state Senator Leroy Johnson, generally regarded as one of the master politicians of the South. In Lewis' opinion, traditional black leaders like Johnson had "abandoned the struggle they had pioneered" by refusing to support black candidates like C. B. King. Such politicking by black elected officials tended to divide the black community and deprive candidates of potential strength. For example, if all 400,000 registered black voters in the state had gone to the polls and voted as a bloc, C. B. King could have been the first black governor of Georgia, or at least the Democratic nominee. King, regarded as a brilliant, scholarly, and humane black attorney, had received very little support from black leaders. Julian Bond was one of the few elected officials who had endorsed him.

After leaving Lewis' office I went to see Bond at his house. He was preparing for another fast-paced speaking tour, this time to New York and other places in the Northeast. What bothered him about the election was that blacks in Georgia had not developed a political strategy comparable to that of Dr. John Cashin in Alabama. "It seems to me," he said, "that what Cashin has done in Alabama is what black political activists should have been doing in other states. It's almost impossible to change the Democratic Party from within in the Deep South. You really have to set up an alternate structure, as Dr. Cashin has done. We should have seized the moment to do that after our victory at the convention in Chicago in 1968. We had the momentum then, and the mistake was not to use it to establish an alternate political party. I think we're living now to regret it."

Bond had spoken at the Congress of African People in Atlanta recently—he and Richard Hatcher were among the few black *elected* officials invited—and had suggested that blacks around the world might come together in an international political party.

"The black elected officials' conference in Washington a year ago and the Congress of African People this year—they're really unrelated to each other," he told me. "The Congress of African Peoples was really a continuation of the old black-power conferences, just under a different name and a slightly different ideology

—the ideology of Pan Africanism added to the ideology of black nationalism. The black elected officials' conference was something I'm sure there's going to be another of and another of, and they'll all basically be about the same thing. As long as they're sponsored by foundation-connected groups, they're not going to get into any partisan politics, and they'll just be about technical subjects. They won't have any ideology connected with them, which is really, I think, a bad mistake. At that conference a year ago, we talked a great deal, particularly Southerners, about the formation of another political party, on the model of Dr. Cashin's National Democratic Party of Alabama. But a year later, nothing's been done about it."

In Alabama, Dr. Cashin was leading the ticket of a distinct political party whose 171 candidates all were running on the same platform. "He suffers from the same kind of splits in Alabama that we do here in Georgia," said Bond, "but the difference is that he has a political vehicle to push his candidacies and his ideologies. Whereas in Georgia, none exists. If there's a clash between Senator Johnson and myself over C. B. King or Carl Sanders, which there is, each of us has to depend on the force of personality to prevail. Cashin, on the other hand, doesn't have to depend on his personality. He has an organization."

I asked Bond about the need to form coalitions with other groups, mainly whites, and he replied, "You have to play coalition politics at the top. But at the bottom, particularly from the Southern perspective, you don't. Coalition politics, I think, always weakens at least one partner in the coalition, rather than strengthens both partners. The old coalition between black people and labor is an obvious example. We have always gone down the line with labor, on everything it wanted, but labor hasn't reciprocated. Labor stood for the civil-rights bills, but when it comes to getting black people into the trades and the crafts, it's a closed shop."

From "coalition" politics we turned to "ethnic" movements which Bond said had to be "built from an ethnic basis, on up to the top. . . . That is, it has to be an inverted triangle, with a small base, and hopefully widen out to the top. The further up you go, the more diluted you become. But down at the bottom, you can have your strength. And if there had been any kind of reasonable organization in this state, we could have turned out a big vote for C. B. King. I mean, that's power. And if the organization had been built, then C. B.'s votes would have been transferable to another candidate. We could have said to Carter or Sanders, 'Now, you can have these votes, either one of you, if you agree in advance that you will do certain things.' But they're not transferable, or deliverable, because we weren't together."

Thirteen

1.

In Detroit, blacks increasingly were complaining of brutality and general harassment by a police force that was almost totally white. Perhaps the biggest issue, therefore, was the establishment of a police review board run by civilians. A petition to have such a proposal put on the November ballot was circulated in the black community, but it fell short by a small number of signatures at the last moment.

At the outset of his campaign for mayor, Richard Austin had supported the review-board proposal. Many of his advisers felt that in doing so he had made a serious political blunder. He needed white support to win the election, they reasoned. If most whites were violently opposed to a civilian review board, Austin should oppose it also. It was a classic dilemma for a black politician —should he support the needs of his own people and risk losing white votes, or should he cater to the whites and risk being labeled an Uncle Tom?

When the matter failed to get on the ballot, everyone in the Austin camp heaved a sigh of relief. On the other hand, it was state Senator Coleman Young's opinion that the review board as an issue would have helped Austin's campaign, not hindered it. In Young's view, it was better for a black candidate to stand for something important to his people, even at the price of further polarization of blacks and whites in the city. Better to create waves in support of something than to attempt a delicate, cautious course through deceptively placid waters. Better to campaign on the review-board issue for all it was worth, risking a rise in racial animosity for the sake of something important to blacks, who would then be motivated to pour out to the polls.

Aside from that, the white police union actually became the leading political force in opposition to Austin's candidacy. The reason the cops had gained such influence was not difficult to determine: It was just possible that white people, in their fear of black crime and in their panic before the specter of black political ascendancy, were now willing to abandon all pretense of democracy and delegate their weakening control to the white police force. "Let the cops run things!" had become a familiar slogan in Detroit. In the minds of many whites, the election of a black mayor would render the police ineffective against street crime— as though blacks somehow had less interest than other people in being protected.

Bolstered by their new rise in popularity, the cops had been encouraged to do an incredible thing. The all-white police union had formed a political alliance with all-white, antiblack homeowner and business groups. The head of the police union said he was now dreaming of the day in the near future when policemen would not only enforce the laws but help make them as well. Utopia would come when the cops' money and influence would elect policemen to the Common Council and the mayor's office. Those elected, in turn, would make sure that the police would be allowed to do anything necessary to maintain law and order in the jungle. No civilian elected official would tell *them* what to do.

All this only reinforced the widespread belief among ghetto folk that white policemen were their enemy, standing for suppression by the white middle-class. It was felt that already the police had too much power, even under Mayor Cavanaugh.

"The police run this damn town already," Senator Young exclaimed. "The police union is the only armed political party in America. They're completely out of control. There's an overt attempt by police officers to take over political control of this city. Their militancy is a call to arms against a black takeover of Detroit. At the same time that we blacks are getting into politics to gain power over our own destiny, the police are looking to get control. They are the chief threat to the political system here, and in the nation, too. The police move for political power is a conscious attempt to frustrate the democratic process. Here in Detroit, in the near future, the blacks will be the majority and the police the controlling minority."

And now, before the September primary election, the police union announced its support for Sheriff Roman Gribbs and an all-white slate of ten candidates for city offices. Blacks in Detroit were more than 40 percent of the population; they came into contact with policemen more often than most people did, and yet the police union itself had supported not a single black person who was running for public office.

"How could they be so insensitive?" said one black leader. "Do they *want* a civil war?"

2.

In the heart of Detroit's black slums, a man named Frank Ditto often prowled the streets in a dashiki, keeping a lookout for any misbehaving white policemen. If the civil war ever came, thirty-nine-year-old Ditto would be leading the fight from one side. Publicity and rumor about this black man had aroused fear and hatred in many white hearts, a fact which amused him more than anything else.

As director of the East Side Voice of Independent Detroit, Ditto was a moving force behind several "black pride" projects in the slums. He ran a black-uniformed corps of more than a hundred black youngsters who patrolled the streets, escorting people through the crime-ridden neighborhoods and protecting threatened storeowners, both black and white. Ditto's youngsters also reported on the behavior of local police, and they helped to clean up the neighborhood. Ditto had organized a Political Education Project, a junior version of City Hall which was made up of black teen-agers from his area.

"His kids had an affair for me one afternoon," said Richard Austin, as if he had just become aware of Ditto's activities. "It was an outing, and I spent an afternoon with them. Boy, you talk about a disciplined bunch of kids—whoo! Now, they're in a very rundown part of the city, but those kids are extremely well-behaved and disciplined. They're all ages, and the older kids sort of shepherd the smaller ones. Ditto's not trying to please anybody in Detroit, just those kids. I don't imagine he tries to please *them,* as a matter of fact. He just tries to give them something to hold onto, something they can have pride in."

I went to see Ditto a few days before the primary election and was greeted at his storefront by several young men with black berets and girls with large Afro hairdos. Ditto, a husky, bearded man, wearing a white shirt with the sleeves rolled up, strolled out of a back room and invited me to come inside. He sat behind a desk and asked one of the girls to bring us some coffee. He was quite relaxed and friendly and soft-spoken, far from his image in the press as a fire-eating militant and irresponsible agitator, and the look in his eyes suggested more than a hint of the sociologist, of the amused intellectual. He seemed to be aware of a thousand ironies involved in the business of being a black militant.

Ditto's view of Richard Austin was in the larger context of Stokely Carmichael's statement that "every Negro, or colored person, is a potential black man."

"I don't see Dick Austin as being as much of an Establishment Negro as it might appear," he said. "The possibility of becoming black in mind, heart, and soul is quite evident in Austin. I have heard out of his own mouth, 'I'm beginning to see a different light, now.' So, I see the possibility of that potential finally emerging in him."

Some black kids walked past the storefront window, and Ditto waved to them. They smiled back and disappeared.

"And Austin readily admits that some of the old political hacks, black ones, were more of Establishment-type people, and he has withdrawn from them. Any support he gets from them now is because *they* feel they have no other alternative. So, that's the way I see Austin.

"But it's not really Austin that I have problems with—it's the goddamn System. And he just represents that. He's no different from a white man or an Adam Powell or a Richard Hatcher. It's the *System*. Hatcher is good, but there still haven't been so many political goods delivered. Until they begin to get additional colleagues, mayors and Senators and Congressmen and so forth, and until more and more blacks actually begin holding office, the political System just won't work. I don't give a damn if a guy is the strongest, most nationalistic, or militant person that blacks have known—if he doesn't have sufficient support, then you're just out there begging. Or banging your head. You're constantly out there fighting, but you're not chipping away too much. You need many, many people chipping away. That's the only way that black people can get any meaningful good out of politics. The way I see it, Austin *does* raise the level, I think—he restores some faith in black people in the *eventual* viability of politics.

"But realistically, as I see it, politics will deliver when I begin to live it on a day-to-day basis, as other ethnic groups have done. When I'm not dependent entirely on others. I think it's unfair to take Austin or any other guy and say, 'Okay, black man, we're gonna put you in there and we want you to change things.' That's bullshit. It's unrealistic, it's unfair, and you're defeating the guy before he even gets a chance to move. If Austin becomes mayor of Detroit tomorrow, he'll only be worth the salt that goes into his bread if I, and other blacks, support him on a day-to-day basis. Not only me but every other black man who cast a vote for him."

He paused, and we listened to his police radio, which enabled Ditto to hear how the police were responding to calls in this neighborhood.

"Dick Austin has ventured out of the so-called Establishment, and he's begun to listen very carefully to what is being said here in the black community. And he's been able to *receive* that and to understand the hopelessness. I think he now understands, for example, that you can't separate or divide black people by their economic status, or by education or whatever. Black people are black people, period. The rich, the educated, the poor blacks— they still suffer the same goddamn problem of inequities and repression. And Dick has felt the pain of racism. Even as a county auditor or whatever, he's been reminded every day that he's a nigger. I think this might have come home a little closer to him as a result of him getting out into this area here. He met some awfully angry people. He saw how determined these young people are, how well-disciplined. He saw for himself that all he's read and heard about us in the papers isn't necessarily true. He sees now that we have to take a good look for *ourselves,* and not depend on secondhand information from the press. The media points out the sensationalism and ignores the facts completely in most instances. So a person really has to get out and investigate.

"Until all pieces and bits of this suppression and discrimination and so forth are eliminated, we have nothing to crow about, and we can't talk about how good things are or how much better things are getting. I think that this is what Austin is beginning to relate to more. More than perhaps he did in his earlier years."

I asked Ditto if he thought an Austin defeat would cause a great deal of anger among blacks. "If Dick isn't elected," he replied, "I don't think there will be any tremendous disappointment among blacks, except by a few. I think the overall masses of black people will say, 'I told you so. He couldn't get elected.' You can't be too disappointed if you've lost so much faith in something to begin with."

3.

The sun was bleeding orange and yellow behind a curtain of gray fog and pollution. On the sidewalk outside a huge auto plant, workers were filing out at the end of a shift, while others, carrying sandwiches in paper bags or metal lunch boxes, arrived for the start of a new shift. Still other workers, black and white, young and old, were lined up along the sidewalk, sitting with their backs to the dull-yellow brick wall of the plant. Many were in T-shirts, and some wore baseball or golf caps.

Dick Austin arrived by car, jumping out without his jacket, and he started shaking the first of a hundred hands.

He slapped a black man on the back and said, "Hey, John! How're you doing?"

"Good, good, good. What's you up to?"

"Well—I'm running for mayor."

"Oh! Well, good! That's nice!"

"Hey, glad to see you there! Hi, I'm Richard Austin, running for mayor. . . . How're *you* there?"

Most of the black workers smiled when he went to shake their hands, some pausing to offer encouragement. The white workers were also polite, but many walked by as if he weren't there.

Several stops later, in the evening, Austin arrived in a white residential neighborhood far from the inner city. Six hundred Polish people were crowded into a school auditorium, men in shirt-sleeves and women in sleeveless dresses. They were restless, now, because the big event of the night had just happened. Mary Beck, the law-and-order candidate, had given one of her rousing speeches. They had stomped their feet and shouted and applauded wildly and now, tired and hot from this orgy of thinly concealed antiblack emotion, they settled back to size up the black candidate. Austin was charming, polite, looking like a professor of sociology, and they listened in silence, gazing dully toward the front of the room. Austin used the word "Negro" instead of "black" this time, and he spoke of the need for Federal money, better housing, increased public safety. The women fanned themselves while the men shifted impatiently in their seats.

"I believe," said Austin, "that shortages in housing lie at the root of much of the problems we have in this city. I'd like to give you a concrete example. If any of you have the time, you might drive down one of the streets in the ghetto, where it is so over-populated—"

There was an almost audible gasp, a dread silence, a vacuum, as if all six hundred people had drawn breath at once, sucking in every inch of air from the sweat-filled room.

"—and where the homes are intolerable, in weather like this. When it gets hot, it's impossible for the people to remain in those places, so they go outside. Not inside for air conditioning, because there is none. So they swarm out on the streets, with nothing to do, many with no skills of any kind to be of service in the present labor market. . . ."

The people were still frozen in position, perhaps out of fear, perhaps because they didn't want to listen to this kind of talk; so Austin, sensing the mood, carefully shifted back to safer ground, retreating with the skill and grace of a man who had learned just how far one can go before his listeners will turn off their minds. At the end, they applauded, but it was clear that few, if any, would vote for him.

"I thought they gave us a very nice reception," Austin said afterward.

Still later in the night, the car sped to the northern edge of

Detroit, which Austin half jokingly called "the last frontier." This was one of the wealthiest sections, a very exclusive, high-class neighborhood. Inside one of the mansions, punch and coffee and cookies were positioned on the cloth-covered dining-room table, and the wealthy white guests mingled with each other nearby. Avant-garde paintings of ghetto life hung on the walls, along with romanticized black faces arranged in collages.

Standing in the center of the living room, surrounded by faces eager to show affection, Austin spoke in a low tone, almost a whisper.

"Some people aren't sure whether the city is ready for a black mayor," he said. "They're not so sure that you ought to encourage it. Don't let them talk you out of this splendid opportunity to make democracy work."

The faces nodded, smiled, frowned.

"In other cities where the people have been given the opportunity, they voted for the best man even though his face happened to be black. It happened in Gary and in Cleveland. And then later, in Los Angeles, where the black population is only 17 percent, Thomas Bradley, a black man, was able to get *47 percent* of the total vote. And this meant that an awful lot of fair-minded whites were willing to consider the candidate on the basis of merit, even though he was black.

"Here in Detroit, where the population of blacks is more than 40 percent, we should have an even better chance to win. For many years in this city, black voters have been extremely fair-minded in supporting white candidates. Blacks have demonstrated over and over that they don't just vote for black, but for the best interests of the city. We have supported white candidates, and now we expect whites to consider a black candidate who is the best qualified."

4.

"Hey, Austin!"

The voices of small children greeted him as he emerged from the car in a black neighborhood. Inside one of the houses, a dozen women sat around fanning themselves. A few men leaned against the wall in the background, looking somewhat uncomfortable.

The women had prepared some ham and cheese for the candidate, and he tried to eat as little as he could without hurting their feelings. One of the black men came forward and handed him an envelope containing eight dollars collected from the neighbors. Austin was so grateful he could hardly speak.

"Thank you," he mumbled, staring at the envelope in his hand. "I know what this means. . . ."

Then he walked around the street in the semidarkness, going up on the porches to chat with other black folks. He was followed by a little girl in a party hat.

"The community is responding beautifully," he said to someone whose face could not be seen in the shadows of the porch.

In other black households, Austin was able to laugh easily and feel at home. "I want you to know," he told one group, "that I'm getting fairly good support among our white friends. They're giving us a good *reception,* anyway. And I want you to realize that I don't change my tune in the white community. The things I say to them are the things I say to you. Because we're *all* interested in the same things, like schools, police protection—"

"That's right, that's right."

"I've lived here a long time, and I'm one who really knows how the other half lives."

"Yes! Yes, you do!"

"Because I *was* that other half."

"Right!"

"And I know how *I* lived. And I don't want any child to have to go through what I went through in order to get along in this world. Really, it's too much to ask of anybody."

"That's right, Mayor Austin."

"It's no wonder that so many of our young boys and girls fall by the wayside. It's too grueling an undertaking. So we have to improve the life possibilities of these young people. If we don't, if we wait anymore, the more we lose, the worse our crime rate is gonna be, and the more of them will be available to be attacking people on the streets. And it never ends! They have no skills, no work habits. . . ."

"This is our home!" cried one of the black women. "We *believe* in this city! We want to make it a decent place to raise our families!"

The others in the room nodded their agreement, one woman adding, "We want the same as what the whites want!"

"That's right," Austin injected quietly, as if the secret had just been revealed. He became excited over this revelation and bent forward in his chair, whispering: "*They* don't think they have adequate police protection, and *you* don't think so either, do you?"

"Nooooo!"

"Let me ask you something, Mr. Mayor," said another lady.

"You notice," Austin interrupted with a broad grin, "how she calls me 'Mr. Mayor' and I respond?"

The sound of their laughter filled the room.

"I don't know if you're aware of some of the things that go on, Mr. Mayor, because you're a gentleman. You're a very cultural person, and I'm sure you travel in such nice circles, so I guess you're *not* aware of some of the problems in our neighborhood, being the high-quality person you are, but . . ."

Dick Austin strained to listen, his whole body leaning forward, and one could wonder how much he was saddened by the invisible wall that this woman seemed to have thrown between him and the group so suddenly. Was he, or was he not, one of them?

5.

On September 9, more than 330,000 people were casting ballots in Detroit's primary, choosing two candidates to run for mayor from among the list of twenty-eight names.

At nine o'clock that night, television crews were setting up cameras and lights in the big ballroom on the Detroit Hilton's second floor. Austin, his wife Ida, and their twenty-six-year-old daughter Hazel had been out all day in separate cars, visiting the various polling places. When they arrived at the hotel, Austin slipped into an elevator and headed for a staff room. He was composed, smiling. "I just want to wash my hands and face, and collect my thoughts."

Austin's three-room suite filled up with an assortment of people, some watching the TV set and most of the others sitting or standing with drinks in their hands. One black woman on the couch said loudly, "There are some people in the black community who *want* the System to fail! A suicidal tendency exists! They believe you have to bring the System *down* first. Now, I'm hoping the system *works,* mind you, but if it doesn't, I'll be ready to join in to bring it down! But let's *try* the System!"

At eleven o'clock a huge crowd on the mezzanine floor cheered wildly at the news that Richard Austin had led the entire field of candidates. He was several thousand votes ahead of Sheriff Gribbs; Mary Beck was trailing in third place. Austin came downstairs and made his way through the happy crowd to the platform. An electricity born of hope and a sense of goodwill pervaded the room. "You're the new mayor, all right!" someone shouted as Austin climbed to the platform in the glare of the lights.

"I am extremely gratified at the response that we've received, from all over this community," he said. "We've been saying that when elected we'll be the mayor of *all* the people, and not just *some* of the people."

The crowd roared. Whites clapped, raised the victory/peace sign with their fingers; blacks raised their fists. For a moment, it all came together, almost like the old, we-shall-overcome days of the Movement.

"With your continued help, we will give the people of Detroit an experience in democracy that they have never seen before!"

They were reeling, reaching a peak of euphoria. One elderly black woman wept. The young blacks raised their fists up, down, up again. Austin watched this, smiling; he hesitated for a few moments and then, as if the invisible chasm between himself and the militant kids were closing, he raised his own black fist into the air, holding it up for the cameras as waves of emotion thundered from below.

6.

"Happy days are here again," they were singing. A sea of white faces milled about below the lobby of the Pick-Fort Shelby Hotel across town. Their candidate, Sheriff Gribbs, had become one of the two nominees.

"If Austin becomes mayor," said a pretty blonde girl wearing a straw hat with "GRIBBS" on the side, "he'll put a feather in every Negro's cap. There'll be another riot for sure. Mayor Cavanaugh gave the most of anyone to the Negro, yet they rioted."

"They're so cocky *already*," said her girl friend. "Just think if they had a colored mayor!"

"If Austin gets in, the population will decrease for sure."

"I'm a secretary downtown, but if Austin got elected, I'd think seriously of quitting and moving away. I really would."

The crowd glanced up at the new voting totals which been put on the blackboard:

> Austin: 124,941
> Gribbs: 105,640
> Beck: 71,065

It was clear to everyone in the room that all, or most, of Beck's votes would go to the sheriff in November, making him the winner.

In his speech that night, Gribbs announced that he would not change his "moderate" philosophy in order to attract the conservative groups that had supported Beck's thinly veiled racist platform. What he failed to add was that he didn't need to woo the Beck supporters, because they now had nowhere else to go. Whether he liked it or not, he was now the candidate of the racists—and as a politician, he liked it.

But what had happened to the so-called white liberals who had been counted on to vote for the best qualified man? Why had they voted for Gribbs? Austin, a man who had been committed to serving "all of the people" for so many years, had managed to receive only 7 percent of the white vote. In some white neighborhoods his vote fell to 2 percent. Across Detroit, voting patterns showed a city divided; in precinct after precinct, whites had voted for the white man, blacks for the black. Richard Austin had become the first black man ever to be nominated as a candidate for mayor of Detroit, but the victory left a sour taste in the mouth. If liberal white people could not bring themselves to vote for Austin, who was militant by no stretch of the imagination, then there was not a black person on earth for whom they would vote.

Fourteen

I had begun to form a picture of Richard Hatcher as a man continually struggling with himself to keep looking at the world from the point of view he formerly had as one of the "little people"—to keep remembering, no matter how fast or high he climbed, that his own identity lay in being mentally down at the bottom. It bothered him in no small degree, for example, that many blacks simply couldn't trust one of their own who had "made it" through the established channels of social or political success. It was a reflex reaction, really, for them to become suspicious of anyone, including a black man—no, *especially* a black man—who operated from a seat of power. Perhaps more important than any single achievement of the Hatcher administration in Gary, to him personally, had been his ability to maintain the trust of the majority of his own poor, black constituents. He was still within their reach.

Hatcher mentioned to me what he called a "schizoid attitude" that had existed for a long time in the black community, and it occurred to me, as he explained, that he was really talking about his own experience. A black family would work hard to make it possible for at least one of the children to go away to college, and all during high school the neighbors would encourage him to study hard, do well, "and when that same child would go to college, go through all the struggle and everything else that it took to do that, and maybe get a professional degree, and come back as a lawyer or doctor or something like that, the same people would then be highly critical of that person, saying, 'Well, he thinks he's better than the rest of us.' And that would be true whether that person actually did think he was better or whether he didn't. And it shows up in politics, too."

On way it had showed up in politics, for Hatcher, was the fact that five other black candidates had run against him in his primary campaign for the Democratic nomination in the mayor's race. A substantial segment of the black community had been opposed to him at the outset.

"A lot of the guys that ran the crap tables, the women who operated the houses—oh, they were really actively out working against me," he recalled. The result was that Hatcher's victory wasn't nearly the solid "black mandate" that many people assumed it was, and once he took office, many of the blacks who had expected him to act in their favor were bitterly disappointed, accusing him of what he feared most, that "he thinks he's better than us, now."

"They figured," Hatcher said, "that after all, 'Hatcher's black, and we're black, so he's gonna help us out.' They didn't make any evaluation of whether it was right or wrong, or of what the long-range ramifications for the city were. They just expected me to do something, and when I didn't do it, then they'd say, 'Boy, that Hatcher's really not what I thought he was. I'd never vote for him again.' The same people that might have worked very hard for you as a kind of hope, a new hope for them—once you're actually *in* office, and doing the very things that you said you were going to do, they say, 'Well, who does he think *he* is? What's he mean that he's gonna close this town down?' These are the same people who said, 'Boy, this town is really corrupt. It needs action.' They're the ones who come and say, 'Well, I got this little place over here, and I want to make sure I'll be able to operate,' and that sort of thing. And when you tell 'em it can't happen, then, man, they're really *angry* and *upset* with you. And there were people, for example, who said, 'There are some terrible slums in Gary. It's really bad, these slums, and nobody wants to do anything about 'em. But if we can get Hatcher elected, *he'll* do something about these slums. *He'll* tear 'em down.' Now, some of those same people are complaining that we've torn down all those buildings! They wonder why we haven't built new housing on the site, like, within two weeks. The same people! It's a kind of interesting thing."

(One evening in Chicago I met a young black man who told me that as far as he was concerned, Hatcher was "screwing his own people." When I asked him why, he replied, "Because he closed up all the crap tables." I was able to understand how those engaged in illegal activities could feel angry at Hatcher for closing their operations, but why was this young man, who was unaffected by Hatcher's actions in Gary, so bitter? Weren't the crap tables actually hurting the majority of black people? Or was life in the ghetto so far removed from the reaches of the System, was the spirit of the people so utterly destroyed already, that by preventing their crimes we were removing their source of comfort? Was a crackdown on gambling and vice as destructive as would be a crackdown on religion? Were the crap tables as important in their way as the churches in theirs? The thought came to me that Hatcher's reforms were like the removal of old adhesives in order to get to the wound; the process was painful, and therefore many patients would prefer to have their wounds left untreated rather than undergo the ordeal of having the bandage ripped off. Or was it like the cripple who doesn't want to walk alone because by now he is too fond of the crutches? He will not let go of them easily, because they have become such good friends over the years of his infirmity. And so it might have been true that Hatcher's zeal to correct conditions in Gary was having at least as traumatic an effect upon many blacks as upon the worried whites.)

But if Hatcher was possessed of an inner fear that by some unconscious process he would move beyond the grasp or trust of those whom he simply called "the people"—that he would in some way cause them to feel he had become too big for them—he had developed a personal philosophy or standard by which to act. And in turn he was able to trust that "the people" would not let *him* down. If *he* keeps the faith, then they must, too. On one occasion he described his campaign this way:

> We had faith in the people. We had confidence in them. We
> knew that if we fought for them, if we spoke for them, stood

up for them, voiced their most hidden desires, exposed their oppressors—we knew that if we did all of this, and if we did not let the people down, they would not let us down.

We waged that kind of a campaign, and I want to tell you something beautiful. They did not let us down. They did not let themselves down.

In other words, he had entered into a kind of compact with "the people"—he had given them not only hope but responsibility to react not in narrow, selfish terms but over the long, frustrating haul. He told me, "Despite all of the things that have happened to me, all of the real disappointments that I've had, I have an overriding, probably almost an irrational faith in human nature. In the basic decency of human beings, whoever they are. That, all things being equal, they will do what is decent as opposed to what is bad. But people tell me that that is the most naïve attitude in the world to have, because people aren't like that. People act out of self-interest only, they say, and that, given a chance, they would more likely do the thing that's bad for themselves than the thing that's good. But I don't believe that, and one of the encouraging things, to me, has been that, whenever I've really been willing to put that sort of thing to a test, it's worked out."

It made Hatcher something of an austere person, this keeping-the-eye-on-the-target philosophy, because it went beyond politics and into the kind of situation where people had to be either for or against what he was trying to do, and that held for blacks as well as whites, especially for blacks who were still tied to the Democratic Machine.

"Many of those blacks were benefiting from the Machine," Hatcher said. "Maybe not greatly, but they were getting some kind of benefit, and many of those benefits have been cut off since I've been in office. Not just for them but even for people who supported me, because we aren't playing the game that way anymore. You don't just hire a guy, for example, because he got two hundred votes for you. Great if he got the votes, but is he qualified for a job? If he's not, you can't hire him, period. So now he's angry at you. But overall, as I say, I still have faith and confidence that, if you do what you honestly believe to be right, if you really try to work *for* people, in the final analysis the people will support you."

There was an unseen tension in this process, this painful ordeal of working to remove old and greedy cancers, and Hatcher acknowledged this when he added, "They may not *like* some things that you do, but in the end they'll support you."

2.

At some point in his life, Hatcher had learned to put practicality above anger and frustration, when possible, and it has served him well as a tactic. Perhaps the pivotal incident had occurred while he was in senior year of high school in Michigan City, in 1951, when he worked in the kitchen of a local restaurant. In the retelling, the incident has taken on overtones of significance that may be exaggerated, but Hatcher himself refers to it as an example of what has molded his thinking since then.

To begin with, he realized that not all blacks obtained even kitchen jobs at the time, and that he had been hired only because the local merchants valued him as a member of the school's football team, that most sacred of Midwest institutions. At any rate, one afternoon a black couple came in the restaurant and sat in a booth, only to be refused service. Suddenly aware of the restaurant's policy of discrimination, Hatcher ripped off his apron, threw it down, and stomped out in a fury. When he got home and told his father what had happened, the elder Hatcher persuaded his son to go back, swallow his anger and pride, save the much-needed money from his salary, and *then,* having achieved a personal goal, return and try to correct the restaurant's policies.

After much arguing, Hatcher took his father's advice ("You gotta go back, go back and swallow that stuff and keep working," he recalled his father saying), and later he did return. First he went back to the restaurant and worked through the year, saved his money, and went off as a freshman to Indiana University, and then, in the summer of 1952, he returned with several friends to stage the first sit-in in the history of Michigan City. Within a week they integrated the restaurant, and years later, Hatcher received a letter from his former boss *thanking* him for what he had done. Apparently integration was so profitable that the owner was able to expand his business to a whole chain of restaurants.

It was one little event of the civil-rights movement—although in 1952 the actual "movement" hadn't yet begun—that tended to form a basis for some optimism within its participants, Richard Hatcher included. And so, although he now carried within him a genuine rage, he was in fact a product of those years when young activists had learned to push, slowly but persistently, toward some achievable goal. And in his own life, paralleling the restaurant incident, Hatcher's goals have always been first personal, then social. He held down a number of jobs to get through school—waiting on tables, working as a psychiatric aide at a mental hospital—and was helped out by a small athletic scholarship and even by a collection taken up by the parishioners of his church.

"I learned," he told me, "that you have to do whatever it takes to make it, personally, on your own, so that you don't have to take any kind of injustice. That's why I went to law school [at Valparaiso University in Indiana] after college; because I never again wanted a job where somebody was telling me what to do. That may have been a distorted view, but by the time I was sixteen or seventeen, the only impression I had of a superior, or a boss, was a guy that tried to kick you in the pants every chance he got and who worked you and didn't want to pay you, and all those things. And I just made up my mind that I was gonna be my own boss."

After law school, in 1959, he moved to Gary to live with an older brother and practice law in East Chicago—Michigan City was a dead end for black youngsters, he said—and during a three-year period he became an attorney for the Young Adult Council of the NAACP in Gary, got involved in a lawsuit against the school system, charging *de facto* segregation, and later worked to combat discrimination in hospital and housing policies. "Just one thing led to another," he said, and the move toward political activity was an inevitable result.

"It really hit me, in about 1963, that with all we were doing, marching and picketing and demonstrating and all, things weren't changing very much. If anything changed at all, it was very slow, and not very much was happening. That's when we really took a look at the political situation in Gary and realized that the black community had been electing mayors and councilmen, and all of that business, just routinely, but they had never *selected* any of those people. They were always candidates that were *handed* to the black community, and yet *because* of the solid black vote, those candidates were the ones that got elected! And so we thought we'd try to reverse that procedure, and have the black community participate in the selection of the candidates as well as in their elections. And that's when I ran for the City Council."

Hatcher and several other young blacks, "out of that frustration," formed a voluntary political organization called Muigwithania ("We are together," in Swahili), after the name of Jomo Kenyatta's newspaper. With this group as his political base, Hatcher defied the Machine and ran at-large for the council as an independent Democratic candidate, receiving more votes than anyone had ever gotten in a primary race for the council. He won election in the fall and within the first year was selected by his colleagues as president of the council, an unprecedented honor for a freshman member. "One of the things I tried to do while I was a councilman," he told me, "was to continue to speak up for the people. I was sort of an irritant to the Establishment, you might say." In other words, political activity was an extension of his involvement in the civil-rights movement; it was not an end but a means to continue clawing away at the System. But by 1967, having been unable to make any kind of real change in the lives of "the people," Hatcher took the step that was to make him a national figure.

3.

Virtually no one believed that he had a chance to beat the Machine, first in a primary and then in the November, 1967, election, and on one occasion Hatcher told it this way:

> Some of us said to ourselves, "How is it possible to ever beat all of that power, all those jobs, all that money?" The campaign started with a small core of people. There were many

doubting Uncle Thomases. They said the time wasn't ready yet. We said, "Ready or not, here we come."

The first hurdle was to beat the incumbent Democratic Machine candidate, Mayor A. Martin Katz, in the May primary. Usually both blacks and whites had united at the polls to elect whomever the Machine was backing, so Hatcher first had to awaken his own people to the need for a kind of political revolution. The word went out to the "little people" in Midtown: "Take the Man's money but pull the lever for Hatcher." The result was a surprising display of grass-roots power. Seventy percent of the blacks showed their independence by voting for Hatcher, and a conservative white candidate pulled almost half the white votes away from Katz—an incredible combination of events—and Hatcher emerged as the Democratic nominee.

At this point he should have been assured of victory against the Republican candidate in November, since Gary is so heavily Democratic, but he wasn't playing the Machine's game, and so it turned against him. Not only was he pledging to clean up the town, but he was also making it clear that as mayor he would make his own appointments, not the Machine's. It was this stubborn, independent stance, probably even more than the color of his skin, that made Machine boss John Krupa withdraw his support. Saying that Hatcher was "not the right kind of Negro," Krupa, the Lake County Democratic chairman, cut off Hatcher from all campaign funds and in fact gave them to the Republican candidate, if such a contortion of the two-party system can be believed. Then he started attacking Hatcher for not having lived in Gary long enough.

"I got here as fast as I could," Hatcher replied.

Krupa then announced that Hatcher was "underqualified" for the job of mayor and implied he was a Communist since he hadn't disavowed the public views of Rap Brown, Joan Baez, Stokely Carmichael, and even Marlon Brando. At one point he was offered $100,000 to drop from the race.

When the Democratic Machine swung its weight behind Hatcher's white Republican opponent, the issue of race was not far behind. Many of Gary's working-class Democratic voters much preferred a white man to a black one, no matter what his politics or personal morality happened to be. Boss Krupa pointedly suggested that "Hatcher has to sell himself to the white people of Gary." One of the many implications was that under a black mayor the whole town might burn down. Hatcher doggedly went into the alien white neighborhoods and visited the supermarkets, but many whites refused to listen.

"I'd go to the mill gate," he said to me, "and the white workers would walk up, look at me, and just ignore my outstretched hand and walk past. It was really something. Or I'd walk down the street and see people turn their heads or refuse to speak. . . ."

At times, exasperated, he would confront them verbally with the fact of his blackness, perhaps to embarrass or shock them: "I know you haven't heard a word I said. All you see in front of you is black. But if, by some miracle, race was ruled out and I and my opponent were considered only on qualifications, this election wouldn't even be close."

Cut off from all political funds and unable to finance his campaign, Hatcher, against the advice of many of his supporters, took out an expensive full-page advertisement in the distant New York *Times,* appealing for funds from around the country. "For God's Sake, Let's Get Ourselves Together," screamed the ad, and eventually the money came in, and the campaign was solvent again, enabling Hatcher to buy the necessary billboards and so on. Not to be outdone, Krupa offered money to anyone who would tear down Hatcher's posters. And being the Lake County circuit-court clerk as well as party chairman, Krupa even refused to provide extra registrars for the black Midtown area. When Hatcher set up volunteer tables on the sidewalk, Krupa threatened jail sentences and fines for fraudulent registrations. And right before the election, it was discovered that thousands of fictitious names had been added to the white voting rolls and that some five thousand black names had been removed arbitrarily. Even after that plot was thwarted, some of the voting machines in black precincts started jamming mysteriously on election day.

> The Machine poured a half-million dollars into the race. Money flowed like wine, and wine flowed like water. But the people wouldn't sell out. In the quiet of the voting booth, they voted the Man right out of office. And the real hero of

that campaign was the little man, and his name was Every-
man. He may have had a third-grade education, maybe not
even that much. He may have been on relief, or living in a
housing project, but that man, that little unknown man,
woke up on election morning, he dressed, he drank a cup of
coffee, and he trudged his way to the polls. And he voted
against hypocrisy, he voted against an ugly system, he voted
against his oppressor. He voted for me, but he did so only in
a symbolic sense. He really voted for his children, and his
children's children—those romping around in overcrowded
living rooms, and those yet unborn but still to come.

Hatcher was elected by fewer than two thousand votes, receiving
some 98 percent of the black vote (a jump of 28 percent since
the primary) and picking up about 13 percent of the white total.
It was a political miracle if there ever was one, and on election
night, while the Indiana National Guard stood by in case of
trouble, he pledged to "remake" the city and to "lead the way
for the whole country to follow."

"We shall prove," he told his followers, "that diversity can be
a source of enrichment, that at least the people of one city in the
nation have decided, finally, to get themselves together."

No political allies marched with him into City Hall the following January (1968), and that accounted for much of the troubles
he encountered afterward. Would diversity become a "source of
enrichment" or would black political power only hasten the day
when Gary would become an all-black city?

4.

To get to the mills, it is necessary to drive through the all-black
downtown, but a steelworker and his family need not live there.
Many of these families, tied to the mills but wanting to escape the
racially changing inner-city neighborhoods, had sold their houses
and bought new ones out in a place called Glen Park, where they
now were making a kind of last stand against the advancing
blacks. Glen Park is a flat, neat, tidy, clean, quiet, dull sort of
suburban area of about five square miles and perhaps forty
thousand people, primarily descendants of Central Europeans,

who live in modest houses set on well-kept lawns that contain orderly amounts of trees and shrubs and children. It is an island, really, a white man's retreat from the turmoil of the times, and in fact if you're *not* white, then you're already too black to have come here. The folks in this section went heavily for Richard Nixon in November, 1968—Democrats though they are—and George Wallace nearly did better than Hubert Humphrey. The year before, only 9 percent of the people in Glen Park had voted for Hatcher who, since his election, had been trying to convince them that he was their mayor as well as the blacks'.

Glen Park, when I visited it in the summer of 1970, seemed not unlike many other residential neighborhoods. It was separated from the rest of Gary by an interstate highway, the polluted Little Calumet River, and as Hatcher once put it, "by perhaps some several generations of social thought." At any rate, there existed a movement by residents of Glen Park to "disannex" it from the city—it had been annexed in 1910—and thereby make the separation complete. Their project began after Hatcher had become mayor, and though their stated motives were economic, there was little question that racial fear dominated their thinking. Hatcher himself saw the separation movement as a futile attempt on the part of worried, panicky whites "to escape the challenge of the times" and also as "a blunt and costly response to black realization." Other Hatcher-inspired phrases were "a white reaction to black ascendancy" and "an embryonic American version of apartheid," take your choice.

A woman in Glen Park named Mrs. Pauline Schwegel had been trying to help Mayor Hatcher undercut the disannexation movement before it reached what undoubtedly would become a long legal battle in the courts. As chairman of the Glen Park Information Committee, Mrs. Schwegel had organized informal kaffeeklatsches between Glen Park residents and Hatcher. She had published a leaflet to promote her feeling that disannexation would mean "bad economics, bad government, and bad morals."

"It will not solve the racial problem in either Gary or Glen Park," the pamphlet advised. "Disannexation from Gary does not mean disannexation from Indiana or from the United States."

I drove out to Glen Park to meet Mrs. Schwegel, heading south on Broadway, a street reminding me of downtown avenues in places like New Rochelle or Mount Vernon, outside New York City. It is the main street but a shabby one, and at one point I waited while a freight train rumbled leisurely across the road, a common occurrence and one of the monster's many ways of exerting its authority over the inhabitants of the city. While the scent of the mill drifted into the car on this hot afternoon, I thought of the faces I had passed along the way—strong, hard faces of men and women, the same faces which had cheered Bobby Kennedy's passage through Gary in the spring of 1968, during the Democratic primary campaign. The assassination of Martin Luther King had occurred not many weeks before then, and Mayor Hatcher had confronted a group of black students who had stormed out of school. Hatcher had persuaded them to turn back and reenter the school. Strange, with the tension that existed in this violent steel-mill town, that these same hard faces, belonging to men and women who so distrusted Hatcher, had cheered so loudly and vigorously for Kennedy.

"Kennedy and I talked about the war," Hatcher told me. "We discussed what it was doing to the cities. And generally, we talked of some of the hopes we had if he became President."

When the freight train disappeared and I drove on toward Glen Park, thinking of words like "disannexation" and "secession," I was reminded of how much hope there had been that Bobby Kennedy could unify America. Now, the mood of the nation had changed, and Hatcher was on his own.

I arrived late at Mrs. Schwegel's little rectangular yellow house. She was a charming lady, a young sixty-two years of age, wearing a colorful, flower-pattern dress that seemed to blend perfectly with the yellow walls and carpeting of her living room. She spoke of Hatcher's "integrity" and "honesty"—virtues apparently in short supply among Gary politicians.

"Both my husband and I voted for him," she said. "He's made some mistakes, I guess, and he'll make more. But that's to be expected, isn't it? He came to our meetings, and he really impressed people in that kind of intimate situation. It's not even so much what he says, but how. He's honest, and he won't sell out to the Machine, but it may be too strong for him. So he might not win the next time, I don't know. The Machine will run an Uncle Tom against him, that's for sure."

(The current thinking was that the Machine would put up a Negro candidate in order to split the black vote away from Hatcher, enabling a white man to emerge the winner.)

When we got to the subject of disannexation, Mrs. Schwegel produced a four-page, single-spaced, typewritten letter, copies of which, she said, had been sent "at random, to a thousand homes" in Glen Park. The letter, unsigned, carried the headline "The Black Intrusion."

"Hello, Neighbor," it began. "Have you ever tried to look out your kitchen window and picture a black neighbor next door?

"Neighbors, please take warning," it went on. "Allow the present black power structure to have its own way much longer, and they will destroy your white heritage along with our country."

"So," Mrs. Schwegel said, "that's what it's all about. It's really that simple."

She handed me another letter, this one signed by the chairman of the disannexation movement, Robert K. Stephenson. Writing to the professional and business people of Glen Park, Stephenson came directly to the point:

> We believe Gary and Glen Park should be two separate cities.
>
> We believe Gary is simply doing nothing more than dispersing its slums, and we do not relish receiving our promised share of them.
>
> Your present clients and customers will find this situation intolerable. They will leave Glen Park and Gary.

"You know," said Mrs. Schwegel, chuckling, "Stephenson won't even say Hatcher's name. He spells it, instead. He'll say, 'That H-a-t-c-h-e-r,' and go on from there. Also he won't say the name of Martin Luther King Drive, either. He just calls it 'that road.' "

Mrs. Schwegel had received several obscene and threatening phone calls because of her association with Hatcher, and at times she had required police protection. One day she was scheduled to go on local radio and was told by an anonymous caller, "If you go down there, you won't get home alive." She went.

"Of course," she told me, "Hatcher gets those kinds of threats all the time, which is why he has a bodyguard with him. He cer-

tainly wouldn't be alive today without one. . . . He probably
feels very much alone. And suspicious, too. I think he feels that
people who do something *for* him must be looking for something in return. And he's probably right. So, he's always on his
guard. . . .

"One night after a meeting, we came out on the sidewalk, and
Mayor Hatcher was smiling, so I said to him, 'Look, Mr. Mayor,
I'm not doing this for nothing, you know. I'd like a favor.' Well!
I wish you could have seen the expression that came over his
face! It was as if I had physically struck him. He replied, 'What
is it that you'd like, Mrs. Schwegel?' So I told him that my son was
coming home for Easter and would like to meet him. Would he
join us for breakfast? Well, he was so relieved! He said, 'If my
schedule allows it, I'll be over for sure.' And he did come over,
too. He and my son spoke French to each other over breakfast."

As I was leaving, Mrs. Schwegel stood at her front door and
gestured outside toward the other houses on this quiet, sun-filled
little street. She said almost in a whisper, "Only two homes around
here are open to me, now. Not that we'd ever been real close to
the neighbors, but they used to speak, and now they don't. I suppose it really doesn't matter. . . ."

5.

As I drove out to Broadway and then back toward Midtown, I
recalled something Mrs. Schwegel had said—something to the effect that maybe the country's race relations have been like a bad
marriage, that maybe we've tried to live together and found that
for different reasons, neither side is ready yet.

"So maybe we *have* to separate for a while," she said with great
reluctance. "And later, when we're ready, we can try living together again."

At first I had thought the analogy a plausible one. Blacks needed
to strengthen themselves politically, economically, culturally;
whites had to search their hearts and change their attitudes, make
some commitments; and then maybe we could come together on
some new level of maturity and understanding. But as I continued into the black downtown of Gary, I was reminded that

we have *been* separated all along, and it occurred to me that "separation" now might mean something beyond what Mrs. Schwegel had meant. Separation may be the necessary means to an end, it may be inevitable, the only way of ultimately coming together. But then it also would seem that we're headed for some bleak prospects in the near future if we don't work things out now, that there is some terrible price to be paid for this growing division, a secret price much higher than the mere burning down of buildings.

Fifteen

1.

Having remained in the shelter of Kenneth Gibson's storefront headquarters for too long, I decided to pay a visit to the other side. I emerged from the doorway and proceeded across Broad Street in the dark, then walked through Military Park to the Robert Treat Hotel, named for the fellow who had swindled the Hackensack Indians out of the land upon which Newark was built. Mayor Hugh Addonizio was hiding out somewhere on the eighth floor.

I stepped from the elevator and moved quietly down the corridor. No sounds of bubbling enthusiasm came forth from this side of the political war; indeed, there was only the dull silence of worried men huddling behind closed doors. Number 833, to be exact, at the far end of the hall. I stepped into the room, suddenly feeling that I had entered the suite of the Mob by mistake. A slip of the senses, perhaps—the Mob!—but then, I was in Newark, now, and, thinking of the trial, I wondered how much truth there could be in this intuition. Perhaps I was more accurate than I knew; indeed, three months later, after Gibson was elected and firmly settled in the job, the New York *Times* would carry the following message:

> The country's newest black Mayor and his aides are discovering that they have inherited a city government even more

corrupt, more debilitated by years of fiscal mismanagement and more thoroughly riddled with resilient forces of greed and ambition than they had expected.

Mr. Gibson's caution, friends say, has become mixed with an apprehension about what law-enforcement officials tell him is a thoroughly entrenched structure of organized crime in the city.

Yes, the reporter felt as if he had entered the chambers of the Mob, the Syndicate, the Mafia, whatever. Here were the sullen faces of men who were into some serious, secret business. There were six or eight of them, all with dark, greasy hair parted on one side and slicked back on the other; there was no joy here, no excitement, only the feeling of cold panic and calculated brooding. No one spoke a word as I came into the room. The difference between Gibson's headquarters and this one was the difference in the campaigns—these men already had something and were trying to keep it, while Gibson's people were experiencing the first flush of hope for the future. I watched the hard faces of these fleshy men and began to understand some small corner of their desperation. If they lost this election, they would lose everything; they would find it impossible not to turn away from the victors out of bitterness and pride. They had gone through too much of the process of cynicism and hatred, they had churned up too much cold greed within themselves, and therefore, if they lost, they would be too humiliated to look the black winners in the eye. The damage they had done to the soul of Newark was impossible to calculate.

"If *we* vote, *we* win," announced the Addonizio poster on the wall. A suffocating silence hung in the room, and I noticed that at least two of the men were, in fact, policemen. The only female in the room was a young secretary who was on the phone, taking down the results of a news poll that showed Addonizio ahead. She looked up and said to the silent, hefty men, "Only one white in eight is expected to vote for Gibson." They all nodded, not with joy but with the expression of a group of gamblers who had placed all their possessions on this final bet. "If *we* vote, *we* win," the poster insisted. A cowboy movie was on the soundless television set, right in the middle of a shootout. "Turn it up," said one of the husky cops.

At last, my presence in the room was noticed, and a tall, thin, black-haired man grabbed my arm and whispered, "Let's step out in the hall."

The man pulled me by the material of my jacket, pacing up and down the narrow corridor of the hotel, and when I twisted loose, we stood facing each other.

"Who are you?"

"I'm writing a book."

"What about?"

"Politics."

"Okay, but what's the *theme* of the book?"

"I don't know. I'm in the process of finding out."

"Listen," the man said, now affecting a confidential tone, "for all we know, you might be one of Gibson's goons."

"Goons?"

"You know—hired by Gibson to come over here and disrupt things."

After being checked for weapons, I was allowed back in the room.

2.

Mayor Hugh J. Addonizio came out of an adjoining room, looking refreshed despite the heavy circles under his eyes. A short, pear-shaped man, he evoked an image of one of those hairless and feetless dolls which, when tipped over to one side, are able to spring back up immediately. And indeed, Addonizio was nothing if not resilient. He had been commuting to Trenton for his trial during the daytime and campaigning for reelection by night; and his wife was in the hospital, suffering from emphysema. The chunky, bald mayor was smiling, however. His pale skin, if not exactly gleaming, was clean, and I imagined for a moment that the little mayor had been slumped in a hot tub all that time, while his strategy men had been sitting around on the edge. The mayor's thin lips formed a sardonic smile as he came into the room. He was wearing a neatly pressed dark-blue suit, a light-blue shirt, and a silver tie, and his large ears seemed to jut out from the sides of his head like a pair of wings. He kept one hand tucked in a pocket of his suit jacket and, head leaning forward, he started out of the room and down the hall, followed by all the silent and beefy men. On the way down in the elevator he stood next to a giant of a man who wore a gun on his belt. Addonizio suddenly looked rather small and babylike next to his bodyguard, like a fallen Humpty Dumpty who was still waiting for his body to self-destruct at any moment. He nudged the big man with his elbow and said, "Hide that thing. You frighten me." He was joking, of course, because the gun was the symbol of what this whole election had come down to. At this moment, however, I could not help but like Addonizio somewhat. There was something in the way the little desperate mayor looked so composed and relaxed, in the way he spoke under his breath and smiled around the lips and eyes, in the fact that he alone in this group still maintained a sense of humor, that made him a likable character.

In many ways, I thought, Addonizio was like America itself. Like *white* America. Steeped in corruption and finding himself struggling to keep afloat, he was, like white America, not without an impressive past on the surface, the way the past is set down in the textbooks of American history. The son of Italian immigrants, he had been a football star in high school and college; when discharged from military service in 1946, he had been promoted to the rank of captain and held a variety of medals for bravery in action; he had been a Congressman for seven terms and mayor of Newark for eight years. Moreover, Mayor Addonizio had been a *liberal,* a champion of civil and human rights! America! Filled with contradictions, neither all good nor all bad, and like white America, Addonizio may not have known who he was anymore, may not have believed in his own guilt; for when a man defends himself in public as "Hughie" had been doing throughout this campaign, he can begin to believe the lie. Even tonight, he held in his hand a printed speech to be delivered: "I am, of course, innocent of these wild and slanderous charges. . . . Each day, I listen with a sense of profound shock, for I still find it hard to believe that such fantastic charges could be brought against me or even taken seriously. . . . So let them bring their charges. Let them tell their lies! So long as we stand together hand in hand, *there is no man, there is no charge,* and there is *no force in this land* which can defeat us. Indeed, I stand before you tonight *proud* to be mayor of Newark. And proud of the scars I bear." (The italics were his, not mine.)

Two nights before, the mayor's voice had cracked with emotion and his eyes had filled with tears as he discussed the "persecution" he was facing. "You all know how important this election is to me . . . to my family . . . my wife . . . my children," he said, and as his voice broke, he stepped back from the microphone and wiped his eyes. This was followed by a huge roar of sympathy from the white audience and cries of "We want Hughie! We want Hughie!" Reporters spoke with sarcasm and humor about "the night Hughie cried."

Also in the speech he now carried was more of his continuing attack upon LeRoi Jones and the Black and Puerto Rican Convention which had nominated Gibson: "We are not talking about a simple political change—we are talking about a *radical revolution,* planned, financed, and controlled *not* by my opponent but by the men around him who have no use for democracy and no use for us."

Addonizio's strategy was the most blatant example of the use of the Big Lie that I had ever witnessed at close range. The blacks, because they had gotten together as an independent political force, because they were working within the system and succeeding at it, were pictured now as the enemy. Unified black politics could only mean a "radical revolution." If the oppressed ever seized power, surely they would become the oppressors. White power had created the black slums (and also had created *white* slums as well), but no matter, black power was bound to be worse. Deny the truth of your own failure by calling it a lie, and then create a more fantastic image, a *real* lie, to take its place. The fear of LeRoi Jones must have been as real as the fear of the devil himself. The myth of blacks raping white women if Gibson were elected was as acceptable as the myth of the Yellow Peril. Indeed, the easiest way to instill loyalty to a corrupt cause was to create an unspeakably horrible enemy. The reporter had glimpsed Jones walking into a parking lot in downtown Newark. White businessmen had stopped in their tracks to stare at the Black Devil. He was a thin little man, the way the little green devil had appeared in the textbooks of religion. One could imagine Jones standing there with a pitchfork in his hand, smiling. Did Addonizio really see him that way? One thought not, just as one suspected that the ministers of religion did not fear the devil as much as they appeared to—they had exaggerated hell.

But the worst part of the strategy was its changing of the rules now that blacks had begun to play the game. "Let's face it, and let's face it honestly," Addonizio was to tell his supporters this night. "My opponent and the man he calls his adviser—Mr. LeRoi Jones—*slammed the door in our faces!*" And this display of outrage was to be delivered before groups of Italians who had made ethnic politics a way of life!

Of course, Hugh Addonizio was fighting not for the survival of the city but for his own. It was a sad spectacle, really, and one could feel sorry for him if the health of a government and its people were not at stake. He was the fallen liberal, now in concert with racists and divisive politicians and crooks and Uncle Toms.

This was the Friday night before the Tuesday election, one of the last crucial evenings of the campaign, and I went with Addonizio to eight or nine of his stops, all in white neighborhoods, a long blur of appearances whose repetitive images became lost within one distinct impression. There was a buffet dinner in the Italian North Ward, where the mayor shook hands and spoke, and where men patted his back and women kissed his cheek. Then he went to several crowded, stuffy storefronts in white working-class sections of Newark, where out in the streets men and boys leaned against parked cars and drank from soda bottles or beer cans. They cheered when Addonizio's limousine pulled up to the curb, and inside, men in shirt-sleeves and women in haircurlers stood up and roared as he strode into their midst. In front of the P. Caposelese Club, I spoke with a sixteen-year-old boy who assured me that Gibson's candidacy was "Communist-inspired."

Inside O'Hara's Clipper Ship, a restaurant and bar, the man introducing Addonizio told the crowd, "I want youse people here to know that we're one-hundred percent behind Calvin West, who is running for City Council again." The crowd, mostly construction workers and their wives, applauded politely for Calvin West, a black man. They were told that Calvin West's presence on the Addonizio ticket proved everything the incumbent mayor had been saying. *They* were the forces of integration, while Gibson stood for separation, racism, and hatred. Never mind that Addonizio had virtually abandoned campaigning in predominantly black neighborhoods while Gibson was carrying his campaigning to all sections of the city. Never mind that Addonizio was inflaming fears by seizing upon the specter of black militancy, warning that his loss could signal the beginning of a chaotic and even violent black takeover of Newark. Because Calvin West proved otherwise.

Back in 1966, Calvin West had become the first Negro at-large councilman in Newark. Councilman West, thirty-six, was one of Addonizio's closest friends; in fact, he and another black councilman, Irving T. Turner, had been indicted for corruption along with Addonizio's administration. Calvin West was a "cooperative" Negro, probably the leading candidate for mayor in 1974 under the "timetable" which had existed prior to the emergence of the new black politics in Newark. The blacks in Gibson's headquarters had said that Calvin West had "sold his soul," that he was a "house nigger," and one could only guess at the depth of the man's private thoughts about himself and his unlucky position. West had been one of the few successful black men in Newark politics, he had played the old game, had done what had been expected of him, and now perhaps it was too late for him to change course. Repudiated by the leadership of the black community, he was forced to choose between dropping out of politics altogether or remaining to defend himself until the end. Having chosen the latter alternative, he was standing up in front of all-white crowds, night after night, and condemning Gibson and Jones.

"Yes," the speaker was telling the crowd in O'Hara's Clipper Ship. "We're supporting a black man! But Calvin West is a *good* black man!"

With that, I found myself laughing, and Addonizio, who was waiting impatiently with the prepared speech on his lap (at times looking as if he were uncomfortable with the tone of his own campaign), glanced up and smiled. The mayor and I shared this brief moment of truth, and I, without thinking, winked in return.

3.

They were all up there on the second floor, in a long rectangular room, as many people as the place could hold. Mostly they were Italian working-class people, and at first I was reminded of crowds at professional football or baseball games, at boxing matches or at the race track. They were sitting at tables drinking beer out of mugs and eating hot dogs; they were sweating because of the heat and mostly they were bored with the speeches. But every once in a while, whenever a speaker raised his voice in anger against the enemy, they banged their fists on the tables and roared the way the crowd did in the play *The Great White Hope* when the Jack Johnson character went down for the count.

Down in the street there were dozens of men hanging about, somehow wanting to be close to the action but still too hot and too restless to go up and listen to the same old political crap. But then a sleek black car pulled up along the curb and a certain electricity went through the night air. Bouncing from the car was Anthony Imperiale, his stomach pushed way out and his black hair slicked up on the sides—his face much younger than I had expected it to be—and the crowd on the sidewalk rushed to follow him inside and up the stairs.

"This I don't wanna miss," said one man as he pushed against the bodies heading upstairs behind the vigilante.

"Hey, Tony's here!" they all said as he marched into the second-floor room to the head table at the far end. The man was a kind of urban populist, a nondoctrinal leader who probably could not have controlled whatever he started. In the papers they referred to him as the "white militant" from the North Ward, but in fact he reminded me of Jackie Gleason playing Ralph Cramden, an ineffectual, decent sort of fellow, a blustering, confident loudmouth with, naturally, a heart of gold. When he spoke, it was in language that Newark's large, poor, Italian community understood. He spoke in the language of the people, and his voice croaked and brayed until a lesser throat would have given out.

In this election, he said, it all boils down to "an American running against a Commie group."

"I cannot sit by and forget what they've done to decent people!" he shouted. "I don't go to church, but I pray to God like He's with me every day!"

A sympathetic heckler in the crowd answered, "You could never do anything wrong in your life!"

"I sat down with my wife," Imperiale confided, "and I says that, well, I been called a racist, a bigot, a fat pig—but that was only because they couldn't eat as good as I could—and I been called everything under the sun. But I'm doing what I wanna do because it's in my *heart* to do it.

"Gibson is endorsed by Communism!" he went on, shouting until I thought his head might burst from the strain. "They're not gonna destroy our city! Over my dead body!"

The blacks and the Commies, he said, had a three-part plan to destroy Newark. First, the riot; then, the educational system was disrupted; and now, a complete takeover by the election of Gibson as mayor.

Of John Caufield, the former fire director who had endorsed Gibson, Imperiale said, "He couldn't urinate on a match! He couldn't even be a dog catcher! He'd have to catch himself first!" Then, shouting at the absent Caufield, he added, "You scum of the earth!

"Gibson calls himself a structural engineer," Imperiale continued. "I say he's a structural bullcrapper!"

Then he quoted LeRoi Jones' alleged statement "Slit the white man's throat, rape, burn!" Now addressing Jones, he screamed, "Well, you come up and fight! I'M WAITING FOR YOU!

"I say all this as a councilman, as a citizen, and as a vigilante! You've got to fight! How in hell can you look in your children's eyes if you don't fight? Fight for your lives! If Gibson was a good man, I'd work for him! But this is Communism versus democracy!"

4.

I remembered the election in Los Angeles the year before, when incumbent Mayor Sam Yorty was able to defeat black City Councilman Thomas Bradley on the basis of a direct appeal to racist fears. Like Addonizio, Yorty had resorted to such a campaign because it was the only kind left for him to run. Yorty's eight-year incumbency had been scarred by corruption and lack of attention to the sprawling city's ailments. Prior to the runoff election, Yorty had received only 26 percent of all the votes cast. Meanwhile, Bradley had led the field of thirteen candidates with 42 percent.

Running scared, Yorty pulled out all the stops and was able to bring out nearly every conservative voter in Los Angeles to the polls. In a city where less than a fifth of the population was black, Bradley deliberately played down his color, while Yorty never let the voters forget it. Not only was Yorty doing this to cover up his own administrative failings but in order to effect a reversal of the truth: He charged *Bradley* with running a racist campaign, and apparently many voters believed it.

Bradley, a former L.A. police lieutenant with twenty-one years on the force, was still in the position of having to prove to many whites that he was in favor of law and order. Yorty predicted that, if Bradley won, the police morale would drop. "If Bradley wins," he said, "the nation's third-largest city will be turned over to black militants and white radicals. . . . The anarchy that began on our campuses now threatens to make inroads into our city." Bradley was depicted as "antipolice" and also as the unwitting tool of insidious radicals, including Communist Gus Hall, who had endorsed him.

In the end, Yorty won a third term by defeating Bradley, 53.3 percent to 46.7 percent. Mayor Addonizio obviously had studied the results from Los Angeles as an example of how effective it could be to exploit the racial issue with fervor—and now, on election night, the question was whether that tactic would also prevail in Newark.

5.

I had spent the night before election day in the company of newsmen assigned to Gibson, who went around the city visiting his various storefront headquarters and making last-minute pep talks. We rode through Newark's shabby neighborhoods in the dark, past vacant lots and boarded-up buildings and stores, over cobblestone streets in the heart of the 1967 riot area. One of the big questions was whether "ignorance and apathy" in the black slums would be the factor that would defeat Gibson. Some of his volunteers had reported that blacks to whom they had talked were uncertain as to whether they were "qualified" to vote in the runoff election, since they had voted already in the primary. And some blacks thought the election had already taken place and that Gibson was mayor!

So Gibson stood before each group of workers, facing them in almost military posture, asking them not to let down throughout the following day, when the polls would be open. "I'm asking you to give one day of sacrifice for four years of peace and harmony in our community," he told them. "You'll get a release from the degradation and oppression and corruption of all these years. . . . You'll be proud of yourselves! . . . The campaign has degenerated on the other side, but we must work to keep this city together. . . ."

I spent the following night with the whooping, stomping crowd at the Terrace Ballroom, where the victorious Gibson shouted, "When Robert Treat founded the city of Newark over three hundred years ago, I am sure he never and you never realized that some day Newark would have soul!" Meanwhile, Addonizio's supporters in a restaurant in the North Ward, hearing of their defeat, turned on the newsmen and viciously attacked them. They surrounded the wooden platform on which the television cameras were mounted and then overturned them. They threw bottles, glasses, and chairs at the reporters and beat on them with their fists, and later, while the blacks were marching in victory toward Military Park, bands of white youngsters roamed through the streets, yelling, "Kill the nigger! Kill the nigger!" I had missed the whole scene in the restaurant and felt sorry about that, having been deprived of a chance to see the face of the opposition at such a revealing time. Indeed, they had attacked reporters like me, so I undoubtedly had missed out on a physical experience as well. They were mad at the media, and their anger was something to be understood if Newark was ever to be healed. In their view, the media seemed to be partial to the blacks, and that partiality had been deepened and made hateful by the lack of understanding of, and compassion for, the poor whites. The blue-collar worker, the white factory worker, the construction worker, the redneck, the hardhat, or whatever he is called—he was a victim of the old political Machine, too, although his mind had been clouded by appeals to his fears of communists and blacks. The media had not helped the oppressed of both races to see their commonality, and so the media were attacked for being on the side of the white liberals and the blacks, and now it was left to Kenneth Gibson to guide his city out of the wreckage of the past, to point out, as Hatcher was trying to do, who the "real enemy" was.

Sixteen

By midafternoon the rain started falling down on the Mississippi River, splattering down on the old wooden bridge across the water from Vicksburg to the northeast edge of Louisiana, and it fell down on the miles of green cow pastures and farming fields that stretched away from the riverbank. I was making my second visit to Fayette, Mississippi, but instead of heading straight down on U.S. 61 I swerved west over the narrow bridge and drove sixteen miles into Louisiana toward the sawmill town of Tallulah, which up until 1965 had been one of the meanest Klan centers in the country.

I was planning to look up a man named Zelma Wyche, who had been elected town marshal, or police chief, the year before. He was the only black elected as the head of a police department of any sizable biracial town in the South, although the reason for his victory was simply that blacks were nearly 70 percent of Tallulah's twelve thousand population. Before going to Chief Wyche's office, however, I paid a call on Sheriff R. Mitchell, who was sitting in his office over in the Madison Parish courthouse.

Sheriff Mitchell's father had been a member of the Klan, and he himself had been wearing a lawman's badge for nearly nineteen years. The blacks were slowly taking over Tallulah, which was actually a village, and soon they would be making inroads into the larger parish, or county. In the process, "law and order" was getting so out of hand that Sheriff Mitchell was thinking of retiring.

I wanted to know if there was any cooperation between himself, a white sheriff, and Zelma Wyche, the black chief. After all, cooperation between law-enforcement agencies was important in order for each to be effective.

"I'll tell you the truth," said Mitchell. "I've gotten no cooperation at all from that cotton-sacking Nigra. He's just an uneducated nigger. In fact, he believes in *breaking* laws, not obeying 'em. He was sentenced to a prison farm for kicking in a door and hitting a white citizen, in a restaurant. Well, that's what *they* want, so that's what they have. I seldom see him. And when I do, it's just a nod, that's all. It's a real bad situation."

The sheriff mentioned that there had been a burglary in a local saloon recently, and that Chief Wyche had conducted hardly any investigation at all. "They don't know what *to* do," he said with sadness in his voice. "His people think he's gone and done a big investigation, but he hasn't done a damn thing. He just loves to agitate. He's not really a good law-enforcement officer, and he never will be. He's actually *opposed* to law and order. Why, he released a Negro woman who shot a boy. Kept her in jail a while, and just let her go. No explanation, no nothing. I have no use for him, I'll say that."

2.

It was still raining when Chief Zelma Wyche returned to the tiny Tallulah police station that afternoon. He was wearing a black raincoat and puffing on a huge Roi-Tan cigar, a tall, muscular black man with a moustache and a powerful but low-keyed voice. He invited me into the back room, where he hung up his raincoat, revealing a pale-green shirt, and relighted the cigar. He had been a barber in a black neighborhood of Tallulah for about forty of his fifty-two years. A combat veteran of World War II, he had married a schoolteacher, and they had raised two children. While on the one hand he had "never lost a fight except once, when I was recovering from typhoid fever," on the other hand he was chairman of the deacons' board at a Baptist church. The road to his current job had been filled with fighting and preaching. As he put it, "The only way I could stay out of jail was to become chief of po-leece."

When I recited some of the things that Sheriff Mitchell had said about him, he flashed a big grin and then said, "Seems *he's* the one that don't like law enforcement. *He's* the one who let folks run wild through the years, doing all wrong. Beating people up in jails, killing 'em in the jails, chasing 'em down in cars, no prosecution, killing 'em—you know? Yeah, black *and* white people. And he was a deputy during the time some of those things happened. And no one's ever been brought to trial for it. So *they* is the ones who are against law enforcement."

By this time, Zelma Wyche had settled into an easy chair and the smile had left his face. "It's been the policy of Southern whites to paint a picture that's derogatory to the black man, and to try to make *themselves* look good," he said, looking me straight in the eye to see whether I was following him. "It's been their *policy* to make the black man look bad. That's what he's doing, see. You can get *no* favorable comments from white people here about me. And why not? Simply because I'm seeing that the law will be enforced, and enforced *right*. The laws of the land are the laws of the land. And individuals who are directly concerned with law enforcement, through the years, have *not* enforced the laws. They have all kinds of ordinances on the books that are in violation of state and national law, and yet they go around and try to *impose* these laws and inflict the damages of these laws upon poor and helpless and defenseless people. And those helpless and defenseless people happen to be black. And *I* happen to be black. No, I don't like the way he enforced the law. Uh-unh, no, because they enforced it *partially*. We checked the records over at the courthouse back in 1966, with a court order, and we found one single white man there, with a felony on him, and the books on the others were all black people. All the arrests are black! All the felonies are black! Disenfranchised black individuals, but no disenfranchised white individuals. No, I don't go along with the way *they* enforce the law."

3.

If the history of black suppression in the South could be traced directly to the way its laws had been enforced through the years, then the fact that a black man was now chief law-enforcement officer of Tallulah, Louisiana, represented a reversal of history whose impact—upon blacks and whites alike—could hardly be calculated. "Blacks feel easier, now," Chief Wyche told me, "because they know we're gonna treat 'em right. Black *and* white. No officers have been beating people over their heads since I been in here. No officer has shot a man. And no one has gotten *away* from us who we've tried to arrest, either."

No doubt many white folks had expected Wyche to use his office—or misuse it—in reverse. That was the biggest fear of all whenever a black man gained power, especially the power to use a gun while wearing a badge. It was a fear that grew directly from the truth of the white man's past, from his own self-knowledge— a fear of black revenge.

And that fear was probably heightened when not just any black man became police chief but one of the toughest blacks ever to make a stand in a Southern town and live to tell about it. In a place where the Klan walked around openly in their robes and shot black people down in the streets, Zelma Wyche was the most active and noisy agitator for racial justice. As far back as the late 1940's, he had been trying to get blacks registered to vote and had been in court and in jail several times on charges stemming from civil-rights activity.

"Growing up here," Wyche said, "I've seen the Klan go around burning, killing, raping, castrating. I've seen the wrongs that were heaped on black peoples here. By law-enforcement officers! I've seen people shot down—one standing right next to me! For nothing! Just because they were black, and just because the white man had the gun."

One time, five white men put guns in Wyche's face, and he dared each one of them to pull the trigger, calling them cowards. "There's never been fear in my heart, not of white people," he said. "I knew, all through the years, that the law was against me. I had no fair chance, no day in court. Therefore, I took my time.

And I worked up my plans. I worked on 'em for years and years and years, until I got individuals behind me, supporting my movement and things I believed was right. And when the time was right, we struck."

When Wyche led marches and demonstrations in 1965, the Klan stepped up its activity. "They burned down Moses Williams' tire shop, the Klux did. But Mitchell didn't tell you that, did he? He don't tell you about all the demonstrations we were in, and how we were put in jail here, how he sent me to the prison farm, for nothing! But he kept me in jail, and people put guns on me, threatened my life, my family. They 'don't know nothing' about nothing nobody did. Moses Williams' tire shop, burned! They burned Irving's grocery! They burned Niley's grocery! They burned a church out there! They burned down Willie Haynes' house! They burned up Gil Ford's store! They found nobody! And then when they said they *did* find a man, the one that burned down Moses Williams' tire shop, the man was dead! The Klux had had a shoot-out here in the countryside, and then they come and say that the one that burned it down was the one that got killed. How d'ya like that?"

(When his tire shop was burned down, Moses Williams turned away from the flames and shouted, "White folks, you can burn me out but you can't turn me 'round!" Through a loudspeaker on the street, Zelma Wyche roared, "White folks, you've burned us out for the last time! You burn us one more time, and we're gonna burn you right back!")

"The burnings were all in 1965. The Klan was still organized then, having their meetings out there in the country. They came to town in robes over here by the courthouse. Came in from out of town, meddling. They were gonna run us out of town. But they're dead since '65, because they found out that we were not afraid. They came here to scare us with their white sheets on, you know? That don't excite *nobody*. As I've said before, the Klux was nothing but a dirty man under a dirty sheet. That's all. They didn't even have the nerve to show their faces. It never excited me. Never."

(One time the Klan came to town, 150 strong, in pickup trucks and old cars, using walkie-talkies. Wyche and his black friends outwitted the Klansmen by using their *own* walkie-talkies and breaking in on the Klan's channel. The men in robes and sheets suddenly heard Zelma Wyche's voice: "Yeah, old Klan, we're watching you, and we've got you trapped. You don't know where we are, but we've got our eyes on *you,* and we just might not let you escape. How you feel now, old Klan?" The night riders beat a hasty retreat.)

The marching and demonstrating were for just about everything, from tearing down the "For Whites Only" and "Colored Entrance" signs to securing school integration and better jobs. "Every inch of the streets within the city limits is blacktopped, now, through our efforts," said Wyche. "We got lights in the black community, too. We have no blacks on the City Council, yet, but we done it all through *force.* We threatened 'em, through economic boycott. We had a bond issue to fix the streets, and some of the whites said they were going to vote against it. So we threatened 'em: 'You flunk it, and we'll flunk your business!' That was the only way. We'd boycott the whole town if they didn't pass it. And so they passed it, and they fixed all the streets."

(Many whites chose to close down their businesses rather than hire black employees. "Man," Zelma said, "some of those people were just mean, mean, mean. They just weren't gonna do right even if it meant crippling the whole town.")

4.

I told Chief Wyche that "politics" was my subject, and Wyche, who has no trouble talking, replied, "Okay, let's talk politics for a while. Politics governs the country, the world! And as politics goes, so goes the individuals who are controlled by politicians. The destiny of the individuals *under* the politicians lies in his hands. So therefore, we established a political base, here in Madison Parish. We did this years ago, even before we could cast a single ballot. We established this base, we got together, we formed our organization, and we got things set, lined up, *planned* our strategy for when that day came along when we would be given the ballot. We would know *how* to use the ballot."

Prior to December of 1962, not a single black person in Tallulah was registered to vote. Wyche remembered that during World

War II, when Roosevelt was running for relection, he and other black soldiers had stood there while the white soldiers went to cast their absentee ballots. Back in the United States, he fought for fifteen years in the courts for the right to vote.

"They had one little criteria set up," he said. "And if anybody had had nerve enough or guts enough, or enough moral respect for anybody, all he had to do was say, 'Yeah, I know that man.' And they could have signed us in as registered voters. But *no* white person did. All you needed was one registered voter to vouch that you were who you were. That I was Zelma C. Wyche, a citizen of Madison Parish, a pastor here in Tallulah, a veteran of the war, fought for the country—and nobody knows him! No, I'm not bitter—but I don't like what happened to me, you know? And I'm gonna do something *about* it. I'll keep *on* doing something about it. I *made* the plans, along with other conscientious black men and black women here. We planned this, and we're gonna see that it works! Politics—I'm *in* it. I'm in it to stay."

Wyche said that he and his followers had "tried moderation" in 1966 by determining to work for only two seats on the City Council. After that effort was unsuccessful, they changed tactics. "We found, then, that the whites in this community did *not* want black people in office, even though we were trying to be fair. And since that time, it's been our objective to take every seat that we could take—and when it all boils down, we're gonna take *every seat* in the village *and* the parish. And Mitchell's job will be at stake. We lost with a white man running against him for sheriff in 1967, but we're gonna beat him in '71. If it takes a white man to do it, we will. In April this year [1970], we had the election all wrapped up in the village. We ran a black man for mayor, and three for the City Council—an all-black slate. And we had it won, right up until twelve hours prior to the election."

At that point, according to Wyche, the district judge issued an injunction against all election commissioners, forbidding them to assist any voters unless they swore that they could neither read nor write. However, when the black folks went to the polls, they were asked to sign their names. Most of them did so, although that was the extent of their ability to write in many cases. When they then asked for assistance in the voting booths, they were requested to swear that they could neither read nor write.

"How can I swear to that if I just wrote my name?"

"Well, then we can't give you any help."

So, many blacks went inside their polling booths, knowing for whom they wanted to vote, but unable to cast an effective ballot. "That's how we lost," Wyche said. "They knew who they wanted to vote for, but they couldn't read the names! So they didn't know how to vote for the right candidates—and some of 'em lost by only eighteen votes."

Wyche was careful to point out that he had built his base "politically and socially" as opposed to economically. "There's no record of nobody giving me money," he said. "It took twenty years to get black people involved. They were afraid to come to meetings. It took years and years. The only way we can make it now as black people is to do it in a group. Politics will not be enough, but this is the beginning of change. We are the voices of the black communities, the black elected officials are, and these voices *will be heard*.

"The judges, sheriffs, prosecuting attorneys, chiefs of po-leece, your mayor, City Council—they *never done anything constructive* to help people over the years. *That's* where all the fault lies. Because those individuals who've been elected to serve and look out for the people have neglected their jobs. They looked out for a certain *class* of people, and they left the others out. And those that were *really* left out were the blacks. And a *lot* of poor whites. But I don't live in the past. I don't, but those whites would do anything to bring back the old days. They'd even kill. But I'm not going back. They can kill me, but I'm *not going back*."

5.

After coming into office, Wyche equalized his police force at six white and six black officers. What's more, his cops usually patrolled in integrated, two-man teams. "I wasn't going to have any of this business of whites arresting whites and blacks arresting blacks," Wyche said. "My policemen are just that—policemen—and everybody might as well get used to that fact."

When I mentioned Sheriff Mitchell's comment that Chief Wyche had released a supposedly guilty black woman from jail, he shook his head. "No black woman shot a boy," he replied. "Maybe Mitchell was referring to the case where a black woman *cut* a boy. I could have predicted that he'd bring that up. But no warrant was issued for the woman's arrest! My office didn't see her commit the crime, and nobody came up to press charges against her! I kept her in jail about three days, then I turned her loose. What was *I* supposed to do? *I* didn't see her cut the boy. But Mitchell hasn't told you about the cases where I *have* arrested people doing wrong. I got his court filled up now, over there. And I've got about 90 percent of the felony cases in that courtroom. They come from *me* apprehending the individuals and turning 'em over to the sheriff for the district courts. So if he's complaining, he just don't like *me,* that's all."

Chief Wyche said that the sheriff's deputies could make arrests within the village limits only with his permission. "But they do it *without* my permission," he complained. "Because the justice of the peace, who is a racist and a segregationist—when people make out warrants against people in the city limits, he gives those warrants to the sheriff! And the sheriff or his deputies, they go out and make arrests in my territory, which is wrong! And they do this just because I'm black. So why should I be so much in love with him? He's doing *me* wrong, indirectly.

"People of the other race," he continued, "say that I will not enforce the law. I *will* enforce the law. If they think I won't, let the white folks break it. Or let the *black* folks break it. But don't come up with some trumped-up charges, saying an individual did this when he didn't do it, you know? Or making false arrests or arresting people without warrants or breaking into peoples' homes, into their privacy, or dragging people out and beatin' them before they get 'em into the jail—no, I'm not gonna *do* that. I *know* what to do with 'em. Every law they violate, there's a fine to be levied against 'em. I levy the fine!"

As one example, Wyche pointed out that recently he had "put the biggest fine that had ever been put through that court, on a *black* man." The story of this one arrest was somewhat involved. The black man in question was a truck driver passing through Tallulah. He was drunk, and he pulled his truck to a stop directly atop the railroad tracks. One of Chief Wyche's officers came by in a patrol car and walked to the side of the truck in order to tell the driver to get off the tracks. The driver couldn't hear him, became frightened, and jumped from the truck, leaving it on the tracks. Naturally, a train was coming, so the officer jumped into the truck. By the time he had rolled it off the tracks, the truck driver had gotten inside the patrol car and driven off. The officer flagged down a passing motorist, got in the front seat, and gave chase. They overtook the police car at a signal light and the drunken truck driver, now on foot, was apprehended. This resulted in a $550 fine for the black man, the largest amount possible.

"And they say I won't enforce the law," Wyche scoffed. "Had he been white, I'd have done the same thing. Sure, I enforce the law. But I don't enforce it like *they* want it enforced. I only enforce it *right*. The laws on the books that are in violation of the Supreme Court decisions—they're *not* laws, as far as I'm concerned. And as far as that burglary in the saloon—I *am* investigating it. What's Mitchell doing about it? I don't know any burglaries that *he's* solved that weren't almost solvable themselves. This one is a tough case, there ain't any clues. You can't just pull in everybody in town, like they used to. You'd have a lawsuit on your hands. You have to give a *reason* for doing certain things in law enforcement, now."

6.

One of the most important aspects of Wyche's new job was the necessity to maintain the confidence and respect of his own people. "In the past," he said, "the only way the policemen gained respect was to use brute force. The power of the gun, the black-jack, the riot stick, the dogs—that was what kept the people in their places. In my case, it was the people believing I was right. And I'm not gonna let them down. They got rights, now. They're free, now, young and old, and I have their respect."

Among younger blacks in particular (but among all age groups as well), a fierce hatred of policemen had been built up over the years, and this hatred, this lack of respect, was what Sheriff Mitchell had referred to when he had told me about the "breakdown of law and order" he was facing. That breakdown was probably very real. "The sheriffs have lost the respect of black folks," Wyche said, "and they can't gain it back."

(A good deal of that respect for law-enforcement officers was lost during the demonstrations and drives for such simple goals as the right to eat in a public restaurant. "You had these racist policemen coming in with clubs, beating people over the head, in peaceful demonstrations," Wyche remembered. "You sit down in a cafe and ask for a meal, and instead of the policeman coming in and enforcing the Supreme Court's law, he arrests *you*. The person that was supposed to have been arrested was the one that denied you the service! But the first person that comes in and whips you is a policeman. Was that law enforcement?")

It was understandable, but perhaps an irony as well, that if respect for law and order was to be regained from the black community, it would have to come from black officers like Wyche. A few days earlier, about five hundred black youngsters had gathered, preparing to fight among each other, when Chief Wyche confronted them and told them to go home. When they moved, he recalled, "I realized that they had respect for me as an *officer*, not just as a black man. They wouldn't have moved for a white sheriff except for violence, with clubs."

7.

Until 1965, Zelma Wyche had been a violent man, one who reacted to threats and intimidation by fighting back, and with his powerful build (he weighed 150 pounds by the age of eleven), he was able to hold his own. "In the spring of '65," he said, "I turned nonviolent. I didn't fight no more. Threats, curses—I took it all from those whites. They called me everything, and I'd say, 'God bless you, Brother, I'll pray for you.' I never carried a gun when I was marching, and I took all the guns away from the others, made them leave 'em behind when we marched. See, I was the hunted—and the hunted always knows where the hunter is."

If it wasn't mandatory, he said, he wouldn't even wear a gun as police chief. "I wouldn't need one," he explained, " 'cause I can talk my way out of anything." By way of contrast, on his first day in the police station he found a big strap with five "tails" attached to it, and a large hammer. "I guess," he said with a chuckle, "they were too lazy to beat folks with their hands."

Wyche, who has very litle time for modesty, called himself one "of the new breed" of black politicians and police officers. I was reminded of Alphonso Deal, the task-force policeman from Philadelphia whom I had met in Memphis with Charles Evers. As "administrative assistant" to Evers and as "director of public safety" during his year in Fayette, Deal had tried to mold the town's seven-man police force into a "new image." One of his recommendations was that the Fayette cops lay down their guns, and although Evers supported the proposal, it was voted down unanimously by the Board of Aldermen. (However, in July, 1970, the board did pass a gun-control ordinance making it unlawful for citizens to carry firearms except on their own property.)

Deal was disappointed that he hadn't been able to strip the Fayette cops of their guns. "I felt," he said, "that, since we had an all-black government, we could also have a police force that the people could trust. We could have a town where there'd be no resentment toward the police and therefore no need for them to carry weapons. Force begets force. And these black guys had seen that white people supported their police with guns, so they figured that they needed guns also. My idea was that as long as we're having a 'new day' in Fayette, why not a 'new day' for law enforcement, too? Anyhow, policemen should really be involved in *services* more than crime prevention. In this particular town, it might have worked."

Although discouraged about the guns, Deal had made some progress in other areas but not before an upheaval, so to speak, in the ranks. Not long after he came to Fayette to train the policemen, they all quit the force. Two returned, and Evers had to replace the other five, including the chief. The new department of seven inexperienced black men apparently went along with Deal's "reforms" only after much prodding.

"I taught them some rules of courtesy," Deal explained. "I taught them how to keep good records and make out reports, how to direct traffic. Some of them were overweight, so I urged them to trim down. And they resented me coming in with these ideas."

Part of the trouble, Deal offered, was that the new black cops unconsciously had wanted to emulate the style and behavior of their white predecessors, including the white sheriffs. "None of them had been policemen before, naturally," he said, "and so the only image of cops that they had was that whole thing—the white guys with their big hats and big guns and big boots. So *they* wanted to swagger around, look mean, and bust heads, like the white cops had done! I urged them to be better than that— but you can see what white society has done to us. Some blacks still think that whites are the *only* ones who can do the job."

In the fall of 1970, Deal returned to Philadelphia, Pennsylvania, where he had been a cop for sixteen years. A black man of dedication to law enforcement who also involved himself in a wide variety of community activities, he believed that the *lack* of law and order—the kind that goes after the drug pushers and organized crime as well as other sources of social illness in black communities—was as much to blame for the slum dwellers' problems as police brutality. Like many other black policemen in departments across the country, he was working to make law enforcement a "service" rather than an agent of oppression.

As for Zelma Wyche in Tallulah, Louisiana, there was the possibility that someday he would become a district court judge—if *he* had anything to say about it. "I don't know much about law enforcement," he admitted, "but I *do* know right from wrong. I've been studying it for a *long time,* as a *defensive* weapon. During our demonstrations, I studied that ordinance book real good. And I've seen that white judge over there take a peek at *his* ordinance book, too, once in a while.

"I'm up in age, fifty-two years old, but I don't *think* like the average fifty-two-year-old man. And I believe that I will live to see some of the things that are rightfully ours *be* ours. And I know that it'll take a lot of work, a lot of time, a lot of understanding, to get this done. And I have dedicated the remainder of my life to fighting for the rights of people, be they black or white. That's my stand. And if it takes death for me to get out of it, that's the only thing that's gonna move me."

Seventeen

1.

The Board of Aldermen meeting was scheduled to begin at five o'clock, but there was no sign of Mayor Charles Evers and the five other members of his all-black government. The room with the folding chairs and the long table in the rear section of Town Hall was almost empty, anyway; apparently, the white people weren't about to attend these sessions anymore, under the circumstances, and the black people hadn't yet learned the habit of it. The blacks were much more accustomed to going to court.

A few of the town's employees drifted in and out of the room. Aside from that, the only people waiting for the meeting to begin were a middle-aged white couple, Mr. and Mrs. Jimmy Walker, and I. We fell into conversation, and it turned out that Mrs. Walker was the editor and publisher of the little Fayette *Chronicle,* a four-page weekly gossip-and-news publication which seemed dedicated to the ultimate downfall of Charles Evers and the resultant return of white supremacy. And while it was obvious that the Walkers had little affection for visiting reporters from the North, on this occasion they were extremely pleasant and gracious. Mrs. Walker, a short and sturdily built woman, quite openly confessed that she was a major thorn in Charles Evers' side (or hide, perhaps).

"They're late," she said, referring to the Board of Aldermen. "No doubt they're meeting secretly right now, in another room, so I can't hear them. When he first became mayor, Evers said he'd always begin the meetings on time. But see? He never keeps his word. Don't they know that we're out here waiting? I have better things to do than sit here and wait at his pleasure."

It certainly was a reversal of roles. Blacks had been excluded from any involvement in their government all through the years; the white minority in Fayette had been in total control of all phases of the government. And so it must have required a major adjustment of the mind for the Walkers to have to sit there like powerless, ordinary citizens and wait for Evers to come in and begin the meeting. The Walkers were present on this occasion for three reasons, the most practical one being that Mrs. Walker needed some material for her next editorial column. On an almost weekly basis she took Evers to task in her column for a variety of small and large actions or statements which she found improper. Already she had found some appropriate material: the fact that the aldermen were late and the thought that they probably were conducting secret business out of earshot. (Mrs. Walker's column, "Just Whittling," appeared in the *Chronicle* a few days later and began: "Tuesday afternoon I went around to the Town Hall's regular monthly board meeting, hoping to find out just what was going on. The meeting, which should have started at five o'clock, got under way just a few minutes before six o'clock. However, there must have been an executive session up front in the mayor's office for almost an hour—very obviously because I was present and what business went on behind those closed doors were not meant for my ears!")

The second reason the Walkers had come to the meeting was a bit more serious. The Jefferson County schools—elementary, junior, and senior—had opened a while back under new integration orders, and some 2,400 black students were attending while only ten white children had showed up. Most of the white students in Jefferson County had been enrolled in newly created private schools. A number of white parents had taken their children out of school completely, because of their lack of finances, rather than send them to public school with black kids. Meanwhile, Charles Evers had made some statements to the effect that he would encourage black folks to boycott those white merchants who were sending their children to private schools, and

Mrs. Walker and her husband were boiling mad at such arrogance. They meant to give Mayor Evers a stern lecture on how to behave, if he'd only just show up.

The third reason they had come to the meeting was to protest what they perceived to be an atmosphere of intimidation and harassment directed toward Fayette's white population. "We're just a minority and we're scared," was the way one white citizen had expressed it. ("What they mean by harassment," said Evers in reaction, "is that they never saw a black man telling a white man what to do.") Mrs. Walker pulled a loaded gun from her purse and showed it to me. "I hope I never have to use it," she said, and I nodded in agreement.

A lot of the recent trouble had come about because of an article which had appeared in *Business Week* magazine back in July (1970), the first sentence of it being the particular bone of contention:

> When Charles Evers took office as mayor of Fayette, Miss., one year ago, Mrs. Marie Walker, editor of a local segregationist weekly, bitterly questioned whether "niggers will work even if he gets industry in here."

Several days later, a large group of black youngsters marched up Main Street to the *Chronicle* office. They stormed inside and demanded an apology from Mrs. Walker for her alleged "nigger" remark. When she refused, they tore down the Confederate flags lining the walls of the office and called her some unflattering names. Then they threatened to drag Mrs. Walker down Main Street while forcing her to sing "We Shall Overcome." "I don't know the words to the song!" she replied.

A few weeks after that, Mrs. Walker wrote to *Business Week* demanding a retraction, claiming she had been misquoted:

> My Daddy was a Section Foreman on the Illinois Central Railroad and worked a gang of Negroes for over 40 years, and he taught me to respect their position in life and their problems, and he never used the word "nigger" and I was taught not to also.

"I use the word 'Nigra,' " Mrs. Walker told me, "but I surely never say 'nigger.' " ("What's the difference?" asked Evers when I reported this distinction.)

The point was, Mrs. Walker and some other white folks were afraid to walk the streets at night. "She says she's afraid to go home at night," said Alderman Will Turner, "but see, there *had* been a time that, if *we* were to get out there, night or day, they'd of beat us to death! See, that's what she's scared of! She's not lying—she's really afraid. But I'll tell you why she's so scared: because they'd been doing it to us, all these years. See, *they* was in power, and they know that we now have the power to do the same thing back to them. But she shouldn't be afraid, 'cause nothing like that never gonna happen here, now. We not gonna be like they was."

Turner mentioned that Mrs. Walker had expressed fear that young blacks in Fayette were walking around with blackjacks in their pockets. In fact, however, the "blackjacks" she had seen were merely hairbrushes. "She saw the hairbrush handles sticking out of their pockets," he said, "and she just assumed they were blackjacks. That fear she has, it's mostly in her mind. See what I mean?"

When I visited the *Chronicle* office around the corner from Town Hall, the Walkers introduced me to K. C. Hayes, a stooped-over, elderly Negro man who had been with the paper from childhood. "K.C. was raised up by the owners of the paper," said Mrs. Walker, "and he's still here, working for us. He doesn't even know how old he is." K. C. Hayes was an example of something, of how well Southern whites treat their colored, I suppose, and it occurred to me that one of the reasons the Walkers so despised Charles Evers was the way he had shattered the old black-white relationships. If he'd only be a little less *arrogant,* perhaps they would have disliked him that much less. The Walkers saw Evers as an arrogant man, one who misused his power by flouting laws and saying all kinds of things that no "colored" in his right mind should say. Mrs. Walker told me that she had detected a strain of greater "militancy" in Mayor Evers these days, evidenced by his new slogan "You Can't Stop Us Now." Her husband, a state tax commissioner who had run for governor of Mississippi back in 1951, was fond of saying, "If only Evers would learn to uphold the law!"

At last the mayor of Fayette came into the room, trailed by his five black aldermen, and he sat between them at the table, facing the almost nonexistent audience. He began the meeting informally, glancing at Mr. and Mrs. Walker as he asked for a prayer, then for a roll call, then for old and new business. He sat there dressed in a pale-yellow short-sleeved shirt, his arms crossed and his scuffed loafers planted firmly on the floor. The Walkers, seated a few empty rows back, got ready to do battle with him.

2.

For a while, Evers tried to pretend that he didn't notice the Walkers (although it was impossible, since they were practically the only spectators in the room). He spoke about some problems with the new ambulance service and then switched to the matter of budgeting for the upcoming fiscal year. "Every department's gotta submit a budget," he told his aldermen like a father instructing his children. "But we can't spend more than what's coming in. You gotta be careful about that."

When the petty business was over, Evers glanced up, his sad-eyed expression aimed somewhere toward the rear of the room, and said, "Well, the schools are beginning again, and I feel it's our duty to see that our school system goes as smoothly as possible. Some of our children are going to private schools. Well, that's their business. But I can't see how we can allow our young blacks and young whites to grow up without an education. If our white brothers and sisters want to go to private schools, with private funds, we can't do nothing about it. But I'm gonna make sure they don't use any *public* funds to do it with. I wanna make sure that no county-owned buses are taking children to private schools.

"We must encourage all our children to go to school. We're too busy trying to build up this town. If the whites want to leave, we can't control that. But I'm sick and tired of paying taxes for welfare. We got to *educate* people and get jobs for 'em. Each of everybody is responsible to see that their children don't hang around home or on the streets while school is on. Anyone in business with a child out of school—we're gonna close 'em up by boycott. If mothers or fathers are caught keeping children home, we're gonna bring 'em to court and charge 'em with breaking the law. I'm a *working* mayor, I can't sit back with my feet up on the desk. I gotta get out and make sure the money comes in so we can keep on going. We all got to work together—"

And here, Evers looked straight at the Walkers, addressing them politely.

"Mrs. Walker," he said, "you can do a lot of good for this town with your paper."

"Not if you boycott me, I can't," she shot back.

Evers ignored her and went on about how he was trying to bring more industry into Fayette so that more money could be spread around. He rambled on for a little while, but then his mind came back to the Walkers, as if the two white supremacists held a mysterious power over his train of thought. "Are you gonna *give* us the town?" he asked them. "That don't make sense, you know."

"Are you gonna boycott the parents of children in private schools?" Mr. Walker wanted to know.

"No," replied Evers, suddenly looking guilty. But then, recovering, he added, "Any black person who'd spend our money on any white person who won't send his child to school with our children—it don't make sense. Why should I buy his feed? If he wants segregation, why should I trade with him? If I'm gonna stand up for my folks, I gotta speak my mind."

"You're trying to block freedom of choice," Mr. Walker told him.

"*Racist* freedom," Evers snapped. "I think my daughter is as good as any daughter. It hurts me—"

"I agree!" cried Mr. Walker. "To the contrary notwithstanding, I been here off and on for thirty years, but I've helped the Negro race. From the heart! Some of these whites from up North are gonna lead you down the wrong road."

"No, no," Evers said, smiling. "Nobody's gonna lead *me* down a bad road. We're working for economic and political power, that's all. We got to take it away from 'em. Someday we'll be zooming around in jets and in rockets to the moon, while you whites'll still be home talking about niggers."

"You're not getting all the facts," Mr. Walker reasoned, trying to bring Evers back from the moon. "When you accepted that responsibility of an elected official, you promised to respect the law! Now, I don't like some laws, either, but I can't go make my *own* laws."

"Which laws are we breaking?" Evers asked.

"You said—"

"When the law is written," he interrupted, "you got to include us! A lot of laws were written specifically to deny us. So we got to do it on a local level."

The debate simmered down for a few minutes, only to start up again when Mrs. Walker brought up what she called an "animosity toward whites" in Fayette. It seemed to me that the Walkers were making a last stand of sorts; having lost political power, they were still trying to carry on as if the tables hadn't been turned. And perhaps Evers had gotten himself into a situation that forced him to allow the Walkers to maintain this silly dialogue. He had bent over backward to assure the white oppressors that they would not become the targets for revenge by blacks, that their rights would not be taken away as the blacks' had been taken away, and now the Walkers were on his back to make sure that he kept his promise. They were going to see to it that Mayor Evers did everything just right; they were going to demand protection and dignity and freedom; in short, they were insisting upon getting everything they had had before, everything the blacks had never gotten. And Evers looked as though he weren't quite sure how to deal with this new relationship. There was something pleasurable for him in being able to debate with two symbols of the white racism which had so plagued him all his life. Instead of giving Mrs. Walker a cold stare and dismissing her with the verbal back of his hand, Evers seemed compelled to carry on a kind of cold war with her. His mood seemed to change like waves spilling over a falls; he was angry, sullen, full of laughter, proud, meek—all in the space of a few minutes. When Mrs. Walker lectured him, he moped, shook his head, became angry, then cocky, then suddenly like a dog with his tail between his legs, ashamed, then sassy as hell, laughing—he twitched and turned and giggled and became serious, swirling with emotions from the past that conflicted with his hopes for the future, as if he were caught in a web of so many diverse impulses that he could resolve nothing. Had he bent over backward too far? Was he so intent upon proving to Mrs. Walker that he was a good boy that he couldn't shake her off? Was she still wagging him by the tail?

"Mrs. Walker," he asked, "do you really feel there's any animosity toward you?"

"I do!" she shouted. "I came around here and offered to run your column in my paper, and—"

"You ran what *you* wanted to run, you mean."

"No, when I disagreed with you, it was a horse of a different color."

"I don't mind you disagreeing," Evers said. "Look, you're free to come in here, to the board meeting, and express your opinion. Aren't you?"

"But you're lettin' your people boycott me," she answered. "You're denying your own people the right to have a paper."

"But we're delivering it to them, anyway," Mr. Walker added. "We've got night riders—"

"Look out, now!" Evers returned, laughing at the image of the Klan which Mr. Walker inadvertently had invoked.

"We've been here since the Civil War," said Mr. Walker, referring to the *Chronicle*.

"Come up to date, then!" Evers replied. "Bury the hatchet!"

During all of this, the five black aldermen had remained silent, letting their leader carry on as he thought best. Evers brought up the matter of the public schools again, noting that the superintendent, a white man, was sending his children to private schools.

"We gotta get 'em all out of there next election," Evers noted. "We gotta stay so mad till then. No picketing—just get 'em out of there. See, we got the things to take care of business with, now. We got the vote. We can have a brand new school superintendent."

"You gonna crack the whip, aren't ya?" Mrs. Walker injected, and although she was out of order in what was supposed to be an orderly, official meeting, Evers let her go on. "I was afraid to go home last night," she said. "There were cars going sixty-five miles per hour down the main street out there! They were having drag races, I tell you!"

Evers shook his head sadly and said it was a "rare exception" that anyone was able to speed through Fayette and get away with it. When Mrs. Walker persisted in her demand for greater protection, the mayor said, "Mrs. Walker, come on, now—they're not gonna bother you. My folk ain't like that."

"I get phone calls!" she retorted. "And I can tell you there were twenty-five kids out there, walking along and—"

"You scared of 'em 'cause they're black?" Evers asked.

"Just remember that they came into my office that day, and one threatened to kill me! Don't you forget that!"

"Don't judge us all," Evers replied. "I never dreamed the day would come when we'd live to see the day when white people would be so bitter that they'd leave those fine schools."

"Because they're afraid!" she answered.

"Scared to death!" Mr. Walker added.

Taking the offensive, Evers broke in, "You were quoted, Mrs. Walker, as saying that the 'niggers' wouldn't work anyway."

"But I didn't *say* that," she said.

"You destroyed us inside," Evers pleaded.

"How?" she wanted to know, and the mayor wearily rubbed his bloodshot eyes, making no answer.

"Your Northern brothers," Mr. Walker noted with sarcasm, "they're leading you astray. Those writers who come down here—"

"You can't run away from it!" Evers challenged him.

"I ain't running nowhere!"

Their debate was interrupted at this point by Ferd Allen, who at sixty-seven was the oldest of the new black aldermen. Allen had been somewhat reluctant, at first, to run for office against a white man. "I was so scared that I trembled whenever nobody could see me," he said of his initial involvement as president of the local NAACP chapter. And now, sitting there in his white shirt and suspenders, Allen decided to inject a little spirituality into the proceedings.

"Let's bury this hatchet," he said. "Let's bury it right where

it is. Let us work together for one common goal. We can disagree—but let us all remember that we're God's children.''

"I think I'm due an apology," said Mrs. Walker.

Her husband added, "Even one of those white hippies you
had in the Town Hall said you've gone too far."

Evers replied, "With all respect, we got to stop provoking
people into saying things. We got to try to come together and
build this community. We got the same feelings that you got,"
he told the Walkers. "The same thing that hurts a black man
hurts a white man. But the whites don't see that. They think
we're just a tool, an animal. We got to eliminate racism and
hatred, and now that we've taken over we're gonna give you
justice. . . ."

When the meeting finally broke up, Evers declared, "Okay,
well, it's been *really* enjoyable," and everyone laughed, even the
Walkers.

3.

Evers left town for a few days, so I was able to pass some time
in Fayette without trying to gather material. I was staying in
the small nine-unit Evers Motel, next to the Evers Restaurant
and Lounge, and I drove down the small strip of highway called
Main Street to the Medgar Evers Shopping Center, paused to
look at the Medgar Evers monument outside the Town Hall,
and stopped in to see the Medgar Evers Health Clinic. Without
Charles and Medgar, Fayette would have been just one more
stretch of scenery along the journey from New Orleans up to
Baton Rouge, to Natchez—then passing through Fayette, with a
sign announcing, THE ALL-AMERICAN TOWN; EQUALITY, JUSTICE,
FREEDOM, BROTHERHOOD—to Port Gibson and on up to Vicksburg
and Jackson. In Fayette the white sections were laced with
paved streets while the blacks still lived in houses with roofs of
tin and tarpaper, the shacks supported by concrete blocks surrounded by paths of red dust and mud and overgrown, thick
vegetation, sweltering under the heat. The average education
here was less than five grades; the incomes were less than six
hundred dollars per year, on the whole, and the unemployment

was up around 65 percent. I walked around the tiny shopping district along the only main street, visiting the stores and shops owned almost entirely by white people, and I walked over to the small park with its traditional Confederate war memorial across from the baroque, red-brick county courthouse and jail. So much had changed, but then, so much was still the same. The black folks could walk around now with almost complete safety, yet they had little more money with which to enjoy their new freedom. I remembered Alderman Turner telling me about the first time he and other blacks had set foot on the park grass across from the courthouse: "We got on that grass and, oh, man, we climbed up there, and we didn't know how to act! First time I'd been on that piece of grass! We'd used to see all the white kids there, but we couldn't ever go on it. We had the *right* to go there, but we couldn't. It's owned by the county, see—and once we took office in the town, the county took all the benches out of the park, and we haven't seen 'em since." So now, the county park was empty; by depriving the blacks of the benches, the whites had deprived themselves of them, too, just as they had deprived themselves of the brand-new public schools.

One night I went to a "mass meeting" of Fayette's black citizens held in a church, and old Alderman Allen got up in the front to tell the folks: "We've come a long ways, and we've got a long ways to go. Now, this goes for everybody—teachers, parents, and everybody else. A loaded wagon don't make any noise! An *empty* wagon makes a *lot* of noise. And you don't hear anything from the other side, do you? You can hear a pin drop!"

What Ferd Allen was trying to say, it appeared, was that while the whites were keeping their children from school, they still might be planning some sort of comeback. Allen's thought was that the economic aspect of private schools would bring many white children back into the public system—but the blacks had better beware of any move to bring back segregation. Alderman Allen's mind was still plagued with the recent past; he was still remembering that old fear he had experienced when he had first become head of the local NAACP.

"And you know," he was saying to the half-filled church audience, "on these party lines, you don't know who's listening in—which is why we have to have these meetings, to talk about our business in private. So let's be careful and try to stay together. We are solely responsible for our children, our young people. The white man has given us a splendid opportunity to educate our young ones, but they're waiting to see what move we'll make. So let's make the right one! The weapon of the mighty dollar might bring our white brothers back to the schools, as well."

After making a plea for patience in the matter of new industry and jobs, Allen sat down, and another man came up front and said, "Before we got our right to vote, we kinda *belonged* to the white man. And they had to look out for us. Whatever we got, they gave it to us—hogs, pigs, chickens, or whatever. But now, we have died, been shot at and everything, and we *earned* the right to vote. So now, the white man isn't responsible for us no more. And if we want anything, we have to get it for ourselves."

Near the end of the meeting, it was agreed that the black girls in the choir should not parade through the streets, chanting and singing. "The time for marching is past," it was said. "Just because we're in power, now, it's no call for marching through the streets like before. We wouldn't like the white folks to do it, so we shouldn't either, unless it's absolutely necessary."

It was agreed that in 1971, if still together in their politics, blacks could take over the Jefferson County educational system and run it themselves. "We got to start at the trunk of the tree in order to climb it," said Ferd Allen, who had an appropriate metaphor for just about any situation at all.

The South was very different from the North, as this meeting demonstrated. One could not imagine such statements being made in a church in Harlem, for example. And perhaps the difference explained why Charles Evers himself was probably the most enigmatic black politican I had encountered. From other prominent blacks I had heard some harsh criticism of Evers. It was said that he was a wheeler-dealer out to amass a personal fortune; others said they just didn't like his style, the earthy, folksy way he was always telling newspapermen and TV audiences that "we got to *sell* love to people, let 'em know that love *is* stronger than hate," and so forth. And indeed, whenever he came up North with this message, white liberals tended to fall all over themselves with adoration and gratitude and, yes, money, and they tended to forget (if they ever remembered) that, because of their own racism in the North, the plight of the inner cities was getting worse. One morning Evers appeared on Martha Deane's WOR-Radio program in New York, and between the two of them they nearly melted every radio set in every liberal's apartment in Manhattan, so hot was the gush:

> I'm delighted to have you here,
> Your Honor.
>
> Thank you very much. It's just
> like comin' home. And I appreciate
> every moment of it.
>
> Well, I appreciate your coming to this
> program, and I always have.

Martha Deane was no Mrs. Walker, but still Evers did not forget where he came from. When Deane expressed amazement that the mayor of Fayette had been able to arrive at the studio on time, in view of his busy fund-raising schedule, he replied, "Well, you know, Martha, in Mississippi they teach you how to move fast; if you want to stay alive, you gotta move fast and know when to move," and one could only imagine black militants in Harlem and Bedford-Stuyvesant, if they listened to such programs, vomiting all over their radio sets. Evers could come to New York, talk about Southern segregation and how blacks "ain't gonna hate their white brothers no more" and receive thousands of dollars in donations from white liberals; but the same kind of response to a guest from the slums of New York itself would probably require another riot.

Charles Evers, no matter what widespread attention he was getting across the nation, could never be a militant black like those in the North. His roots were in the rural, dirt-poor South, and therefore although he had been through long periods of hatred and despair in his own lifetime (he and Medgar had once planned to kill two whites for every black man they had seen murdered, and Charles recalls how as a youngster working in the kitchen of a restaurant he had spit on the white folks' hamburgers before serving them), still he had grown up in those churches among black people like Alderman Turner and Alderman Ferd Allen, and he was more at home trading verbal points with Mrs. Walker than he was on Martha Deane's radio program. How else explain why this champion of integration told his white town attorney, a woman, and a black Fayette policeman that they could not marry and continue to work for him? His explanation was, "I know how people feel, here. I know the resentments. There's enough tension, enough problems as it is, without adding that. I've nothing against intermarriage, but not now, not here. It's too soon." (The couple left Fayette and married outside Mississippi.)

Evers finally returned to Fayette during my stay there, and we walked up a sloping field of tall grass near the motel, to where some horses he owned were grazing under a hot sun. I asked him about the accusations against him that he was trying to build up a personal fortune. He reacted swiftly and with anger and even hurt, perhaps. "Why can't I be a millionaire?" he asked. "They call me a capitalist. Well, what's wrong with that?" Besides, he went on, to be really free you had to "own something" in this world. That was why he had organized cooperative stores owned by local blacks in places like Natchez, Port Gibson, and Hazlehurst (near Fayette), at twenty-five dollars a share. "Black people have to share in some of the fruits of this country," he went on, lecturing me.

When I mentioned the Congress of African People which had been held in Atlanta, he dismissed the subject with a wave of his hand, mumbling, "They wouldn't invite me to that kind of thing." He was angry, hurt, proud, full of contradictions, a larger-than-life man whose home was in the Deep South country of Mississippi, the state of which he probably would run for governor some day, and he was too busy trying to build something good out of the South to stop and wonder whether he was following the correct style or trend of the moment. I brought up Mrs. Walker, and he commented, "The Walkers, they're not really so bad, you know." (No, she just doesn't like *him*, that's all.) "Did you know," he asked, "that I often go out to their home for breakfast? Or dinner?" (No, I hadn't known about that. Why did he do that?) "We still talk to each other around here," he said. "The South can be a good place, someday."

I had seen a photograph of the Walkers' house, a white mansion with large pillars in front, located about three miles from town. I thought over the relationship between Mrs. Walker and Charles Evers—it seemed that the white bigot tried to score points in her newspaper column while the black mayor retaliated with veiled threats of boycotts or other war-game tactics; and then they both sat down for breakfast together for a rest.

"In that meeting we had," he said, "did it sound to you like I was Tomming? Did it?"

I replied that I wasn't sure, but certainly there were some people who would say he had acted like an Uncle Tom.

"No, no," Evers said. "There was no Tomming in that. Cussing at her wouldn't have done any good. You just believe me— there wasn't no Tomming in that meeting."

Eighteen

1.

Poor Richard Austin. He had nearly everything going for him except the personal "charisma" of a Carl Stokes on the one hand or the grass-roots strategy of a Kenneth Gibson on the other. I had an image of him climbing into bed each night after long hours of campaigning and saying to himself over and over, "I am the most qualified, I am the most qualified." In the way in which he viewed himself as a politician, he was not unlike Thomas Bradley. Both men tried to play down their race—or, another way of putting it, both forgot to stress the fact of their blackness as an issue—and therefore many blacks, especially younger ones, branded them Uncle Toms. "We want Bradley to run as a black man so he'll win as a black man and everyone will know it" was the way a young Bradley volunteer expressed it in Los Angeles. "People of Tom's era," said Sam Williams, Bradley's campaign chairman, "try to prove themselves as men first, as people with the qualities and talent that society is looking for. Tom is standing out independent of his color. This is the image that most Negroes are still really looking for."

And if one were to look at the Detroit campaign through Dick Austin's eyes, how qualified, or how *over*qualified, should he have been in order to receive fair judgment? The Detroit *News* was editorializing, after the primary, that "there are no great shades of difference in the abilities of Austin and Gribbs."

Even the more liberal *Free Press* had been suggesting that the
two men were "equal in ability." Were they kidding? The only
voice in the wilderness with enough courage to speak against
this myth was Columnist Judd Arnett of the *Free Press:*

> If both candidates for Mayor of Detroit were the same color
> . . . it is the view from this outpost that Richard Austin
> would win the forthcoming election in a gallop. . . . I have
> believed this since the primary campaign opened, but have
> been too chicken-livered to put it in words. . . . A reading
> of Mr. Austin's professional, political, business and civic af-
> filiations waters the eyes and boggles the imagination. Doesn't
> he ever go home? . . . For what little it may be worth, it is
> my opinion that Richard Austin is the best-qualified candi-
> date for Mayor I have seen in Detroit in ten years, and in all
> likelihood the finest municipal candidate I have come upon
> anywhere, ever.

Austin's victory in the primary may have been hollow, but his
real accomplishment was the uncoiling of black political power.
It was the greatest display of unity and strength ever put on by
the black community, which had begun moving in this direction
ever since the 1967 riot; indeed, the riot may have been the
single springboard. Many black leaders, however, had sat on
their hands during the primary campaign, preferring either a
more militant black candidate or none at all. Some even tried
to undermine Austin's efforts among his own people. But he
demonstrated that he could get blacks to the polls; his showing
in the primary generated much admiration among blacks, and
they, above all, resented the suggestion that he and Gribbs were
"equal" in ability. They knew that as an "equal" candidate,
Austin could not hope to win, and they were determined now
that he get a fair hearing in every white household of the city.
Even if he got all of the black vote in November, which was
unlikely, he would still need at least 20 percent of the white vote
in order to win. His main task now was to make strong inroads
into white neighborhoods. "That's where we have to sell him,"
one of his aides told me. "The whites don't know yet that Dick's
such a solid guy." In the seven weeks of campaigning that re-

mained, could he raise his white-vote percentage from 7 to 20? His task was to convince thousands of white folks that a black man can be a responsible, effective mayor, and beyond that, perhaps he could convince some of them that black leadership in fact had the best chance of unifying a divided city. Would they listen, would they comprehend this point of view? He proposed television and radio debates with Gribbs, in order to get into thousands of white homes that he otherwise would be unable to enter.

The rest of September went by, then all of October, and the campaign rambled on toward election day, November 4, 1969. Gribbs was wearing a two-sided mask, the sheriff and the liberal. He presented the image of a man whose soul was tortured by having to talk up crime, crime, crime; yet he did so with increasing ease, especially after a *News* poll showed that "of all the problems Detroit voters are concerned about, crime in the streets and a soaring crime rate are far and away the most worrisome." Enter Firmness, the new, fashionable panacea for our urban ills. The sheriff decried "lawlessness" and "permissiveness" and accused Austin of being "soft" on criminals. "Order and justice under law" had become the new code signal in Detroit, and rosy-cheeked girls in miniskirts and chubby young men in plaid sports jackets were applauding.

On September 28, the first Detroit *News* poll showed Gribbs way ahead with 46 percent, Austin with 38, and 16 percent undecided. The *News* acknowledged, "The black-white split for these two candidates clearly shows that Detroit voters are polarized along racial lines." And the sheriff kept insisting, "Race is simply not a relevant issue."

"Gribbs has had a badge for only eighteen months," Austin sighed, "and he's trying to ride that badge into the mayor's office." Austin wanted to talk about fiscal reform and Vietnam and the "root causes" of crime, and about the fact that in a city of so many blacks "it's a disgrace to have less than 10 percent black police officers on the force. . . . It's no wonder that large segments of the black community do not relate to the police department as they should." In reply, the sheriff reminded everyone that Austin had supported the petition for a police trial board and charged that the black candidate didn't even "recognize" crime as a big issue. Austin wearily repeated that he had been willing to *let the voters decide* whether to have a civilian review board for police. "No sane person in America is for crime," Austin said at one point (as I remember it, he said that in the company of some friends, and it came out somehow as exceedingly funny). "Gribbs is focusing on one issue," he added, "an issue guaranteed to lower the intellectual level and raise the emotional level of this campaign." With infinite reluctance, Austin tried to convince his white audiences that he was equally concerned about law enforcement, that in fact black people were probably *more* concerned about crime, and that they were definitely more *affected* by it.

In early October, the Urban Alliance dropped its rating of Gribbs from "good" down to "acceptable"—and it hiked Austin's rating up to "superior" with an endorsement of "strong support" for his candidacy. The alliance added that Austin had "steadily demonstrated his wide-ranging knowledge and experience in public affairs."

The Detroit *News* editorially endorsed Gribbs—"Both Are Qualified, But We Choose Gribbs"—and pointed out that the sheriff was the best man, in view of his badge, to ride in and clean up the town's lawbreakers.

Then the *Free Press* surprised a lot of people by announcing: "Between Two Good Men, We Choose Dick Austin." "Mr. Austin's comprehension is deeper," the editorial noted, "his concern greater, his ideas larger, more imaginative and better thought out."

But by October 19, the second *News* poll showed very little change in the citizens' own attitudes. Perhaps the polarization was now feeding upon itself like some sort of self-generating disease. Gribbs was still holding a substantial lead, but his percentage had dropped from 46 to 44; Austin's had dropped from 38 to 36; and the "undecided" vote now represented 20 percent instead of 16. *Something* was happening, all right, and the most optimistic way of looking at it, from the vantage point of the Austin camp, was that a full 20 percent of the voting population could be swayed. Still, Dick Austin was quietly despairing over this latest poll. Riding in the car to another campaign stop, he said, "I can't help feeling that we're doing better. We've campaigned so long and hard in the white community. . . . This is really the most anguishing moment of all. After all our work, there's absolutely no change in the distance between Gribbs and myself. My main concern now is not to worry our supporters. . . ."

Repeatedly Austin was being asked by newsmen—and by Gribbs, too—to disavow black militants. ("Yet nobody," he remarked to me, "is asking Gribbs to disavow the white racists.") Austin would complain, "Nobody wants to hear my views on taxes. They insist on viewing my candidacy in a racial context." "And anyway," he said on another occasion, "we can *learn* something from the militants. Their voices *should* be heard. They have the right to speak out, the same right that any other citizens have, and we must allow them an opportunity to register their dissent. This is the way we reduce tensions in the community—by letting whatever feelings exist come out in the open, so we can examine them and find solutions."

A young black policeman was sitting in the back seat of Austin's car as we rode through a downtown street one afternoon. He was in plain clothes, acting as a personal bodyguard for Austin. Suddenly he said, "You should see some of these young kids on the force, now. Afro hairdos, no regular cops' uniforms—you could easily mistake some of them for Black Panthers."

There was a silence in the car as Austin pondered this observation for a while. At last he said, "That's a good thing. Today's police force has got to be reflective of the community. The young kids have got to see themselves on the force."

Perhaps his strongest emotions during the campaign were directed toward the young, both white and black. He was genuinely moved by the new generation's spirit of openness, of enthusiasm for each other and for life, and he seemed to hunger for their affection. He often remarked that the young people were "the great hope for this country," a cliché, perhaps, but when Austin uttered it, there was a feeling of something more than frivolous romanticism. Austin said it with reverence and also nostalgia for something he had missed in his own life. It was as if the campaign itself, by bringing him into contact with so many youngsters, unexpectedly had filled a void in Austin's period of growing up. He had entered a corner of the land of youth, where brotherhood seemed possible, and this alone had been a deep fulfillment for him.

One day during the campaign he told his driver to stop so he could get out and greet an integrated group of high-school boys and girls who were joyfully raking leaves in the midst of a rainstorm. Austin rushed from the car and shook their hands. The kids, dripping wet, were not of voting age, but he wanted to thank them, to show his appreciation just for the fact that they were smiling and working together in the rain, to thank them for their existence in a city that sometimes seemed so filled with the deadening weight of misunderstanding and apathy and ill will.

2.

The third and final Detroit *News* poll was published on November 2, two days before the election, and it came like a thunderbolt out of the sky. The *News* reported, "Richard Austin has taken a slight lead in the final poll, but an amazingly large undecided vote means that Tuesday's mayoral election is too close to call." Austin was now the *front runner* with 42 percent; Gribbs trailed at 39; and the undecided percentage stood at 18. An additional 1 percent of the voters said they would write in Mary Beck's name. "The most marked trend," observed the *News*, "is a shift of Gribbs voters to Austin."

Leaning back in the front seat of the campaign car, Dick Austin sighed, "Well, I think we've turned the corner. The machine is rolling, and I just hope I don't put any sand in our wheels." He was pleased by the new poll but also puzzled. "We were supposedly trailing by eight points only two weeks ago!" he exclaimed. "I can't help believing there was some hanky-panky in that previous poll."

Whatever the case, the newest results were possibly damaging; some of Austin's aides felt the poll was a "deliberate gimmick" to get conservative white voters aroused enough to come out in heavy numbers to insure a Gribbs victory (or, perhaps more accurately, an Austin defeat). But that was unlikely in the extreme, although indeed the published poll probably had such an effect. For the first time, it had dawned upon people all over Detroit that they might in fact wake up Wednesday morning with a black man elected to lead them.

It had also dawned on the cocky Mr. Gribbs; it was apparent from the grim look on his face as he strode into the Channel Seven studios for the next-to-last televised debate. He wore a pink shirt and his freshly combed hair glistened under the lights; with victory slipping from his grasp, his mouth twitched involuntarily as he turned to face Dick Austin and attempted to smile. Once on the air, the sheriff launched an attack upon Austin, who sat there in a light-brown suit and calmly tried to hold his ground. "Crime is the number one issue!" said Gribbs. "I'm liberal, but I'm firm! My opponent is permissive!" Austin reiterated his theme that the major issue was the "total health of our community."

Afterward, Austin tried to hold in his feeling of excitement. The sheriff had blown the calm image of the Marlboro Man; maybe he was aware that many white voters had seen through the polish of his style to the shallowness beneath.

(Almost as if to give Gribbs a helping hand, the police department hurriedly announced that 56 murders had been committed in Detroit during October, more than in any single month in the city's history, and the newspapers, again almost a bit too eagerly, printed this frightening statistic along with their reports of the campaign.)

Despite his new position as the apparent front runner, Austin continued to examine his own performance. "I'll admit," he said almost to himself, "that perhaps I haven't been as specific as Gribbs on some issues. I haven't sent up as many trial balloons." (Gribbs had issued a "nineteen-point program" although at times he couldn't remember more than three of the points; it was sheer public-relations gimmickry, but I think his staff actually believed that such a list of proposals proved he was the better man. I wondered what they would have thought if Austin had mimeographed, say, a twenty-point program. The fact was, Austin's entire approach to the campaign was different; he could not afford to play the game that way.) "I *could* have sent up more trial balloons," he told me, "but I can't run the risk of it.

It would be more damaging to me than to Gribbs. All I'd have to do is send up one silly idea, one faulty proposal, and I'd be dead."

"Because you're black?" I asked.

"Of course! So, I'm cautious. I've got to walk softly."

Paranoiac as this view may seem, he was probably right.

3.

They held the last televised debate on Sunday night, and once again Gribbs was on the attack. This was his last chance to jolt those wavering white voters who were just beginning to imagine a black man as mayor without conjuring up visions of a wild-eyed militant leader bringing the city under siege. Gribbs the "moderate" man had a lie in his pocket; he had brought it with him and was ready to drop it like a bomb on the wounded, racially torn city that Richard Austin was working so diligently to heal.

The handsome sheriff leaned in toward the television viewers in living rooms all through the suburban sections of Detroit, and the following exchange took place:

> GRIBBS: Frank Ditto and others have entered Butzel Junior High School and brushed by the school principal. Mr. Ditto, that person who has disrupted the schools, *now is on Mr. Austin's staff*. When my opponent is so tolerant as to put a leader of those kinds of functions on his staff, it indicates a vast difference between him and myself.

> AUSTIN: I don't know where Sheriff Gribbs got the information that Mr. Ditto is a member of my staff. Mr. Ditto, as I understand it, is employed by a group of churches. . . . He is not on my staff. He is a supporter.

But the lie was spoken, the appeal to fear had been made and transmitted. There was no way to repair the damage done. A fragile trust, which Austin had earned from cautious whites all over the city, had been severely undermined. Later in the debate, Sheriff Gribbs faced the cameras with a look of satisfaction

and said, "I am confident that if all the people who want to see
Gribbs mayor come out and vote, I will win." The implication
was clear, and the campaign was all over except for the *News*
headline on Monday, the day before the election: "GRIBBS SAYS
FRANK DITTO AIDS AUSTIN."

4.

"What I'm doing during the campaign, with these kids down
here," Frank Ditto told me, "is merely trying to bring about
greater awareness of the kind of responsibilites of power and
authority that officials have. What are the powers of a mayor?
Who does he have working for him? Who is actually responsible
to him? And so forth. What we're doing is educating. . . .

"Perhaps I have more faith in people than in anything else.
No one—in my head, in my soul—is more angry, no one is any
closer to just out-and-out hate, no one is more determined, than
I am—but I realize that if I get so carried away with my anger,
if I let that be my barometer for action, I can get too easily side-
tracked. . . .

"I think I've discovered the real meaning of brotherhood, the
real meaning of democracy and freedom. I know what it is because I've been denied it almost all my life. You have no idea—
and this is very hard to tell—I mean, you have no idea about the
denial of these things. Whatever little bit I have has been acquired through my own fortitude, my own drive—and whether I
get it or not depends on me. *You* can't instill self-respect in me.
I mean, there's no way possible that you can respect me if I don't
respect myself. I've been so affected by this white racism that I
have looked in the mirror and asked myself, or almost asked
God, 'Why did you make me black?' This is for real, man. This
is no dramatic-ass, motherfucking bullshit. It's a reality. I lived
that. And many times I've said to myself, 'If I weren't black, I'd
have it made.' Shit, *now* I wouldn't trade this blackness for nothing in the world! I wouldn't! And when I look into the faces
of my little kids down here, I see that pride, you know? And it
just overwhelms me. . . .

"But now, this is really a meaningful life. I'm not interested

in adventures of going up to the moon or making millions of
dollars or wearing silk shirts or suits. I'm not concerned with
that. . . .

"I have to struggle just to tell you, to give you some idea of
how I feel about giving way to just utter frustration, hopelessness, powerlessness. I have to struggle almost every day to keep
from getting myself a rifle and just killing white folks. It's not
easy, even now. Man, the shit the white man has put me through,
the stripping of all my manhood and my pride—and *blaming* me
for that situation. It's a bitter pill that's not easy to swallow.
He's told me that my people were lazy, and then I find that
they've worked from sunup to sundown and never got a fucking
penny. He told me that they were stupid, my people, that they
didn't have the capability to learn, and I found out that blacks
performed the first open-heart surgery, that they laid out Washington, D.C., and so on—all of these things, and this white guy
had convinced *me*. I was working like a goddamn slave, every
day, and he'd tell me, 'Man, you're lazy, you don't want to work.'
He'd say, 'You don't have any capability of learning, you don't
know how to learn to read, or to decide whether you're happy
or unhappy, or whether you want to be free or want to be controlled.' And I was almost convinced! That's how completely
black people have been destroyed. That's the thing the black
community is facing today. We have to tell our own brothers,
'Man, you're *not* inhuman. You're *not* lazy. Look at your own
goddamn work record! Just look at it! Does this say you're lazy?
What kind of job do you do? Do you bust your ass while somebody walks around in a suit and gives orders?'

"I've been on welfare. My family was broken up because of
welfare. They said, 'We can't feed your wife and kids as long as
you're in the house.' So I either had to watch my wife and kids
go hungry, or . . .

"We should be able to say, 'This police officer isn't fit to be
a policeman in *this* community. If you think he's a fit police
officer, take him in *your* community.' We want new job opportunities. We're entitled to them. They're long overdue, and the
dividends will be put back into this country to make it a great
country. That's what black people are saying.

"I check myself on this time and time again: What is to keep me from becoming a reverse racist? The human quality in me says, 'Man, you have the experience of man's inhumanity to man, and you know what the bitter fruits of that are. But could *you* be that low?' No, I couldn't. The new manhood that I have discovered would never let me stoop that goddamn low. Never! I damn near hate white folks, man—and you included. Not because you've done anything, but because you symbolize something. But I would never attack you unnecessarily. If I caught George Wallace in the middle of five hundred other blacks, I wouldn't throw a stone at him. . . .

"Can you imagine that I, as a little boy, never saw myself as being anything other than the lowest kind of somebody? The lowest would be a bootblack, and the highest level of achievement that came across my mind was being a hotel clerk. Can you imagine that? I never dreamed of being a doctor, a lawyer, a mayor, a Congressman—and my greatest ambition was to be a goddamn hotel clerk. I saw myself running an elevator, carrying stuff up to white folks. Those were my highest aspirations. . . ."

5.

It was raining in Detroit; it had poured for most of the day. White and gray smoke was pushing its way up in thick columns from the Motor City, but the heaviness of the smog and pollution and fog seemed to be pressing all the ugliness back down into the spaces between the dull buildings. People were hunched over, many of them heading for the polls. You could wonder if it made any difference.

The elderly Negro maid who was cleaning up my hotel room said, "Oh, I got my special man to vote for. I can't get to the voting booth fast enough."

Naturally I assumed she was talking about Richard Austin, and I had visions of this old woman, after a day of cleaning up the rooms of white folks, plodding in the rain to cast her vote against the oppressor, whispering, "Right on!" under her breath. Yeah, she was gonna vote for Richard Austin to lead her out of the darkness.

"I'm going with Mr. *Gribbs*," she said proudly. "I cleaned up his room in this hotel one day, and he put some bread in my pocket. So I says to myself, *'That's my man!'*"

I made a note to please stop jumping to conclusions.

As the cab driver pulled up outside the Detroit Hilton that evening, he said the blacks, if they won, might go haywire and wreck the place. Strange, but I would have thought they'd become more violent over a *loss* than a win. Maybe the cabbie felt that blacks were used to losing.

Thousands of people were crowded into the second floor of the hotel. The whole spectrum of attitudes and styles seemed to be present; there were tough-looking street kids in jeans and denim jackets, and they rubbed shoulders with stylishly dressed members of both the black and white middle-class. Perhaps a third of the crowd was white.

You could see the excitement and hope on the faces here, and you could feel it mainly among the blacks. Because of Dick Austin, they had achieved a new level of political awareness and unity and stature. Austin had brought them along with him every step of the way. Of course, he probably hadn't convinced them all, and at times I could see in his expression the agonizing knowledge that time to unify the city was running out. If only the militants would put their trust in him, if only the open-minded whites would give him a chance to do now what might not be possible later, if only enough people would understand that the conflicts in Detroit—between old and young, white and black, rich and poor—could best be resolved in the leadership of this quiet, friendly man who symbolized the upward struggle of a solitary Negro to make it, both economically and socially, in America.

I had picked up a copy of the *Free Press* and now read that Detroit's high-school students had held their traditional mock election. They had "elected" Dick Austin over Gribbs by nearly two to one, which must have pleased Austin a great deal. Historically, the pupils had reflected their parents' views, but in recent years, according to the newspapers, the youngsters had shown a much stronger liberal trend than their parents.

White policemen were worried about a riot happening in this hotel. They seemed more concerned about protecting the hotel than the candidate. Meanwhile, dozens of off-duty black officers had volunteered to protect Austin. As his prospects for victory had gone up, so had the fear of violence from either extreme. One black cop in plain clothes told me, "We have one man assigned to watch each black militant in this hotel. But we're also worried about some crazy white racist coming in here with a gun."

Gribbs took the lead at 9:30, and forty minutes later NBC-TV predicted that he would be the winner. At 10:30, wearing a blue suit and red tie, Austin came downstairs, made his way through the crowd, and announced that it was "too close to call." Few people could hear him. He was smiling, so you had the feeling that NBC could go hang its prediction.

Later, up in Austin's private suite on the sixth floor, the small gathering seemed painfully subdued. People were trying to show their concern, their sympathy, but Austin would have none of it. He kept smiling, and they left him alone with himself. His wife Ida and his daughter Hazel, in blue and yellow dresses, sat on the couch watching television. There was a report from Gribbs's headquarters, showing a great amount of jubilation. Mrs. Austin sat very still, trying to conceal her emotions. She had been married to Dick Austin for thirty years; they had lived in their three-bedroom colonial on Oakman Boulevard since 1956; their daughter was a medical technician at Detroit Memorial Hospital and was studying for a master's degree. ("Ours is a quiet generation gap," she told me about her relationship with her father. "He's usually right.") They had lived through Dick Austin's struggles for a long time, and now there was nothing they could do for him except wait.

"All hell's gonna break loose," a woman said, but to no one in particular. "If this goes down the drain, God help Detroit."

"I wish," a young man said, "that white people could learn to put the survival of the city above race."

They were bitter, and now that Dick Austin had disappeared into another room, they felt more free to express their anger.

"It's what it'll do to him, personally," someone whispered. "It'll kill him."

Austin was restless. He moved back into the room, wearing

his light-blue shirt, and he stood in front of the TV set, which was showing some man-in-the-street interviews filmed earlier in the day. Austin sat on the edge of a chair and leaned toward the set. His aides were running about with voting results and projections, yet for the moment Austin himself was absorbed in what the people were saying on the television. Then he stood up and quietly retreated into the adjoining room.

"This is the first time," said a young man with an Afro haircut and dark glasses, "I've done something that I thought was worthwhile. Working for Dick, I mean."

Nobody answered him. Congressman John Conyers, Detroit's leading black political figure, was standing in the room now, looking very young and self-assured. In 1964, he had beaten Richard Austin in a Democratic primary for the Congressional seat he now held. The primary had been a bitter one, fought in an almost all-black district, and Conyers had come out on top by only 38 votes. Since then he and Austin hadn't been the closest of political allies, but Conyers, during this campaign, had given Austin his support. The television announcer was saying that Gribbs "apparently is going to wait for Austin to make a concession." Conyers muttered, "Don't hold your breath, buddy."

In the other room, Austin was holding a sheet of paper with some figures on it. "All we know for certain," he told me in a soft voice, "is that 470 out of 1,111 precincts are in." He was holding on a bit longer, while his aides moved around him glumly, and at last he sat down with them to work on his concession speech.

Just past one in the morning, he stood downstairs facing his supporters and told them, "You have waged with me a magnificent battle. But we now must accept the verdict of the majority of Detroit voters. With nearly all precincts and over 500,000 votes, seven thousand votes separate us. Despite the disappointment of not winning, I cannot regard this as an inglorious defeat. This campaign brought together forces that never before coalesced in our city. We raised issues, critical issues, in a forceful and logical fashion—and people listened. Together we have achieved a level of unity never before attained in our city. . . ."

6.

Frank Ditto left the Hilton Hotel and headed for the Pick-Fort Shelby, where the sheriff's victorious supporters were celebrating with cold sandwiches, beer, and polkas. Gribbs had acknowledged victory at 1:30 A.M., and now everywhere he moved in the hotel he was accompanied by at least ten sheriff's deputies and off-duty Detroit policemen. In fact, the hotel was swarming with plain-clothes cops who were acting as self-appointed bodyguards and bouncers. The victory was theirs as much as anybody else's—and the cops did not hesitate to claim credit. The police union had endorsed Sheriff Gribbs, its members had helped to register voters, and today they had transported people to the voting booths, and they also acted as pollwatchers. Moreover, the Detroit Police Officers Association had topped the entire list of major contributors to the Gribbs campaign.

Ditto walked into the hotel wearing a windbreaker that had his name written across the back in bold letters. He moved through the crowd of white faces, giving people what he called the "stare treatment," and now almost everyone was aware that a "black militant"—in fact, the very man whose name the sheriff had invoked at the last hour to arouse fear and backlash—was in their midst. Confronting a group of men in the hotel, Ditto said evenly, "Where's Gribbs?"

Suddenly a police car pulled up outside, and two uniformed officers rushed in. Then another car arrived, and still another. Now more than a dozen nervous, anxious cops were clanking around in the hotel lobby, surrounding Frank Ditto, who could barely conceal his amusement. "These people," he said, "they believe their own propaganda." With only two well-chosen, harmless words, Ditto had just triggered the unreasonable fear that lay at the heart of Gribbs's success, and had just brought about Sheriff Gribbs's first moment of law and order as mayor-elect.

7.

Out of 511,766 votes cast, Richard Austin had lost by only 6,194, a margin of less than 1.2 percent. It was the closest mayoralty election in the city's history, and a switch of only 3,000 votes would have reversed winner and loser. "One more week and he'd have won," his aides were saying. "Time ran out on him." In the short time given to him, he had more than doubled—nearly tripled—his white support around the city. He won about 18 percent of the white vote, but it was just not enough. Given a little more time, he might well have changed a few more minds and become the first black mayor of Detroit. Not that he ever did relish being a "black" mayor with the narrowness of vision which he felt such a term implied.

It was generally conceded that, had he been white, he would have won in a landslide. However, perhaps because of the final *News* poll showing him ahead, perhaps because of Gribbs's untrue charge that Ditto was a member of Austin's staff, whites came out in droves to defeat the black man. Some 75 percent of the registered whites came to the polls, as opposed to less than 69 percent of the eligible black voters, and that undoubtedly made the difference. The black turnout was high, relative to the alienation that existed, but in the 1964 presidential election, when Johnson ran against Goldwater, 80 percent of the black community had turned out to vote. Many blacks blamed their own people for Austin's narrow, painful loss. They pointed to the fact that thousands of blacks, more than enough to put him over the top, had failed to come out and vote. Some thought the rain and chilly weather had kept them away; others said that it just proved that despite Austin's magnificent campaign, black people had become too disillusioned by the System to have gotten themselves completely together for this first big opportunity. And of course still others felt that Austin should have run a more militant campaign—and perhaps he might have won on that basis, who knows?—but such a tactic was simply not within his vision of himself or of America. He had wanted to win as a man for "all" the people, black and white, and he felt that in order to do so, he had to improve the image of the black man in the eyes of many whites. When asked to comment on this, he replied, "My appeal to white voters was not as successful as we had hoped. If I made a miscalculation, that was it."

Still others said that white voters had been "turned off" by an Austin advertisement, placed in newspapers by white supporters, which had asked in huge print, "CAN YOU VOTE FOR A BLACK MAYOR?" The ad had continued: "If you can, but you think the other candidate is superior, we respect that judgment. But if you can't, and the reason is color, Detroit is in more serious trouble than most people think." Perhaps this did "turn off" some white voters. If so, it is too bad that a bit of the truth was too big a price for them to pay, for there is no doubt that race was the principal factor in this election.

There was at least one solid victory, due in large measure to Austin's campaign: The Common Council now had three blacks instead of two and six liberal members out of nine. In other words, white voters *did* support some black candidates. "What they are saying," commented an Austin staff member, "is, 'We are liberal, and we think there should be some black representation, but not a black *mayor* yet.' Whites will vote for blacks for lesser positions, but not for the top job." The same old patronizing spirit had been at work.

The election went to Gribbs, but the white rulers will lose out in the long run. They had lost their chance to reach out; they had missed an opportunity to leap into the unknown. Now, the political tide had turned in Detroit, and that was the real message of this election. Blacks were already talking about capturing City Hall for good in the 1973 election year, perhaps aided by a new political coalition with liberal whites, but maybe they would do it all by themselves. In my view, Gribbs was certainly the last Detroit mayor to be elected by a conservative coalition of white homeowner and police groups—and certainly he was the last to win without substantial black support (he had received only 3.5 percent of the black vote). Before the 1973 election, more than half the city would be black; Gribbs was merely presiding over the years of transition. Austin was a "black moderate with a chance of winning," but in 1973 the blacks would be back without his caution, without his patience, without his lowered voice catering to the goodwill of the white community. Next time the blacks would be knocking on the door to City Hall with a much more strident voice, not asking but demanding to be let in. Austin was simply a symbol of the future, of what impended for Detroit; the black candidate in 1973 would be much more militant, but such a man would not be Richard Austin, because that was not his way.

Nineteen

1.

The president of the City Council of Gary, Indiana, was a handsome white fellow named William P. McCallister. One of the council's two Republicans, he was regarded generally as a fair-minded, objective politician, which was another rarity in these parts or maybe anywhere. I met him one morning at his investment office on lower Broadway in Gary, and we rode out toward a meeting between some homeowners and officials of the Sewer District.

"Mayor Hatcher is irresponsible as hell," McCallister said as he drove. "He'd be late to his own funeral. He isn't the greatest at returning phone calls, either. He's so afraid that somebody's gonna ask him for a favor. The way I'd describe him—he's liberal, with militant leanings, and he's impeccably honest. He wants to be clean as a pin. And because he's honest, Gary is receiving Federal funds and cooperation for the first time in years. Of course, Hatcher himself is just not capable as an administrator. He's very reluctant to delegate authority, and he's been known to come late or even miss his appointments altogether. . . ."

McCallister adjusted the tiny American-flag pin on his lapel and went on, "The problem is that so few blacks are qualified for top-level jobs. Hatcher fired a lot of Negroes in City Hall who were on the take, and he was determined to appoint a number of other Negroes, qualified or not. But they had no experience, there was no place where they could have gotten it, and there's no job training for them."

I asked him about the disannexation movement, and McCallister replied, "It's based on shallow thinking. Many white people are worried that Hatcher will neglect them. They're worried about garbage pickup, snow removal, street signs—that kind of thing. And at first, when Hatcher came in, the services *were* poor. The garbage wasn't picked up on schedule, and so forth. The new people at City Hall, they tried hard, but they were all screwed up. . . ."

McCallister said that people became worried when Hatcher spoke to militant groups (although the definition of "militant" in these parts encompasses more viewpoints than in other places). "He spoke at a dinner one night, and there was no flag on the stand, and they said he was un-American—and, for example, one of his school-board appointees, a woman, said she favored school bussing, and that caused a big stir. It's partly a matter of his having to be more careful. At the moment, Negro kids are bussed to white schools, but if the reverse ever came about, it would be the absolute death of Gary. The absolute death! All the whites would move out, and I would, too." And public housing in white areas, according to McCallister, represented "another spike in Gary's coffin. . . . Integration can work, though. The problem will work itself out if people are able to move into the economic neighborhoods they can afford."

The meeting between city officials and homeowners was already under way when we arrived at the Sewer District headquarters. Nearly two dozen white women were sitting in a room while a spokeswoman read off a list of grievances to a group of men seated at a conference table. What struck me about these middle-aged and older women was their look of almost complete helplessness as they pleaded with the officials for help in solving the sewerage and drainage problems in their neighborhood. No sewers had been built when their subdivision had been created many years ago, and on top of that, faulty storm drainage was causing floods in their cellars and backyards. The women, stocky and hard-faced, were wives of mill hands, and they had come to this meeting in desperation. "Just tell us what to do," one of them said in a shaky voice. "We'll get down on our knees, if that'll help, and we'll *beg*." They were in danger of losing their homes, they said; all of what they had worked for was being threatened, and I could not help thinking of Hatcher's phrase "little black people and little white people." These were little white people, all right, and their lives had come to the point where survival was more important than any other consideration, more crucial to them even, I imagined, than race. Their homes, their *possessions*, were literally sinking into a swamp, and now they were doing what black people in America had had to do for generations: they were throwing themselves at the feet of those in power, asking for mercy, for compassion, for alleviation of a condition that had gone beyond toleration.

As a matter of fact, they wanted *special consideration*, under law, for certain city services, and the officials reacted sympathetically. One of them, a black man appointed by Hatcher, stood up and said, "Obviously this situation can't go on, and we promise you that, even if the problem is a long-range one, we will take some kind of action, immediately. That much we assure you."

The women all nodded their heads at this black man. It was a small, insignificant happening in the context of Gary's daily history, but it illustrated, to me, how quickly black-and-white divisions disappear, at least momentarily, when people are in trouble.

2.

Another person I saw in Gary was Carroll B. Harvey, a young black man in Hatcher's administration. We had lunch together in a small restaurant near City Hall, and our conversation seemed to stray in several directions, perhaps because, like many young people who choose public service over the "corporate bag," Harvey's mind travels in global, philosophic orbits at least as much as it moves within the daily bureaucratic labyrinth of local government.

"Environment," he was saying with great enthusiasm as we walked over to the restaurant, "is *the* issue, the golden opportunity, for someone to reach across race and class and unify people. People are tired of conflict, they want a healer—and the environment issue can provide the basis for that. It's *been* an issue in the ghetto, but now it covers all America. . . ."

When I mentioned to him what McCallister had said about the Hatcher administration's lack of efficiency and expertise, he admitted that "for key jobs, there was no one, black or white, experienced enough." "The setup wasn't at all geared to giving services," he said. "Hatcher inherited a completely undisciplined government in Gary. This is true of other small cities, where there's no history of professionalism or civil-service training. City Hall here is understaffed, underfunded, and along comes this tremendous rush of new activity, new programs, and it takes a while to reverse a whole fundamental situation. People have to recognize that.

"The level of criticism automatically goes up when you have a black man running things," Harvey went on. "Where was McCallister the rest of his life? Why so critical now, when in fact Hatcher has redirected everything? Also, he's an idea man, and he has a direction, a purpose."

After lunch we drove into one of Gary's pleasant little residential areas near the downtown, and we went to the home of Bishop Andrew Grutka. The bishop, who lived and worked in this large, handsome, sturdy house, was strolling outside on his front lawn. It was a warm day, and he took a deep breath as he surveyed the quiet residential street. A big man, perhaps in his sixties, with white hair and a reddish glow on his face, he sighed and remarked softly, "All up and down this street, they're moving out." He pointed to several "For Sale" signs perched outside the little homes with their carefully groomed bushes and lawns. "My own *friends* are moving away," he said in a tone conveying both sadness and disbelief. "Most of them are old, and you know what the real tragedy is? The move will kill them. It really will. How can they hope to start life all over again? How can they possibly establish new friendships at their age? No one cares about an old person, not to make a real friend with. You make only a few of those in a lifetime. They're frightened, but once they move, they'll die from loneliness anyway. This is a terrible thing that's happening here. . . ."

As he turned to go back inside his office, the bishop paused, his face brightening somewhat. "You know," he said, "when a Negro family moves in here, the white children in the neighborhood go right out into the street to play with the Negro kids, and you see them all together, black and white. But the adults, they stay inside their homes, and they don't speak to each other at all."

Harvey had come to see the bishop about a new program called Goals for Gary. Mayor Hatcher had appointed the bishop to serve as chairman, a move regarded as politically shrewd, since the bishop's flock included many of Gary's fifty-seven ethnic groups (the program's chief aim was to unite the city's residents in common goals). Harvey and Bishop Grutka discussed their plans, and at one point the bishop stood up behind his desk and leaned his body across it. "Listen," he said to Harvey, his voice trembling in a partial whisper, "in all due respect to Mr. Hatcher, his days of glory are over. Now, even to his own people, he's just another politician, *and he has to deliver.* The kids in Midtown, the street-gang kids, they have nothing to do. If they're just left to themselves, without jobs, with nothing to do, something terrible could happen. I'm very worried, I really am."

The question, if that's what it was, just hung there in the room, and in the space of one hour on a hot afternoon, the bishop had given a capsule view of Gary's double-edged dilemma: a white community frightened of rising black power and a black community desperately hoping that its mayor will have *enough* power to alleviate their condition.

The bishop had made a great impact on me, I wasn't sure why. Something in the way he seemed so involved, so concerned, as if the tumult of the times had finally invaded his own bachelor's life (indeed, his flock formed a sizable flank of the frightened mob that was retreating from the advancing blacks, and his diocese was losing their money, as well), and it occurred to me that perhaps he had undergone a rebirth of sorts at this late hour—and no lonely old man was *he* about to become. I liked the bishop, who rambled over a dozen subjects as we were leaving, but there was still one more aspect of the rebirth to be revealed. He went to his bookshelf and lifted out a plain-looking book, saying that he had been struggling with it for quite some time now, and when he opened it and flipped through its pages, we discovered that it was printed entirely in Chinese. "I can't read a word of it," said the bishop as we stared at the vertical columns of Oriental symbols. "I'm trying to decipher it," he went on, adding something which seemed to have terrifying global, perhaps heavenly, implications, and I was wondering if my journey to Gary, Indiana, which was not large on the atlas, had led to some secret understanding or private unveiling of the apocalypse— symbolized by an elderly white bishop racing against time to crack the code of the language of the people of China.

3.

One Saturday night I went into the Midtown area with a young *Post-Tribune* reporter named George Crile, in order to visit with a small group of black women. Crile was perhaps twenty-four, and he was white, and who knows, one day he may become a nationally syndicated columnist, but for now he was working on the problem of being twenty-four, white, and a reporter for the *Post-Tribune*. He had been on the job for only two months, having moved to Gary from Washington, D.C., because, he told me in a voice not entirely sure of itself, "the action is here." A microcosm of America, nothing better than to put in time at a newspaper in a small city, et cetera, and so he had arranged to see these black women, who would tell him the as-yet-unprinted truth of the ghetto, and he, in turn, would assure them that somehow he would take the message to his editors. . . .

At any rate, my memory of this meeting is full of empty spaces, maybe because one's senses tend to become disoriented, out of balance, from the sudden jolt they receive upon entrance into the black slums. The streets and sidewalks were dark, and we made our way into a building (I failed completely to notice what it looked like from the outside), and climbed some stairs to the second level, which had a few rooms adjoining an open floor, one of which rooms contained the several black ladies.

I am still uncertain as to the exact purpose for which this gathering of young reporter and black women was called, but a clear tension existed on both sides, an uncomfortable wariness hung in the center of the mood, and for several minutes I expected that we would get up and simply leave, some incomprehensible act of communication having been accomplished. Young Crile leaned forward, trying to improvise an approach, and the black ladies, seated around a long table, shifted uncertainly in their chairs. They had the look of captive victims about to be examined for warts.

"I know you're critical of the paper," Crile offered, "but that's why I'm here. I want to be objective."

The ladies stirred uneasily. "Well," one woman spoke up, "we don't *want* you to be objective. The paper is already *too* objective. *We want you to be biased in our favor for a change.*"

The dam holding back the mysteriously coiled tension broke, and wonderful laughter bounced around the walls of the small room. I knew the sound of this laughter, had heard it on other, similar occasions when such tired, frustrated black people had shook with merriment at the mere mention of a glint of the truth. They had become so weary of their own anger that it was almost impossible for them to sustain it anymore. "That's right!" they all seemed to scream at once, and it was a measure of the duration and the depth of their feelings that they would find such humor in the truth of their own condition. (By contrast, the women at the Sewer District meeting had had no need for such laughter; as desperate as their situation was, still it *was* but a situation of the moment and not, as in the case of these black women, a condition of their lives reaching back from before birth to the present and beyond to the abyss of the known future; the laughter in this room was a sound born of a slight madness, a drunkenness of the spirit, and it seemed to reside just a beat away from the darkness of despair.)

They continued to laugh wildly at the truth. "Government programs, they're either here to tear up places, or to bribe people *not* to tear up places." Laughter! "I'm sure the mayor don't know just how the people feel about these programs. We don't get nothing. The money don't stay in the black community, 'cause we consumers, see. The Glen Park people, they stupid to feel that we gettin' money—it just enough money to keep folks scrappin' over it." More laughter, more helpless recognition of the truth. "This money never come in till folks started burning. It just enough to keep us from burning up the frigging place, but not enough to rebuild it." Greater laughter, now. "It true that Mayor Hatcher has put more peoples in jobs. There's more blacks in city government and in these programs, but very little money trickling down to the little people." General agreement, head-nodding. "White people think we're really doing great 'cause of these programs, but you go through a thirty-dollar training period and you get out and there's nowhere to go to work!" "That's right, yeah!" "I'm all for participatory democracy, I think that's great. But I seen some other black women get involved, and in three months they've become the biggest oppressors you ever seen!" A roar of laughter, now—to the point where the woman who made that last remark is now burying her face in her hands and shaking, somehow managing to add, "One of my lady friends said, 'Send me to Model Cities, and I'll do a job for y'all'—and now she's back and she don't even *know* y'all!"

There was a confusion here, that conflicting (or balancing) combination of desperation and humor, and neither Crile nor I really understood it. When we moved in the direction of showing our sympathy or concern or understanding, we wound up with cynicism and laughter. When we ourselves laughed, one of the ladies would plunge us back into the bleakness of the same truth which had just seemed so funny. Back and forth went the mood of the evening in a self-defeating cycle, and it became apparent to me that, unlike the white ladies with the sewer and drainage problems, these black women did not for a moment expect that anything good might come from our meeting, that in fact this was merely one more futile session with some well-meaning white folks (in this case, the well-meaning Crile), and that present in the room was a bitterness and rage whose depth no film camera and no sound track could record.

"We're tired of being studied and studied," said one of the women, referring to the continual forms they were asked to fill out by government agencies and corporations and committees. "The white man needs our money, so we tell our guts!"

Another woman described the frustration of going to meetings where white people come to listen to black people's opinions. "All *I* get out of it," she said, "is to get black and white to understand each other, but what will that do? They'll maybe understand us better, but we'll still be standing here. . . ." She described how she had gone to one meeting at which a film about crime in the ghetto had been shown. "I'm not gonna spend every Thursday night," she yelled to no one in particular, "telling white folks that they oughtta feel sorry for a pregnant girl on an elevator!"

Again, that laughter.

All of which gave me a sense of futility about my own work—I could imagine them saying, "You'll do your goddamn writing, and yet we'll still be down here. . . ."—but I went ahead and asked about Richard Hatcher. What changes in their lives had come about because of his efforts?

"One thing, you *can* go to him, if you can catch up with him. Mayor Katz"—the previous mayor—"would see you comin', and he'd infiltrate through the walls."

Howls of hilarity.

"He's getting Federal money, but it ain't enough. It hasn't filtered down to the people yet. He may talk of all the things he's doing, which is fine, but you come in here, and you find the people are still gettin' poorer."

General agreement.

"I'm from Mississippi," said a plump black woman who was fanning herself with a sheet of paper. "I came here in 1947, and I tell you, *it's worse here!*"

Would you all support Hatcher again?

"Oh, yes! Of course!"

"He's done more for this city in this short time. . . ."

"Mayor Katz used to have a police car parked all night outside the red-light district, which didn't do nothing. But Hatcher came along and tore the whole damn whorehouse down! You don't see the prostitutes standing on the corners, now."

"The mayor needs time to do things. People should support him. He can't do it all by himself."

"Every eye is on that man."

"He's given my son, and other people's sons, a new outlook on life."

4.

They were ambiguous about Hatcher, the poor people were, because at this juncture he was still more of a hope than a guarantee, and because the sins of the past cannot be corrected in four years or maybe not in a decade. And the ambiguity extended down from these black women to their sons and daughters. I attended a dance in the ghetto in Gary—there was a crowd of black kids in a darkened room, they were dancing to the music from a record player while young girls were selling grape juice at five cents a cup—and outside in the front hallway were several members of a street gang. Each of these black youngsters was eager to engage me in some kind of heated dialogue, mainly, I think, because I represented the Establishment to them. Some merely glared at me from a distance for a while, but eventually even they would step forward to say their piece. Perhaps remembering the bishop's worries, I took an offensive role, at times, challenging them with questions like "Are you gonna do anything with yourself next summer?" or "Five years from now, do you have any idea of what you'll be?" God knows what prerogative I thought I had to challenge them in this manner, but it became obvious to me that these young men relished the opportunity to respond and to assert themselves. The main thing they wanted to get across was, as expressed by one of them, "We're not a gang, we're an *organization*. We're not *de*structive, we're *con*structive."

"We don't like violence," another said. "If we did, you wouldn't get home tonight."

What about the Panthers?

"We'll go with 'em when they're right, but we won't bother with 'em if they're wrong."

What do you think of Mayor Hatcher?

"We *don't* think of him, man. He's doing his thing"—right here I remembered that Hatcher had used the same words for Carl Stokes—"and we've got our bag. He's all right—he's just a black cat trying to make it."

Out on the sidewalk, a young black fellow, perhaps sixteen years old, came up to me and said, "Man, don't listen to them guys in there. They don't give a damn 'bout nothing. They don't think past tomorrow. Wine, women. But me? Man, I'm gonna be a doctor. That's right! A doctor! You don't believe me? Hey, you know something? I talked to the mayor right here on this corner the other night. He was standing just over here, and I walked right up to him and said, 'How're you doing, Mr. Hatcher!' And we talked for twenty minutes, him and me, and he told me to stay in school. I told him I was gonna be a doctor. And he invited me up to see him at City Hall, in his office. That's the truth."

"He wants to be a model for behavior," a friend said of Hatcher. "He feels a *responsibility* to do that. He's very much aware that he provides an alternate identity to which black kids can aspire. Hatcher is an alternative to the hustler-on-the-street, alligator-shoes image."

When I discussed this with Hatcher, he again referred to his past, to his family background, making the point that for most black kids "high achievement is possible, but highly improbable, without the kind of family encouragement, and love that I had." He emphasized the role that his father took in the household ("Hard as it was, he was really the man there, and he tried to instill certain basic things") and pointed out that most black kids who get into trouble probably have no father or family stability. "I'm not the most confident individual in the world today," Hatcher admitted, "but I don't think there are many situations that I would panic in. I think I can handle, you know, just about whatever comes along. But I'm convinced that the reason I have that kind of security is because my family gave it to me when I was growing up. They made me feel like I was important and made me feel that they cared about me. And that was really necessary for me, because of the real problems that I had when I was growing up. If that love hadn't been there, I don't know where I'd be now. And I think of all the kids who don't get that feeling of someone caring, and I don't see how they can possibly turn out any other way but insecure, frustrated, and everything else.

"Whatever you say about the Panthers, one thing comes across loud and clear. And that's that pride and that feeling, you know, that 'I'm a *man,* and I can *do* things.' And that's there, you can see it. I'm sure that's what attracts most kids to the Panthers. You find the same thing with the kids in the gangs, here in Gary. I'm always accused of being 'soft on gangs'—sort of like being 'soft on Communism' or something. But a lot of these kids are in the gangs because, for the first time, there's a kind of authoritarian image for them to look at and to relate to. And they have a role, they're an important part of the overall organization. All of those things count for them.

"So being a model for kids, I think that's important. To me, it is. I don't know how effective—I just don't know how many kids go out and really try to be like Mayor Hatcher or Mayor Stokes, but I suspect that many of them do. And for that reason, it's very important that I be very careful about what I do and what I say— and to maintain some kind of, you know, integrity."

5.

I saw Hatcher speak at an antiwar rally in downtown Gary on a hot early Saturday afternoon when the wind was blowing the scent of the mill away from the city, leaving a bright blue sky, and on the way to the rally Hatcher, wearing sunglasses, stopped to talk to a black shoeshine boy on the sidewalk. "Making a lot of money?" he asked the boy, and the two of them walked along for a block, the mayor's arm extended down to the kid's shoulder, and they seemed oblivious of all the passersby.

Inside the small auditorium, white college students, a handful of young blacks, and some older folks filled up only half the available seats. The kids had just completed a long protest march— they had walked through Glen Park and were jeered at and threatened—and now, for their reward, a dull batch of speeches. Hatcher sat up on the stage waiting his turn, and when he finally got up to speak, I realized that he was maybe the only guy in the whole place wearing a suit and tie, a complete contrast to the long-haired kids with their jeans and vests and sandals and general raggedy power-to-the-people-peace-now outfits, but they all stood up in one collective *whoooosh* when Hatcher walked to the microphone. They gave him a long standing ovation before he spoke a word, and he waited up there, modest-looking, *clean* in his crewcut and black suit, smiling a bit as if to say, Please don't make it so easy for me.

"We are being forced to confront what we have become as a nation," he told them, and he talked of "how deep racism in this country goes . . . programs for the poor being cut out while the war goes on . . . time has run out . . . the patient is dying. . . ." And their response was terrific, another standing ovation for the only man in the room in a crewcut and a suit with a tie.

Three or four weeks later I returned to Gary and caught up with Hatcher in the radio studio where he did his talk show. ("Well, Mayor Hatcher, it's good to have you with us today." "Good to be here, Ted.") For the next hour I listened to Richard Hatcher talk, in response to citizens' questions, about his anti-litter program (he didn't read the names of any convicted litterers this time), his junked-car tow-away program, an abandoned store, a new Federal grant, fast cars, pot, uniforms for school crossing guards, sanitation ("Mr. Hatcher, there's an old garage with a whole lot of *debris* right beside my house." "What's that address? Okay, ma'am, we'll get someone out there right away to clean that up. Thanks for calling."), parking, zoning, sewers—and after a while one ceased to think at all about the fact that Richard Hatcher was a black mayor trying to hold together a racially divided city. Maybe this was one way he was doing it. He was so low-keyed here, so unhurried and polite, jotting down names and addresses of callers—he behaved like a tired antagonist who had called a temporary truce. It seemed to me that more than half the callers were white, and they, too, seemed overly soft-spoken and nice. The radio show itself had a strong capability of putting the listener into a solid sleep. Hatcher seemed to want to avoid all controversy during this hour of broadcast, and on the whole it appeared that the callers also had no desire to break the spell. It was difficult to remember what all this black-white fuss was about.

After the show we walked over to the Gary Hotel for coffee—he smiled and nodded at people along Broadway as if to maintain the spell some more—and he commented, "I think people *will* be able to live together, and that color *will* become secondary."

Over coffee, we discussed several things. When I mentioned all the "For Sale" signs in the inner-city residential neighborhoods, he said that many of them had been there for two years.

"Those people not only want to get out, but to make a profit as well," he said. "But some have decided to stay. There was an initial 'I'm getting out,' but now they really don't know how to take those signs down. I think they realize what it means to start all over again somewhere else. For one thing, their expectations of chaos because of my election just haven't come to pass. And because of the employment thing, many *can't* leave. The block-busting attempts by brokers—that's one reason for the signs. Some of those houses have been sold by whites to *other* white people. The signs are still there to give the impression that the neighborhood is really shifting.

"I certainly do worry about the community disintegrating, though. And about people who say I'm only concerned with poor people. But we *do* do things to counteract that feeling. Glen Park gets preference, even—we break our necks to prove it to them. The snow plows go out there *first,* for example. And the police protection is probably better there than anywhere else in the city. The opposition there is really all race and politics. We've put some housing, some public housing, out in Glen Park—the alternative is to go against everything you believe in. Some racists were there at the dedication for one of the housing projects—they stood across the street while I made a speech about how I hoped we could learn to live together—but there've been no problems since.

"See, guys like Stokes and myself, we're paying the price. Any blacks after us won't have half the problems we've had. On the other hand, they won't have that special attention for being first. Without trying to sound like a wise man, I think I understand the antagonistic people better than they themselves do, so I can deal with it. In some ways, that antagonism has diminished, but in others, it's increased. My guess is that things will get better. We're going through a period of great strife. A lot of values are being rethought, and that causes friction, but I don't think it's a permanent situation. I really believe that in a short time we'll be through this. What we're experiencing is the last dying gasp of certain attitudes, myths, and so on. And they're not giving up without a fight. I think we've reached a high point in the struggle. It might get worse until it gets better, but we'll come through. I really believe that we'll stop wars like Vietnam, that we'll get out of Indochina, and learn to live together.

"Even in the darkness of the Nixon administration, there are some bright sides. There *are* some hopeful signs, and we're gonna get through this. Black people have already reached some conclusions about violence. It's been a couple of years since the outbreaks, and blacks have reached a certain maturity. I don't mean to say that everything's all right, but I'm more optimistic than pessimistic. I look beyond, and I see people overcoming these problems. Even the worst bigot is beginning to realize that bigotry is in the past. I just see more cause for hope than despair. . . ."

6.

Hatcher's executive secretary, Ray Wild, had told me that in his opinion Gary was "ten years ahead of the rest of America—racially." The meaning of that statement is still somewhat vague to me, although at the time I just nodded, assuming that I comprehended. I think, however, that Wild was referring to the fact that Hatcher was operating on two levels at once—one for the black community, the other for the total city. Hatcher was no separatist, but he was aware that equality will never come about unless blacks can gain political and economic control of the ghetto. "What black people are saying," he once told a reporter, "is that if you call control of your own neighborhood separatism, then we have separatism all over this country. What's so unusual about people saying, 'We're going to control our own turf'? That's not separatism—that's good old Americanism." On the other hand, he was trying to make it clear to white citizens that his "blackness" had nothing to do with his ability or willingness to serve them. "He could win reelection easily if he ran a strictly 'black' campaign," another City Hall aide told me (although I wasn't entirely convinced).

During his first mayoralty campaign he had declared, "I'm not after black votes or white votes, but rather good old red-blooded American votes." He had campaigned among whites, but his only hope for any kind of white acceptance was in one prosperous middle-class district—and this situation probably would occur again. "I have tremendous hope for Gary," he once said. "There's a greater degree of unity now, and people are beginning to believe in our city again. I've gone into areas of Glen Park where before people almost spit on you. That's how strong the feeling was. And now I see mothers who tell their children, 'There's the mayor. Get his autograph.' " The new signs of friendliness may have been only superficial, but that was a step forward nonetheless.

Even the monster, U. S. Steel, had begun to play a larger role in helping to solve problems in Gary, but only after Hatcher had threatened to reevaluate its property. "They still won't let us look at their books," Hatcher said, referring to his belief that U.S.S. was failing to pay millions of dollars in property taxes. "We demanded to see their books," he told me, "in order to examine their new construction and so on, but they brought in lawyers and even went to court to fight us. We're still trying." And although some pollution controls had been set up, Hatcher admitted that "it's still not enough." (One time he was speaking to an audience of students about how America's corporations "dominate the market and the economy and even set priorities for our society," and although he usually becomes involved in the writing of his speeches, he hadn't checked this one over. The speech went on, "Who can believe that big industry doesn't want to do what's best for the people?" and after reading several more "who can believe" statements along the same lines, Hatcher looked up, bewildered at his own words, and confessed, "*I* can believe it." The students roared with laughter.)

"He came in without the approval of the business or political machines," Ray Wild commented, "and maybe they think all this reform is transitory. Sometimes I have the feeling that they're just sitting back, hoping that Hatcher will just go away."

In May, 1970, John Krupa had breezed in for another term as chairman of the Lake County Democratic organization, declaring that the Machine was now "the biggest and greatest we have ever had." The *Post-Tribune* reported that Krupa "was pleased to be restored to precinct power, particularly in Gary, where there had been some problems. . . . There was little, if any, evidence of Gary Mayor Richard G. Hatcher's supporters. . . ." Already there was speculation that two Negroes would run against Hatcher in the next Democratic primary and that in such an event former Mayor Katz would join the race and try to squeeze out the nomination. Once again it would be a contest between the Machine's money and Hatcher's personal ability to unite the "little people" —black and white—behind him.

It would have seemed much easier and maybe more rewarding for Hatcher to run for Congress or even move outside of politics altogether, but he had committed himself to "working within the System," which had become something of a misleading concept. The concept had been used so often lately that one tended to become dulled by it into the kind of apathy which had been common in earlier, less turbulent years—apathy that resulted from the blind faith that all necessary changes would come about all in good time. "Working within the System" was now hailed by almost all, more out of relief from fear, it sometimes seemed, than out of conviction that it would work. It was hailed by liberals and conservatives alike as an alternative to violence by blacks, students, even madmen and crooks, but it too easily became an unconscious alternative to real change. One suspected that it might have been a coolly conscious plot to give the disaffected only the *appearance* of change. And so if Richard Hatcher was "working within the System," there was the sinking feeling that perhaps we would wake up one morning to find it had all been an unreal fantasy played out on a stage by the manipulated black puppets of an unseen white ruler. But Hatcher was playing the part too well; he had thrown away the old script and seemed to be improvising, producing conflict where the lines hadn't called for it, stubbornly pursuing an objective for which the System was totally unprepared. In other words, Hatcher might have been exposing the false promise in the phrase "working within the System" by working within it for the purpose of changing it into something else; his kind of nonviolent militancy may in fact have been the last exercise of faith by the angry and the damned. The point was, if "working within the System" was to have any validity at all, it had to be carried out with the opposite of dullness and apathy, with an abundance of conflict and turbulence—and someone like Richard Hatcher was likely to work the System's ass off, to the brink of exhaustion and near-collapse if need be, to make it earn its reputation for flexibility (and, for that matter, workability). Too often the System was a poor prostitute, taking the little man's money and spitting on him in return; and if the

System really was a prostitute, then she hated her pathetic customers with a hatred deeper than one could know. But Hatcher was paying out and demanding full service from the old girl, whatever her feelings toward him may have been.

Twenty

1.

> The Republicans know they won't get the black vote, and the Democrats are sure they will, so neither is paying much attention to Negroes this time.

That observation in the New York *Times* by an unidentified politician pretty well summed up the November, 1970, election campaign from the standpoint of a black voter, and on the national level it was enough to make one wonder why blacks still maintained any faith in the System at all. I was reminded of Julian Bond's observation that black politics had to be an "inverted triangle" with a small base that widened out to the top. "Down at the bottom you can have your strength," Julian had said, while "the farther up you go, the more diluted you become." And on the national level, black political strength had been diluted out of sight. The swing to the right in American politics had moved liberal white candidates to the "center" and others across it; most white politicians had found it much more beneficial to talk up law and order while simply forgetting about the blacks. And so it would not have been surprising if every black voter in the nation decided to stay home on election day. "The negative mood of black people and black voters is markedly deeper today than in past elections," Bond had been quoted as saying. Another black spokesman added, "We're sick and tired of voting for crackers and participating in this jive political system. It's a sign of political maturity that we tell the cracker politicians to go to hell." I thought about these comments and decided that if I were black, I might be inclined to withdraw from "working within the System" altogether. What was the use of coalition and compromise if you were only manipulated in order to serve some politician's personal goals? Why continue to choose between two candidates if neither represented my interests or concerns? What was the game worth if winning meant nothing?

Bond had been quoted as saying that there was a deepening frustration among blacks with "national" politics and policies, mainly because of the racist overtone of major campaigns throughout the country, but when one looked farther down the "inverted triangle," it became clear that black enthusiasm for politics was on the increase. No doubt it was a major irony of the 1970 elections that, while the nation seemed to be swinging away from its black citizens, minority politics was making new gains, especially at the grass-roots level in the urban North and the rural South, down at the bottom of the triangle. More than six hundred black candidates in thirty-eight states were running for office. In New York, there were seventy-five candidates, in Ohio thirty-seven, in Missouri thirty-five, in Maryland thirty-two, in Illinois thirty-one, in Arkansas thirty, in California twenty-one, and so on, until one was able to form a mental picture of "blacks in politics" as a vibrant and diverse reality, a movement into the System being enacted on a stage too broad for any single reporter to absorb. And the most activity of all could be found in Alabama, where Dr. John Cashin's independent, undiluted, down-to-earth Eagle Party was running more than 170 candidates for offices throughout the state. The National Democratic Party of Alabama (NDPA) was not an all-black party (eleven of its candidates were white), but it was in fact one of the most advanced black-oriented political organizations in the nation. In terms of having "strength down at the bottom," there was nothing like it. Cashin, the forty-two-year-old black dentist from Huntsville, was the single driving force behind this revolutionary, grass-roots kind of politics that was sweeping across the Alabama black belt.

Aside from Cashin's own race for governor against George Wallace, the NDPA was running candidates for lieutenant governor, secretary of state, commissioner of agriculture, state treasurer, state auditor, and public service commissioner. The Eagle Party had five candidates for Congress, five for the state Senate, and forty-eight for the state House of Representatives; and dozens of other candidates were running for state and local offices in something like thirty counties. Win or lose, black people could go to the polls and pull down the lever under the sign of the Eagle and know they were voting not just for names but for a political party representing their point of view. The Eagle candidates all stood for something, their attitudes and concerns were clear and uncompromising, and in fact the NDPA was the first political party in Alabama to have adopted a platform. Apparently, the major parties had never felt the need to run on issues. The NDPA was a coalition of most of Alabama's 310,000 black voters and those "liberal and radical" whites who cared to join them.

There were some fifteen counties in Alabama where blacks numbered more than half of the total voters registered, all in the black belt, named for its dark, rich, cotton-producing soil, counties like Greene and Hale and Sumter and Marengo and Perry and Lowndes and Macon, where NDPA's local candidates had a real chance of gaining political power of the most fundamental sort. For the rural, desperately poor blacks, the election of a sheriff or a probate judge was more important than having a Congressman or even a President.

And so I decided to return to Alabama, having come to the conclusion that Dr. Cashin's work was at the heart of my journey into the new black politics. For if it were true that the blacks could be used or manipulated or even written off by politicians of both major national parties, such was not the case at the bottom, where blacks had numerical strength. If the country was continuing to divide along racial lines, then it was also solidifying in its division, and, yes, the new Black Nation was being built, ironically, because of the growing separation. What Cashin was attempting to do in Alabama, and especially in places like Greene County, was not unlike what LeRoi Jones and Kenneth Gibson had done in Newark. The settings were completely different, but the strategies were the same. The new black politics was a strategy for survival, a tool for the takeover of the land upon which blacks held majorities, whether that land was littered by the tenements of Northern urban ghettos or by the tarpaper shacks of Southern rural countrysides.

John Cashin's work was an outgrowth of the civil-rights movement which had begun in Alabama. "If that movement was frustrated in the mid-1960's," he argued, "it was only because people were not able to bridge the gap between confrontation politics and electoral politics. The former are emotional and temporary; the latter are tedious but lasting."

If the 1960's was the decade of direct action and street rebellion, then the 1970's could become the decade of massive black political gain—less dramatic and more painstaking, perhaps, but with solid results in the long run; and this new struggle was what Dr. Cashin's new political party both represented and embodied.

2.

The Birmingham office of the Jefferson County NDPA was located in a black section just up the street from the park where Police Commissioner Bull Connor had unleashed the dogs and the hoses on Martin Luther King's marchers in 1963. On this gloomy gray day before the election, there seemed to be little activity going on beneath the small white wooden sign which hung over the sidewalk outside the storefront. An eagle had been painted in black on the sign along with the words "Party of the People." Inside the small office, a group of black youngsters, mostly students from Howard University and other colleges in the South, sporting Afro hairdos and old clothes, some carrying knapsacks, milled around waiting to be prodded into doing chores by a short black woman in a light-blue sweater, Mrs. Merulrine Watkins (who, I later learned, was a candidate for the state House of Representatives on the Eagle ticket). There were several desks in the office, and most of the remaining cramped space was taken up by dozens of large stacks of as yet undistributed *Eagle Eye* newspapers, which had been printed for the party free of charge by the Black Muslims.

"Don't just sit around here," Mrs. Watkins urged the kids every once in while. "There's plenty for y'all to be doing."

A radio on one of the desks was tuned to a local black station, and the announcer was saying that Dr. John Cashin would be arriving soon at the studio in downtown Birmingham. I walked over to the offices of Station WJLD at around two o'clock in the afternoon, by which time Cashin was already sitting behind the glass wall of the studio, hunched over the microphone in order to respond to callers.

"We're gonna clean house tomorrow," a black female caller was saying.

"Thank you, dear," Cashin replied.

"Hi, Brother Cashin?"

"How's it goin', Sister?"

One of the callers wanted to know why Cashin was still so optimistic about the System, and he answered, "There's nothing necessarily wrong with capitalism if it pays attention to the human values of people. I say that people are more important than money, and I always will. I want to see that people don't serve money but each other, and that's what society is all about."

To the final caller, he said, "Tell the folks that all they have to do is pull that straight Eagle lever, okay?"

"Yes, I will. We'll make us a new Alabama tomorrah."

"Okay, Brother, thank ya."

"And thank *you*," the black announcer broke in. "And remember, folks, it take *both* black and white keys to play 'The Star-Spangled Banner.' "

John Cashin came out of the studio on the second floor of the building. In the light coloring of his skin and in the youthful contours of his face he resembled Julian Bond, although he was shorter and heavier, and the sandy resonance of his voice was also similar to Bond's, perhaps reflecting a certain middle-class, Southern Negro background that they had in common. Cashin's Afro hair, the "natural" look, was not as long as Julian's had been during the summer, but somehow he looked like neither a dentist nor a candidate for governor. And if he did appear an older, fuller-faced Julian Bond, he had lost the younger man's regal composure and sense of timing and restraint. Today, election eve, Cashin was in a kind of Muhammad Ali mood, as if at any moment he might be called upon to jump into the ring for fifteen rounds with Wallace. If so, I thought, then Cashin's style would be to dance around his foe, mocking, jabbing, circling, taunting, pounding in and breaking away, always moving and always keeping up the chatter, as he did in a speech later that night.

> I could tell you about my opponent, but I think you already know about George Wallace.
>
> *(Jab!)*
>
> He's a master of the Big Lie technique. He's earned his reputation as being the fighting little judge. He has refined race-baiting to the present state of the art. He's the master race-baiter of them all. I'm running *against* George Wallace —he's running *from* me.
>
> *(Circle, jab, jab!)*
>
> He's built his reputation as a great fighter, but I want you to be sure that you know this—all tyrants are cowards, and George Wallace is one of both! He has to be! It's only a coward that wants to enslave and take unfair advantage of another human being! I know the nature of snakes and the nature of tyrants and the nature of George Wallace! And as it is the nature of snakes to bite, and of tyrants to oppress, it's just like George Wallace to holler, "Nigger, nigger, nigger" when he's in trouble!
>
> *(Left, right, left!)*
>
> Now he's running away! But it's a *black* man that's setting him to running. Just remember that! The very first time he's up against the real thing, he tucks his little tail between his legs and runs! It was his *own* people's idea to challenge me to a debate, and when I rose to the challenge, we haven't heard anything from him since!
>
> *(Knockdown!)*
>
> We have a good chance to elect Isaiah Hayes as lieutenant governor tomorrow! If we elect a black lieutenant governor, George Wallace *can't* run for President. Can you imagine George trying to explain that to all those Klansmen? Every time he left the state they'd say, "George, are you gonna leave Alabama in the hands of a nigger? And a big one, at that? One that's bigger than you, George?"

But now he stood there outside the studio, with no Wallace to debate, no camera crews to film him, no tape recorders whirring, no representatives from the press taking down his every word, he was alone and jumpy and irritated and excited and punchy . . . wound up. We hurried together down the back stairs of the building and walked across the street toward a parking garage.

"Gonna make a lot of money off us folks, eh?" he said as we walked along at a brisk pace. "You're a smart little white boy, ain't ya?"

A few minutes later he said, "Don't mind me talking that way —I may give you trouble from time to time, but that's just my nature. I'm a bit unorthodox, you see."

When we got to the car, he showed me his Magnum .357, a heavy silver gun which he kept under the armrest in the center of the front seat. Cashin had received numerous threats against his life in the last few months. He could be the first black governor of Alabama, I thought, or he just as easily could be shot down in the street like one more nigger.

We rode over to the headquarters on 17th Street, and after he greeted Mrs. Watkins and the kids, we walked around the corner to the Fraternal Café, where black folks sitting around the tables failed to look up or respond when he made his entrance. Somewhat annoyed, probably having anticipated mingling among the tables and shaking hands, Cashin made some loud noises and took a table where he could face the rest of the café, and he seemed to talk louder than necessary for simple conversation. He ordered one of the hot plates on the menu, and after waiting ten minutes he was told by a young black waitress that the food he had ordered wasn't available. Now more annoyed than ever, he fussed and fumed and berated the waitress, finally shouting, "Give me just anything!"

"Anything?" the girl asked meekly.

"Whatever you have, honey, that don't take time to fix. Something you can give me without complications. I'm hungry, and I don't have time."

Cashin could hardly sit still while we waited for his food. Tommy Wrenn, the Jefferson County NDPA chairman, burst into the café and asked Cashin for some money.

"How much?"

"Fifty."

Cashin took a fifty-dollar bill from his shirt pocket and handed it to Wrenn, who then left as quickly as he had arrived. Still waiting for his meal, Cashin jumped up and went around the corner, returning in a few minutes with some of the local black newspapers.

"Some of our folks can be paid to do anything," he said loudly, apparently referring to something he had noticed in one of the newspapers. "But I don't think people are paying too much attention to the Judases anymore. I'm glad to hear it, too, 'cause it's been my life for the past two or three years, since we started out with the objective of putting the Eagle on the ballot." By this time, some of the blacks in the café had overheard and recognized him, and now they listened carefully, still not responding to him, perhaps out of respect. (Although, as it turned out—and this came as somewhat of a surprise to me—Cashin was regarded by many blacks in Alabama as "too radical" for their taste; there was a fear that the NDPA, while it was an integrated party, smacked too much of separatism, and therefore, Cashin was almost as angry with the middle-class Negroes as he was with the white supremacists.)

"Those Judases," Cashin said, his voice rising so that all the blacks in the café could hear, "they're trying to deceive their own people! They're *paid* to deceive us. Paid to divide and conquer us. Paid to control their own people! But I found out something —that there's more of us than there are of them!"

The waitress came with his food, and he requested that I refrain from smoking while he ate. He called the waitress back and informed her that there was some ugly-looking foreign substance floating in his orange drink. By this time, the girl's composure was rapidly disappearing, and Cashin had gained the attention of everyone else in the café.

"*You* wouldn't drink that," he told the girl. "Would you?"

She cast her eyes downward and went off to replace the orange drink.

In one of the newspapers, there was a report that Charles Evers had gone to New York State and had commented that he would vote for Nelson Rockefeller for governor if he lived there. In effect, Evers was declaring that he would *not* support Basil Paterson, a black candidate for lieutenant governor on the Democratic ticket with Arthur Goldberg. When I wondered about this aloud, Cashin put down the newspaper and said, "Who among those candidates running for governor of New York has the most money?"

"Rockefeller, of course."

"Well, now you know why Evers would support him."

"You don't like Evers?"

"Now you get the picture."

(This needed more explanation, because in my view there was great similarity between Cashin and Evers, in terms of their goals, at least. Yet Cashin had come out of the middle class as a member of the Negro elite, from a family background of lawyers and dentists, while Charles Evers had grown up in the poor, rural countryside of Decatur, Mississippi. One suspected that John Cashin had never suffered as deeply as Evers had and that the two men had arrived at their blackness through entirely different circuits; and one also suspected that Cashin was embarrassed by the money he had made as a professional, that he had been struck by conscience at some point in his life, causing him to throw himself into the Movement with a kind of missionary zeal, while Evers, without an ounce of guilt or shame, had made a career out of fighting racism, a career that was inseparable from his own self-development and personal gain. Evers was also a national hero among blacks and many whites, while Cashin was not. One suspected that Cashin's view of Evers was colored by the terms in which he had come to view himself, and that Evers would reply that the reason Cashin could denounce money was because he already had it.)

"Evers isn't any millionaire," I observed.

"Well," Cashin scoffed, "he will be."

3.

During the next three days I came to know and admire John Cashin, and came to understand something of what it must have been like to be the first black candidate for governor of Alabama. The fact that I was the only reporter with him before, during, and after the election, a crucial three-day period for him as well as an historical one for the state itself, was some indication of how frustrating it must have been. Apparently the news media had written him off as a major contender. Not that he himself had any persuasive illusions about being able to win, but in some secret corner of his mind he must have begun to believe that he had a chance. At one point he exclaimed, "You know, I just might win this thing. Man, that'd be one hell of an upset!"

After the meal in the café, we went around the corner and into a barbershop, and Cashin sat up on the chair at the far end in order to get his shoes shined. He chatted with the black men in the shop and was irritated to discover that they had run out of their NDPA sample ballots. Walking back to the storefront headquarters under a sky threatening to rain, he bounded along, nearly getting run over by a car, singing to himself. In the office, he instructed Mrs. Watkins to have the kids run some sample ballots over to the barbershop.

Two bodyguards suddenly appeared, remaining with him for the duration of his stay in Birmingham. One was a tall, thin, young fellow with a wild Afro, a student from Wisconsin of all places, and the other was an older black man in blue overalls and a white T-shirt. (The younger bodyguard stayed with Cashin until the day after the election.) We drove through the streets of town, Cashin driving with the younger escort beside him. "Where's the Western Union office?" he asked, but none of us knew. We pulled up at a light alongside a car driven by a middle-aged white man, and Cashin gestured to him to roll down his window. The white man appeared bewildered and frightened, no doubt wondering why in hell these black men wanted his attention and possibly thinking that now, at last, his moment of confrontation with the other race had come. When the man decided to pretend that he didn't notice the frantic gesturing in our car, Cashin screamed, "Roll that thing down, fool!" Although the man hadn't heard the remark, he did roll down his window, looking as though he had resigned himself to fate.

"Which way to the Western Union office?" Cashin asked him.

Obviously relieved, the man gave us detailed instructions. As we sped off, Cashin muttered, "I don't know *what* it's gonna take for this country to change."

He sent off his telegram and then stopped at a department store to buy three shirts, each seventeen and a half inches around the neck. "I have a thick neck," he noted. "I used to blow the trumpet a lot."

At around 4:30 in the afternoon, we pulled into the parking lot of the black-owned A. G. Gaston Motel (named after a self-made millionaire and philanthropist), and Cashin said he was going to sleep. Nearly four hours later we were speeding off in the night to what was supposed to be Cashin's first campaign stop of the evening. We arrived at a church in a black residential neighborhood, only to find a group of middle-class black men standing around, their meeting already over. Cashin was annoyed enough at the mixup in the timing of his schedule, but he became incensed when he discovered that the leaders of this meeting had distributed the wrong sample ballots—ones given to them by a small opposing Negro group—to their congregation. When Cashin lectured them, the elder blacks stood there in the vestibule of the church like small boys who had been caught stealing—bewildered, apologetic, embarrassed, ashamed.

"It's enough to make you vomit," Cashin said afterward in the car.

Another man with us added, "Just goes to show how far back some of our old folks are."

"I tell ya," Cashin said, "this'll be the death knell of those Toms. Their death knell!"

We sped along some dark lonely roads for a while, eventually arriving at the St. James Baptist Church, where Cashin made his one and only speech of the night. He stood up at the front, flanked by the two bodyguards, one of them now holding the silver Magnum .357 in a small green pouch. I wished I had brought along a movie camera to film the proceedings, because I sensed in the faces of the crowd and in the mood of the night that a moment of some historical importance was unfolding within the walls of this large church. Yes, I would have recorded the faces of the elderly black people who were making their way up the stairs and into the pews, and the faces of the youngsters as well, and I would have recorded the sounds of their singing and praying, for this moment in time recalled other occasions from the past of this place, these people.

Tommy Wrenn, the young black man who was head of the Jefferson County NDPA, stood up in front of the church audience to warm them up, telling them, "This may well turn out to be the greatest demonstration for political representation in the history of this country. You know, I've often said that the Almighty moves in mysterious ways. I just *believe* that something will happen tomorrow!"

A great swell of sound and emotion poured from the crowd, and there was much head shaking and heaving of breasts.

"We're on our way!" Wrenn screamed.

"That's right!"

"In Alabama!"

"That's right!"

"No *longer* will the government be all white! No more!"

The crowd in the church heaved back its own sounds in reaction as if it had been transformed into an echo chamber, a wild Greek chorus.

"This is it!"

"Yeeeah!"

"Yasssah!"

"I just want you to keep the record straight," Wrenn yelled.

"Keep it straight, baby!"

"Somehow or another, I'm gonna be able to tell my grandchildren—that I stood at the podium with the governor of Alabama!"

"*Yeeeeeeah!*"

"There's a political revolution at hand!"

"Well done, Brother!" someone screamed as the voices in the audience rose up in a deafening roar that seemed to threaten to blast away the walls of the church.

"We're on our way!"

"Yeah!"

"And the reason we're on our way is 'cause *a man stood up!*"

"Yah!"

"And I'm *so* happy to present to you—the next governor of the great State of Alabama, John Cashin!"

They all stood up and applauded and screamed as Cashin and Wrenn embraced, and in the emotion of the moment reality had somehow slipped away through the cracks up in the rafters, leaving one with the impression that John Cashin already *was* the governor of Alabama, that the political revolution had in fact taken place.

He gave a good speech that night, which the members of that audience would not easily forget. "Times are changing," he told them. "We see something going on in Birmingham tonight that wasn't happening last year or the year before last. We don't hear those Toms talking too loud no more, do we?"

"Amen!"

"The same message comes from Mobile, Montgomery, in the black belt, up in Huntsville, over in Gadsden and Anniston—and you know what that message is? *That we gettin' together!*"

4.

But "gettin' together" was more difficult than it sounded, and no one knew that better than Cashin himself. There was George Wallace and all that he represented on one hand, the frightened middle-class blacks or "Toms" on the other, and every manner of pitfall in between. Blacks were one third of Alabama's voting population, but to mobilize them into one strong bloc was probably impossible, at least at this stage of their political awareness, even if it *was* already November 2, 1970.

"Our folks have been brainwashed for so long," one of Cashin's aides said to me, "that it's really hard for them to conceive of themselves having any power." This inability to grasp their own voting strength (and its meaning) was especially true in the rural counties where, ironically, the blacks had the greatest potential for political gain. "These folks are voting and joining the process for the first time in their lives," the aide went on. "For most of 'em, this is their very first experience in politics—either as candidates *or* as voters. They're nervous, they're scared of being beaten up or something, and many aren't sure who's telling the truth."

One of Cashin's main points in his speech was that not only blacks but whites as well, especially poor ones, had been brainwashed:

The poor white man has been in the same situation we've

been in. You know—George Wallace tells 'em, "Let old George do it for you, don't worry." But they don't know what ol' George is doing *to* 'em.

This whole situation of a poor, poverty-stricken South exists because of one thing and one thing only. Because a sizable segment of the population has been turned against another sizable segment, and they have fought each other in a racial war filled with hate and bloodshed. And the poor State of Alabama lies crippled, exhausted from all of this conflict. There's no energy left over for productive endeavor! We have *worn ourselves out,* fighting each other.

And only when we black people, one third of the population of this state, come into our own and inject some humanism and some decency and some understanding and some love into this situation, only then can Alabama come into its rightful place. Now America cannot survive, the American Dream *cannot* come true, unless black people make their inputs into the government.

Part of the problem in "gettin' together" was simply the low educational level among Alabama's blacks (somewhere between the third- and fourth-grade levels), a direct result of the separate school system. Most of the state's black people were functionally illiterate, unable to read or write, and therefore the process of voting, of reading a complex ballot sheet and making clear decisions, baffled and frightened them. This was one reason why Cashin had fought so hard to get the Eagle on the ballot. As he explained to the audience in the church:

You don't have to ask anybody for any assistance to vote the Eagle ticket. It's all this "help" we've been getting that hurts. See, you go into those polls, and they got those very, very good white paternalists, or their paid Toms, the poll assistants—and if you're not sure of yourself and what you got to do, you go in with the ballot and you're in there two or three minutes when somebody knocks and says, "Hey, you need some help?" And you're a little nervous, a little uncertain, and you say, "Well, maybe I do need a little assistance." So they say, "Okay, who you want to vote for?" You say, "Well, I want to vote for Dr. Cashin." He says, "Okay, good." And then he pulls that thing for George Wallace!

This is the kind of "help" we've been getting. But you don't need to ask for all that help tomorrow. All you need to know is that the Eagle is on the ballot! And you can pull that lever down and just walk out! It won't take you ten seconds!

See, the Eagle gets you past all of that separate-but-equal education we've had. You don't *have* to be able to read or write, nowadays, in order to vote. You don't *have* to be able to read or write to see that Eagle on the ballot and pull that lever.

Another important task for Cashin was to convince blacks that their own candidates were qualified to hold office. In terms of academic background, Cashin himself was well qualified. He graduated from high school at age fifteen and obtained degrees from Fisk University, Tennessee State A & I, and Meharry Medical College, earning scholastic honors at each institution and maintaining the highest marks at the latter for four years.

Our white brothers have been misled into believing that we're not qualified for office. They say I'm not qualified to be the governor of Alabama. And you know, there's some Toms around here saying the same thing? These are the Judases that need to be done away with in this country!

I got three college degrees! And all of 'em with honors! I make a practice of doing things people say can't be done. I got two college degrees within a week of each other. I have met the competition. I know what I am. And I know what I can do. But the degree that I have worked hardest on is one that nobody can bestow upon me, because it doesn't exist. And that's the one of black political science for the state of Alabama! And I have spent more sleepless hours, I have worked harder for this, than for any of my degrees!

I will put my qualifications up against any of them. But those same Judases who were telling you to vote for Lurleen Wallace didn't say one word about *her* qualifications. I've got three college degrees—Lurleen Wallace didn't have a high-school diploma!

Then Cashin went on to say that the *only* qualification necessary for *any* black person to serve in public office in Alabama was "getting elected." He told the audience to remember that it was "a full-time job just to *be* black" in Alabama and survive.

Don't fool yourselves—don't have anyone tell you that you're not qualified, that you are not cunning, that you are not crafty, because just in order to *survive* this hostile environment in Alabama—and we *have* survived—we've had to be smarter than our white oppressors.

And yet, the "white oppressors" were still exceedingly cunning and crafty. In forty-two of Alabama's sixty-seven counties, white voters were registered in excess of their voting-age population, if such a statistic can be believed. In courthouses all through the black belt, the names of dead people and of those who had moved away were still on the rolls, and therefore many whites were able to vote twice or more. There even were fictitious names on some registration sheets, so that many "absentee" ballots could be cast, usually all in the same handwriting, mailed right at the courthouse itself. In some counties, even if blacks did have the majority of eligible voters, even if they did get themselves together, there was the possibility of losing. It was amazing that those whites who professed to love America could so freely frustrate the democratic process—amazing, until one remembered the depth of racism involved.

5.

The best part of Cashin's speech was when he tried to relate what the NDPA was doing to the civil-rights movement, so that those in the crowd could see clearly how their going to the polls and voting would be an extension of what had begun in Alabama back in 1956. "It all started here," he told them. "It was a little old lady's feet that were hurting down there in Montgomery, and she decided she wasn't going to take any more, and that she was *not* going to get up and give her seat on the bus to a white man. Mrs. Rosa Parks! The whole movement started right there!" Cashin went on to give what he called a "sermon on what one little sore foot can accomplish." He quoted from memory the words of Frederick Douglass in 1857, how the former slave had argued that without struggle, there is no progress:

Those who profess to favor freedom and yet deprecate agitation are men who want crops without plowing up the ground. They want rain without thunder and lightning. They want the ocean without the roar of its mighty waters.

This struggle may be a moral one or it may be a physical one, and it may be both moral and physical—*but it must be a struggle.*

For power concedes nothing without a demand! It never did, and it never will. Find out what any people will quietly submit to, and you have found out the exact measure of injustice and wrong which will be imposed upon them. . . .

For the limits of tyrants are prescribed by the endurance of those whom they oppress.

"A good example is Rosa Parks's sore feet in 1956," Cashin continued, pointing out that it took "only one pair of sore feet" to start the whole Movement. And Cashin particularly enjoyed disgressing for a moment to point out that in Montgomery County at this moment

the man who listened to Mrs. Rosa Parks, the man over there, E. D. Nixon, a retired Pullman porter, an old staunch black man, who is still in the action, the man who took a struggling young minister named Martin Luther King and put him in the front of the Montgomery Improvement Association and made him the world leader that he was—this man, E. D. Nixon, the *granddaddy* of the civil-rights movement, is running for state legislature on the Eagle ticket!

But so much for history. Having brought the whole Movement up to date, having in effect compressed it into this church on this night before the election, Cashin bore down on his audience of emotional black folks as if by the power of words alone he could explode all that history and suffering and emotion into an effective political hurricane that would spread out from Birmingham and roll across the state in all directions.

If you got a shoe that's pinching your foot, and it hurts, and you don't do anything about it, if you hold still quietly for it, then you *deserve* to have your foot hurt!

If you want to change things in Alabama, by God, you're gonna have to do it *yourselves*.

If you would be free, *you* must strike the blow!

You can do it—tomorrow! We're gonna have an uprising of those who have been deceived and sold out for so long—we black people and, hopefully, our poor white brothers as well!

We are going to cast our *own* votes tomorrow, for our *own* people.

Tomorrow is indeed the turning point. It's the day that we cast our vote for freedom! It's the day we make *our* attempt to make the American Dream come true. It's the day that we insist that *our* humanity be counted.

We have come over a way that with tears has been watered,
Treading our path through the blood of the slaughtered.

Now, that's the road I'm talking to you about. *Stony* the road we trod . . . *Bitter* tears shed . . . *Blood*-stained road . . .

And it was our blood, it was your folks' blood, and my folks' blood, it was black blood, sweat, and tears that watered that road we're talking about. But there is a beginning to the *end* of that road in sight, and it's in sight tomorrow! We can strike our own blow for freedom!

At around midnight, we went over to the headquarters in downtown Birmingham, and some of the black candidates sat around for a last-minute strategy session. One man meekly inquired, "What do we say if we win?" In a way it was a poignant question because it revealed that this man, and no doubt most of the other black candidates, had never actually conceived of winning, of the political process working, until this moment.

Being the county chairman, Tommy Wrenn decided that it was his responsibility to answer the candidate's question. "Just don't shoot your mouth off," he said.

6.

At 6:45 A.M. the next day, three or four dozen black people were standing in a long line, shivering in the cold early-morning air of the rural countryside of Jefferson County, waiting for the polling place to open at seven o'clock. Cashin had driven back up to Huntsville with his wife Joan the night before, after delivering his speech at the St. James Baptist Church. A young man named Bill Edwards, a white VISTA worker, waited on line with the blacks in order to vote, and when he finished, we drove upstate together to Cashin's home.

The Cashins and their three children lived in an all-white, upper-income neighborhood of Huntsville, Alabama's third-largest city, in a modern house with a bay-window view of a scenic mountain which now was filled with splendid autumnal shades of orange and red. Cashin's dental office—his practice was still 60 percent white—was located closer to the business center of town, next to his mother's house and across the street from NDPA's state headquarters, which was actually just a small white house. Part of the enigma of John Cashin was this setting, this suburban life style, when compared with his following as a political leader among the rural, poverty-stricken, uneducated blacks. The middle-class blacks in Huntsville did not trust him as did the poorer blacks throughout the state, and among whites in his hometown there was also no great love and affection. Cashin was an erratic figure, emboldened by his own personal accomplishments, and he had pursued his political career with similar zeal. Back in 1964, he and Joan had shown up at the local White Citizens Council in Huntsville, causing much embarrassment during the course of an antiblack meeting. He was not the sort of person who avoided trouble.

At eleven o'clock that morning, he and Joan arrived at the exclusively white Maple Hill Cemetery in Huntsville in order to cast their votes inside the little brick house within the gate. Joan mentioned that a television crew was supposed to be along soon. "Stop trying to please those people," Cashin snapped. "If they aren't here, we're not waiting for 'em."

Two white photographers were on hand in the cemetery to greet them as they emerged from their car. The Cashins entered the house and voted, then came out on the concrete patio, a handsome couple, to pose for the cameras.

'Did y'all know," Cashin joked as the cameras clicked, "that there are four governors of Alabama buried just over there?"

From that high point in the day, as the hours passed by in his house, I began to understand why John Cashin sometimes appeared to be so irritated and frustrated and depressed. As reports came in by telephone from all over the state, it became clear that "working within the System" was still nearly impossible in Alabama. There were eight counties—Sumter, Perry, Hale, Greene, Lowndes, Macon, Wilcox, and Marengo—where the NDPA seemed virtually assured of winning elections, some thirty-six offices in all. The lowest black population among these counties was 62 percent, the highest was 84 percent; yet because of the fraudulent white registration figures and a variety of other forms of manipulation, heavy black turnouts did not insure victory. A great many of NDPA's pollwatchers were untrained, enabling white voting assistants to carry out their usual methods of deception ("Come on, boy, I'll show you how to do it"—and then pulling the "Rooster" lever for Wallace and the regular local Democrats). In some counties, NDPA workers reported that the Eagle levers weren't working, to begin with. A black person would go inside the booth, pull down the lever, and it would bounce back up, recording nothing. Federal observers had come in, but they took no interest in their jobs, many staying only two hours and then disappearing. State troopers were out in droves, generally intimidating black folks who were on their way to vote. Even if Cashin's pollwatchers *were* trained, even if the folks *were* brave enough to go and vote the Eagle, even if the levers *did* work, then there was still the possibility—no, probability—that the trickery would be carried out in the vote-counting procedure, simply by fabricating the totals to show white victories. One seventy-five-year-old black man, an NDPA chairman who was alert to this procedure, was physically beaten up in a rural courthouse when he tried to watch the counting. Some students from Valparaiso University in Indiana, who had come down to help, were virtually chased out of one small town by carloads of white men. As the reports continued to come in, one could wonder if this was really happening in the year 1970. How, one could ask, were black people in this part of the country supposed to keep faith in the System if it could be misused against them in this way?

"It's not just Alabama," a young black man in Cashin's house offered. "I've seen these same things in New York and Chicago."

There had been only the slightest possibility that the white vote for governor would split between Wallace and an independent candidate, A. C. Shelton, enabling Cashin to squeak through with the black and so-called liberal vote. No such thing happened, of course; by seven o'clock in the evening, Wallace was declared the winner with something like 74 percent of the vote (Cashin got 16 percent). Cashin's main objective had been to use his own candidacy to bring out the vote in the black belt, and as the night wore on, it became apparent that he had succeeded, although not as well as he had hoped.

"Well," he said at one point, "it looks like we won Greene and Lowndes, but they stole Perry, Sumter, and Hale. Them crackers actually stole three goddamn counties from us! I swear, we just might take it up to the Supreme Court and get us some special elections."

Cooking dinner for the small group, Joan Cashin stood in the kitchen of her house and said in a low voice, "It just makes me tired of urging folks to work within the System. At times like this, I feel like telling the kids to come on ahead and do their thing. I feel like saying, 'Bring on the militants, those behind us who really *are* militant. Bring on the militants that you accused *us* of being.' We've been sincere about wanting an integrated party, but they call John a separatist and a racist. Sometimes I feel like saying, 'Well, bring on the real thing.'"

What the NDPA did win, however, was significant. In all, the Eagle Party captured twelve new offices (nine other blacks in Alabama also won elections), including a seat in the state legislature, the first time for a black man since Reconstruction. (Another black candidate, running as a regular Democrat but favored by the NDPA, also won a seat in the legislature, and there was word from South Carolina that three blacks had been elected to that state legislature, with support from the newly created United Citizens Party, which had been inspired by the successes of the NDPA and the Mississippi Freedom Democrats, although the latter was not an independent party like Cashin's.)

Cashin's party succeeded in its quest to take over the entire government of Greene County, its full slate sweeping into the offices of sheriff, probate judge, circuit-court clerk, and coroner, plus two school-board seats. Greene County was left with only two white officials, the tax assessor and the tax collector, and those offices hadn't been up for election. And in Lowndes County, blacks were elected as sheriff, coroner, and circuit-court clerk.

"Well," Cashin said, slapping his stomach and roaming about the house, "we got a black probate judge [William McKinley Branch] for the first time in history, and that's something!"

The small group in Cashin's house—black and white college students, friends from Huntsville and party workers, VISTA volunteers—began to break up, some going off to sleep and others heading homeward. By one o'clock in the morning, Cashin was seated at the dining-room table with some of the young people, and it occurred to me that the scene was symbolic of what his Eagle party was all about. Young and old, black and white, rich and poor—the coalition was still possible here in the South, perhaps especially between the young blacks and their elders. There was still a respect for their elders among the young blacks, and the older folks seemed to reciprocate.

"There's a silver lining somewhere in this cloud," Cashin was saying. "The country has gone to the right but not as far as it might have gone. . . . It's a sure thing now that Wallace will run for President, but you can bet we'll have a Democrat in the White House in '72. . . . Only one thing wrong with poor folks—they don't vote. We got to fool 'em into voting in their own interest. Just preachin' and prayin' don't win elections. We need even stronger organizations. . . . Man, those probate judges and sheriffs are some tough sons of bitches. We'll need half a million dollars for the '72 elections. . . . Well, what we got wasn't so bad. We lost, we got our asses kicked—but maybe it takes a defeat to get folks awake. . . . But I don't know how long I can keep mobilizing the students. . . . I hear Andy Young lost tonight. He spent more in his campaign than we did in a whole year for the NDPA. If I'd had his budget, we would have taken those other counties. We spent less than $50,000— that's statewide—for all our candidates! We got a whole lot of promises of money, but they didn't come through. Maybe people thought I was a millionaire, I don't know. We didn't get any- where near enough money. Well, they let us down. . . . The black dentists, they spent all that money in Miami Beach, on themselves, but they didn't spend anything for a movement like this. They get Julian Bond down there talkin' to 'em instead. People give money for personalities but not for movements. . . ."

At around noon the following day, Cashin wrote out his concession statement on a pad of yellow paper:

> The march from Selma to Montgomery continues as blacks achieve political goals in the Deep South.
>
> Political parties that begin at the bottom weather the test of time. That's where we began, but we're moving up.
>
> We intend to be around for a long time. . . .

Twenty-one

1.

During my return trip to New York from Huntsville, I had to stop over in the airport terminal in Atlanta, Georgia, and there on newsstands was the report of Andy Young's loss by 20,000 votes to Congressman Fletcher Thompson. Back in September, Andy had won the runoff to capture the Democratic nomination after a campaign in which he had been smeared by his opponent, Wyman C. Lowe. (Lowe had warned that if Young were elected it would be a "takeover for the Communists and Black Panther elements"—proving, I suppose, that Southern conservatives still have terrific senses of humor.) Andy had come close to losing the September runoff, for as late as two hours before the black Atlanta precincts were counted he was trailing far behind. Then, when the black community's ballots came in, producing a "late-hour reversal," he wound up with about 59 percent of the vote.

Still on the newsstands were some of the weekly black newspapers' editions from before the November election. The editors of the Atlanta *Inquirer* had done just about everything possible to arouse black enthusiasm for Andy's final test at the polls. "GET OUT AND VOTE TUESDAY," went the streamer at the top of the front page, and the banner headline screamed, pleaded, begged, "BLACK VOTERS CAN ELECT OR DEFEAT YOUNG FOR CONGRESS.

. . . INTEGRATED CORPS OF STUDENTS, ADULTS IN PUSH TO 'GET OUT VOTE FOR YOUNG.' . . . ELECTION CRUCIAL TO CITY'S FUTURE." On the left side of the front page was a cartoon showing a black sculptor ready to chip away at a solid block labeled "The New South." Another caption read, "Caution! Open only with the Vote!!!" On the right side of the page was a photograph of Andy chatting with some black students under a tree, a typical pose of him standing there in a white short-sleeved shirt and a wide striped tie. The last line of the caption noted, "Voters have been urged by numerous leaders to 'crawl to the polls' Tuesday if necessary."

Fletcher Thompson had also run a campaign appealing to white fears, and apparently it worked. The Republican incumbent drew most of his support from north and south Fulton County and in Atlanta's white neighborhoods. The white votes needed for Young's strong coalition had failed to materialize, and more disastrous than that, the black turnout was disappointing.

Throughout the period of waiting for the results at Paschal's, Andy could never catch up with Thompson. The Reverend Ralph Abernathy was there, and so was Mrs. Coretta Scott King, but even the old SCLC magic couldn't bring about another last-minute reversal. The *Inquirer* editors had anticipated a kind of mysterious apathy in the black community, and that accounted for the nearly hysterical tone of its preelection issue. It was pointed out that Andy could be elected if 75 percent or more of the registered black voters would only go to the polls, and Young himself was counting on about 80 percent. At Paschal's, there was the lingering hope that the black community's votes, still coming in, would turn the tide. Andy conceded defeat after midnight, and in typical fashion he urged the gathering of students not to become discouraged, adding that they had to learn that "victories don't come easily."

The white-liberal part of the coalition had failed to hold up its end, while blacks had stayed home in large numbers. There were those who would say that Andy, like Richard Austin in Detroit, had placed too much faith in white voters, and that he should have spent his big budget in the black community in place of his massive billboard and television campaign. And per-

haps, they would say, Lonnie King had been right all along
about the necessity of a grass-roots strategy.

I tended to agree with the latter argument. In my opinion,
Lonnie had had the correct strategy but no money, while Andy
had had the necessary funds but the wrong approach. He had
run a good campaign, concentrating on the issues, but that wasn't
enough. Lacking a strategy to mobilize black voters to the polls,
allowing himself to become too dependent upon liberal whites
(and therefore vulnerable to any kind of appeals to racism or
fear), he wound up losing on all sides.

Like Austin in Detroit, like Bradley in California, Andy
Young could be proud of the *tone* of his campaign, but also like
those men, he had forgotten that the black community was the
nucleus upon which he had to depend for victory. This does
not mean that Andy was not sensitive to the needs of blacks in
the Fifth District, nor does it mean that he "forgot" about them
in relation to the issues, but it does mean that he had sought
the coalition at the top—using Julian Bond's image of the inverted triangle—without establishing a strong, black political
base at the bottom. The statistics were incredible—only forty
thousand of the district's 72,000 black voters had gone to the
polls! In other words, there were 32,000 black people, or twelve
thousand more than enough to elect him, who did not vote on
election day.

Several reasons were given to explain why Andy received help
from only 56 percent of the registered black vote. For one thing,
this was the third time they had been asked to go to the polls
during the campaign. Some said that blacks were generally
turned off by politics or that they could not comprehend the
importance of having a Congressman to represent their interests
(and indeed, it was difficult to imagine how Congressman Andrew
Young could have made a fundamental difference in their lives,
at least right away). John Lewis said that black low-income
workers had gone to work before the polls opened and had gotten
off after they closed, and that therefore they couldn't vote. Julian
Bond offered the simple reasoning that many voters were confused by the number of candidates and issues on the scene.

All of this had much less to do with rhetoric and style than
with strategy. After the first primary election I had talked with

Bond, who startled me somewhat by his concern over the minute, practical details of campaigning. Bond, who loved to ponder the great issues of the day, was going on about the fact that there had been no attempt to telephone voters on the part of Andy's staff. "When I ran, my first time," he said with a mild touch of pride, "we telephoned every voter in my district. I had a small staff, while Andy had a much larger one. And his district is of course much, much larger than mine. But he should have made some attempt to telephone all the voters. He had hundreds of volunteers. And he should have done some mailings."

On my way back to New York on the plane, I imagined that on election day a fleet of chartered buses had rolled into the Fifth District's black neighborhoods, and that all through the day these buses—with big "Andy Young" signs on their sides—had picked up voters and taken them to their polling places. That, I thought, is where I would have spent the great bulk of my campaign money—on getting the folks to the polls, on election day itself, when it all came down to sheer numbers. (I was reminded of the special election in Greene County, Alabama, back in the summer of 1969, when black candidates had won their first victories. While people were celebrating, Hosea Williams of SCLC commented, "Personally, I have mixed emotions about the victory. When I think about blacks winning, I say, 'Thank God.' However, when I think about the fact that they only won by 200 votes when they held a 2,000-vote majority, I say, 'Damn us!' I am worried—worried about the entrenchment of plantation mentality in our people. Too often we are too satisfied with too little when we are entitled to so much more." I thought of John Cashin's statement that next time around he would have to "fool 'em into voting in their own interest." And then there was author Chuck Stone's description of Charles Evers' campaign for mayor of Fayette: "On election day, the plodding, sleepy, rural countryside was transformed into a fast, efficient, urban complex of a fleet of cars, two-way radios, and a portable sound system. Volunteers chauffeured elderly or incapacitated voters to the polls. Voting lists were checked constantly to ensure the maximum black voter turnout.")

I would have preferred contemplating much more lofty and profound aspects of the black political scene, but for the moment there was only the fact that Andy Young would not be part of the 92nd Congress, and it all seemed to boil down to that imaginary fleet of chartered buses.

2.

A month or so later I went back to Washington, D.C., now more than a year after the black elected officials' conference, and as I descended the steps to a coffee shop in a downtown hotel, I noticed a familiar figure sitting alone at the counter. I paused, then recognized Richard Austin. He was looking extremely well, sitting there in the near-empty shop alone with his thoughts, eating a bacon, lettuce, and tomato sandwich and reading a copy of the New York *Times*. The only thing missing from his appearance was the red-and-black campaign button that he had worn on his lapel. Otherwise he was the same, wearing a dark suit that I recognized from the campaign trail back in Detroit in 1969.

"Well, how are you?" came the familiar greeting and of course the warm, friendly smile along with it.

I ordered some coffee, and after we talked a while, I told him, "This'll make a good footnote for my book." He nodded modestly. I was referring to the fact that Austin, a month before, had been elected as Michigan's secretary of state. He had come a long way over the past six years, from his unsuccessful Congressional campaign in 1964, to his win as county auditor the following year, to his loss in the mayor's race in 1969, to his recent victory on the statewide Democratic ticket.

Austin had run for secretary of state on a program of "traffic safety, modernized election laws, and government efficiency and economy," issues which could hardly be called controversial when compared to those he had faced in the mayor's race. He had won by a large margin in all areas of the state, proving once again that whites could be very fair-minded when it came to supporting blacks for positions of lesser significance.

"I might even have run for governor," he said. "This would have been the year."

"Why didn't you?"

Well, he explained, he was now fifty-seven years old, and it would have meant another strenuous campaign, one much more exhausting than the recent contest for secretary of state—it was the old thing about black men having had "late starts" in life and therefore lacking the time to realize their full potentials.

There was a sadness in his tone, but overall, Dick Austin was a contented man. He was satisfied with his performances as a candidate, aware of the fact that in the mayor's race he had raised the quality of the campaign and also the level of black political involvement in Detroit. There was little doubt that his performance in the mayoralty campaign had earned him broad appeal among the voters of Michigan—and it was just possible that the hope he had given to Detroit's blacks was the major reason why the city was keeping cool during this transitional period.

"How's Mayor Gribbs doing?" I asked.

"Well, I shouldn't say this—but in Cleveland they say that Detroit is now a 'city without a mayor.' I'm afraid that Gribbs is cutting back on things rather than pursuing programs."

He added, "I'm concerned about my city, but there's not a thing I can do about it now."

Austin reached into his pocket and removed a telegram which had been folded and unfolded several times. It was from Congressman Charles Diggs, who had become Michigan's first black member of the House of Representatives back in 1954. "Invite you to luncheon caucus with Michigan Democratic Congressional delegation," the telegram began, and that was why Austin had come to Washington, D.C.

Smiling, he returned the telegram to the inside pocket of his suit jacket and informed me that he was going to head up to his room in the hotel and get some sleep.

Before he turned to go, he said, "I was what you might call a 'casualty at the beachhead,'" meaning, I gathered, that other blacks would have less difficulty running for mayor of Detroit in the future, because Richard Austin had been the first black man to "hit the beach," so to speak. "In that sense," he added, his grin widening and his face literally beaming, "I suppose I *am* a militant, after all!"

3.

The main reason I had come back to Washington, D.C., was to look up Congressman John Conyers of Michigan. A forty-one-year-old bachelor, Conyers seemed to me to be one of the most articulate and energetic blacks on Capitol Hill. He had been elected for the first time back in 1964, after beating Austin in a Democratic primary by just a handful of votes, and since that time he had assumed an increasingly large role of leadership among his black colleagues—indeed, in the House as a whole—taking strong and responsive stands on almost every issue affecting his constituents, some 80 percent of whom were black, and popping up around the country to lend his influence to candidates and causes relating to black goals. But there was a paradoxical quality involved in Conyers' growth as a Congressman. While on the one hand he had become more "militant" over the years since 1965, he had also become increasingly tolerant, or perhaps "realistic" was the word. It was as if Conyers had come into a kind of wisdom because of the experiences he had gone through on Capitol Hill. One could picture the bright young man, fresh from political victory in the ghetto, arriving at the nation's capital with fire in his eyes, ready to take on the whole damn government, only to find his energies whittled down or at least tempered by the frustrating maze of customs and traditions and machinery involved at this high level of public life. And this confrontation with the realities of the game, so to speak, had somehow given him a broader outlook on the whole process of black political development.

"I have come to understand," he told me, "that there is a necessary process through which you must go, in order to secure political power, even in the black community." We were sitting in his office on Capitol Hill and Conyers, wearing sunglasses, had taken a chair facing his desk rather than behind it. I told him that I had seen Dick Austin in town. It had been widely known that Conyers had been displeased with Austin's candidacy for mayor, apparently feeling that the tone of his campaign hadn't been forceful enough. And yet now he restrained himself, speaking of Austin as if from a distance, as though he could see that

particular moment in recent black political history within a
larger context.

"I've begun to think in terms of tactics and strategy," he said,
"and I've begun to think less of how 'black' a guy is. I've become
more generous with some of the lapses that black politicians
have, and I'm also generous with some of the people who want
to adopt a superblack position. Dick Austin, see, is acceptable.
He is a black guy, but he's not an offensive black guy. The
threat, or the capability, of affronting people, offending them, is
clearly less visible with him than with me. But they're right, to
a certain extent. I mean, Dick was the guy who had to run for
mayor—because if they were ready for any black, they would
have been ready for him. Now, we've been through that. Now,
we can come up with someone who'll take a shade-tougher stand
on the issues. And that's really the process!"

He uncrossed his legs and leaned forward, as if trying to sort
out some things in his mind. "We're nationalizing black politics,"
he went on. "It's important that we understand that. And in that
context, the Tom Bradleys and the Richard Austins *are* important. Because we can't spring from the cement full-blown into
a mature, powerful, dynamic, black political organism. It just
doesn't happen that way. You can be as angry as possible and
have as big an Afro hairdo as you want, but it still isn't gonna
affect the process that we have to go through. A guy may decide
that he's gonna have to blow things up rather than register people to vote, but the process doesn't move. Him blowing things
up may help affect the process that I'm working in, but there
may come a time when him blowing things up may be very det-
rimental to the process I'm trying to affect.

"These things are political. You know, if you look at things
in a political context, as I do almost as second nature, then race
becomes a feature, or a subtopic, of the political thing. It becomes another factor that you consider. It doesn't become the
main factor. Your political objective becomes the important
thing. Then, you add race into the equation. And if you're a
good political student, whether you're a black nationalist or a
white racist, then the tactics, strategy, plans, and maneuvers flow
from that, no matter what you believe in. And we're not very

long on political tactics, because black people haven't been long on the political scene."

As Conyers spoke, I was thinking that the Congress was at the very top of Julian Bond's image of the inverted triangle, and that therefore it represented the weakest kind of political power. All 435 seats in the House of Representatives had been up for grabs in the recent elections, and of that number blacks had won twelve—the highest figure since Reconstruction (three more than the current number), but still just a tiny fraction of the whole.

Those blacks reelected to the House included Conyers and Diggs of Michigan, Shirley Chisholm of New York, William Clay of Missouri, Augustus Hawkins of California, Robert Nix of Pennsylvania, and Louis Stokes (Carl's brother) of Ohio. In addition, Charles Rangel of New York and Ralph Metcalfe of Illinois captured the seats vacated by Adam Clayton Powell and the late William Dawson, respectively. The three new seats in Congress were gained by George Collins of Illinois, Ronald Dellums of California, and Parren Mitchell of Maryland.

Both Mitchell and Dellums wandered into Conyers' office on Capitol Hill during the week I was there, and when each man appeared, there was a stir among Conyers' staff employees. It was easy to understand how Capitol Hill could be a strange, impersonal, even intimidating place, especially for a new black Congressman, and so it was also easy to understand why Mitchell and Dellums had decided to look up Conyers, who could be trusted to show them the ropes and offer them advice or encouragement. If the black Congressmen were to have any sort of influence in Washington, they would have to stick together. Conyers greeted them both warmly, as if to say, "Welcome to the club."

Parren Mitchell had become the first black man elected to Congress from the South since Reconstruction (it seemed that almost every new black elected official was the "first since Reconstruction"). A political-science professor at Morgan State College, Mitchell had won a close Democratic-primary victory over the white incumbent of eighteen years. His district, including parts of Baltimore City and County, was about 40 percent black, and he had won with the support of many liberal Democrats who lived in the suburbs.

Dellums had also fashioned a coalition in order to come out ahead in a district that was only 40 percent black. Unlike Andy Young, Dellums had built his strength at the bottom and had worked from that base. After his election, he said that his campaign proved that "the black community could be politicized."

At thirty-four, Dellums was depicted in the press as being the most "radical" member of the newly elected 92nd Congress, although in person he seemed low keyed and urbane in manner. Tall, moustached, nattily dressed, he sat in Conyers' office and lighted a cigarette, and he mentioned that he, too, was working on a book (everyone, it seemed, was writing a book or having one written about himself). Dellums, who held a master's degree in social work from the University of California at Berkeley, said he considered himself a "new" politician, one who would try to go beyond the "symptoms" of problems in his efforts to represent the people of his district, which included both Berkeley and the black slum of Oakland. In reaction to charges that he was a "radical," Dellum had issued the following reply:

> If it is radical to want a living wage, a decent home, and adequate health care for every American, then I'm a radical. If it is radical to believe that the quality of life in America, the air and land and water around us, and hopes and joys of our lives, are more important than the drive for a quick profit, then I am a radical. If it is radical to want an end to war and violence and destruction, so that we can all devote ourselves to the challenge of peace, then I am pleased to call myself a radical.

During his primary campaign, Dellums had rejected the label "liberal" and had run with backing from Oakland's Black Panthers and on a tough antiwar platform. He carried the black precincts—where there was a heavy turnout—and all of the Chicano precincts, including the largely white precincts around Berkeley, the birthplace of the Free Speech Movement in 1964. The new coalition of blacks, Mexican Americans, students, and liberals which had sent him to Congress was perhaps an indication of how other black candidates would conduct their campaigns in the future.

"But given the statistics involved, with only twelve black Congressmen out of 435," I asked John Conyers, "don't you sometimes feel a bit helpless?"

"Well," he replied, "there's very little that anyone can do singlehandedly around here. Everybody's throwing in their little inputs into the machinery. There's 435 Congressmen and a hundred Senators—that's 535 people who are all tinkering with the machinery—and out of that you get a product. And if the product is a little stronger than one Congressman wanted it, well, maybe I was able to turn my dial just that much. And not just me but a lot of other guys with me, blacks and whites. Each of us had some input into it. So, you have to look at it like that. You gotta realize that this isn't a thing where you can 'seize the moment' politically, and trick 534 other guys into supporting a bill or something."

At this point, Conyers got up from his chair and circled around in back of the desk. He found a sheet of yellow paper and handed it to me. "This letter just came in last night," he said. "Read that."

The letter was from some black university students in Detroit. They wanted to meet with Conyers to discuss plans for the creation of a whole new constitution for the United States, since the current one was "clearly unresponsive" and so on.

"How do you respond to that?" I asked.

"Well, I'm gonna meet with them. They're in my district, and I've got more than a duty to answer that letter. I've got to sit down with them, and go through all the young, black moods that occur on the scene, and see if we can work out a new kind of rapproachement."

"What do you say to them about your own position?" I wanted to know. "I mean, can you convince them that you're being effective?"

"That's something I constantly have to respond to. I always tell them what it is that I've actually been doing, and if that doesn't add up to an accurate answer, then I've failed, by their standards. My job is to try to relate this job to black people, to do so a little bit better, and it takes the form of help to many people on a very individual and personal level. And there's the matter of affecting the legislative process."

Conyers pointed out that he had spent a great deal of time working on a bill that would set up the Equal Employment Opportunities Commission. "So if their response is 'Well, what's the EEOC bill gonna do?' then I've been wasting my time. I have to report to them what I'm doing, and then they have to determine if it's meaningful or not."

During the week that I was in Washington, it was clear that Conyers was doing more than merely "working within the system" in the usual sense. For example, the EEOC bill he had spoken of was being held up by the House Rules Committee, mainly because its eighty-year-old chairman, William Colmer of Mississippi, had the power to keep it from going through the necessary procedures for passage. At the same time, Conyers was meeting with Aaron Henry, chairman of the integrated Mississippi Democratic Party, to discuss a new drive to strip Colmer of his Congressional seniority. One could ponder the complexity of Conyers' job, the tediousness of working his way through the labyrinth, the amount of time spent on working to reform the system as well as to work within it, and it became easier to understand both his pragmatism and the younger blacks' impatience. How long could he continue to tell the black people of his district that, well, there was this one Southern conservative who could hold up everything, even thwart the will of the majority of Congressmen in the House?

On another day, Conyers held a press conference in the Rayburn House Office Building to announce that he was supporting a welfare-reform organization which was "seeking material assistance from foreign countries."

"Can you imagine," he said to me after the press conference, "that we have the poor of this country going to the Soviet Embassy, asking for welfare assistance? See, the race problem in America is becoming internationalized. This is important, because we're now no longer making Washington the repository for the hopes of black people. We're speaking to the *world* audience, now. We're not just talking to the Secretary of HEW, asking him to please give us some surplus food. We're saying, 'World, can you help? Will Russia give us something? Some clothes? Can we get some surplus foods from England? Or Yugo-slavia?' It's a new concept."

According to Conyers' press release on the day of the confer-ence, at least seventy thousand poor children in Detroit were in need of $5 million worth of clothing for the winter. "Until our national priorities are a true response to our national needs," he told the reporters, "there is little else that can happen but that many of our citizens will suffer to such an extent that they will be forced to look beyond their own country for assistance."

"We're going to the United Nations," Conyers told me later. "We'll seek help from the U.N. on some problems that we've not been able to resolve in this country. We're raising the ques-tion of the black and the poor to an international level. We've realized that this is a new forum."

Since the spring of 1970, he said, the black Congressmen had been trying to set up a meeting with President Nixon. For nearly ten months, the President had refused to grant such a meeting, and the prospects were still uncertain.

"We argue," said Conyers, "that he has an inescapable obliga-tion to meet all of the highest black elected members of Con-gress, notwithstanding the fact that not one of them in the House is a member of his party. It's a political question for him, quite frankly. He's got to balance the fact that after meeting with us we could give one of the most critical press conferences against him that he's ever had—as opposed to the alternative risk of re-ceiving massive criticism and raising it to almost the level of a campaign issue, by refusing to meet with us. That's the dilemma he's in."

The strategies and maneuvers seemed to go on and on, and when Conyers would leave Capitol Hill to make speeches around the country, he would remind people of the "recency of black-ness," as he put it, meaning that the new wave of black political involvement was in its infancy, really, and that it was hardly appropriate to condemn the System at the very moment when blacks were getting into it for the first time. "If we haven't tried it, my man," he would say, "then how do we know if it's work-ing or not?"

When black students challenged him on this point, he would counter by telling them, "Ain't *none* of us been black *too* long!"

He'd point into the audience and shout, "You there, how long have *you* had that Afro? Three years? One year? Six months? No, ain't none of us been black so long."

That was the basic message—after all the marches, all the riots, all the rhetoric, all of the weary confrontations over the past years, blacks were just now getting their hands on some of the levers of the System; it was not the end, but the beginning.

Twenty-two

1.

By the end of my "journey into the new black politics," the subject had assumed a much larger place in the fabric of American life than I may have anticipated. Bayard Rustin was writing, now, that the 1970 elections had marked "another major turning point" in the black-protest movement, equal in significance to the Montgomery bus boycott in 1956, the Greensboro sit-ins in 1960, and the urban riots in the midsixties. "If I am not mistaken," Rustin wrote, "the dominant thrust in the 1970's of the Negro movement for equality will be political action."

Prior to the Voting Rights Act of 1965 there had been only seventy black elected officials in the South; now, there were over seven hundred, more than one hundred of them having captured their offices in the recent elections. In the entire United States there were over sixteen hundred blacks holding elective positions at all levels of government. By the summer of 1970, a Joint Center for Political Studies, sponsored by Howard University and the Metropolitan Applied Research Center, had been created to "help black elected officials play a more effective role in government." For the first time, an "institutionalized approach" to the subject of blacks in politics was being shaped on a nationwide basis.

My own approach, of course, had been anything but an institutionalized one. I had allowed my intuition to determine most of my travels and my feelings to decide the direction and shape of the book. And to the extent that I was able to follow this pattern, I was well rewarded, first as a man and then, almost incidentally, as a reporter. Near the end, people would ask me, "Well, what was the main thing that you learned?" My reply was seldom an intellectual one. "The main thing," I'd say, "was the experience itself—meeting the people." My response probably sounded sentimental or evasive or both. But the fact was, I had been drawn toward people rather than politics, which was why, for example, I had chosen to spend time with Richard Hatcher rather than Carl Stokes, with Julian Bond rather than state Senator Leroy Johnson, with John Conyers rather than Senator Edward Brooke of Massachusetts. The people upon whom I had decided to focus my attention seemed to have less concern with "being" politicians than with "using" politics as a means toward some goal. By itself, politics was an empty profession, in my view. The ideal society would have no politicians, no government, no police, no army. Especially no politicians, for life was filled with more important things, and how wrong it seemed for us to become so saturated with political news, with campaign rhetoric, with the machinations of government, rather than with the basic, simple, eternal aspects of being alive. I was not interested in politicians, black or white, but in blacks who had discovered politics as a means by which to eliminate conditions that were intolerable. For such men, for Zelma Wyche, for Charles Evers, for Andrew Young, for Richard Hatcher, for Julian Bond, for so many others, politics was a natural extension of their own personal struggles against racial injustice in this country. These men were not politicians in the normal sense; they were full with life, they were emotional men, not phony actors but men of strength and endurance and compassion and sensitivity.

A romantic viewpoint, friends would say. Wasn't I aware that, human nature being what it was, black politicians would wind up squabbling with each other and promoting themselves just like most others? Well, yes, there was nothing sacred about black skin coloring. The point I tried to make was that there are two types of black politicians—those who see themselves as individuals making their way through the political system regardless of their color, and those who have come to politics first and foremost because they want to help black people. The latter, I argued, were able to see "blackness" as an experience, as a condition, as an attitude, as a concern, as a point of view.

I have tried to think about this "blackness" thing, to think of what it must be like for those who suddenly realize that they have been born into an alien world. What would it feel like to realize that, my God, I am one of a distinct minority, I have been thrust from the womb into a white nation, I am not one of the fortunate ones, I am not privileged, I am in someone else's country, a white country where white men rule, where white men have the power, the money, the votes? To realize that I have been born into *their* nation, where *they* own everything of importance—the banks, the newspapers, the great corporations, the law firms, the government, the land I walk on. It is their land, their law, their culture, their philosophy, their morality, and their corruption that dominates this nation in which I must live. To think that I am at their mercy, that they have the power to love or hate me, to treat me like an animal, like dirt, and who would I turn to for justice when I need it but to them? I have tried to think of this, and I am not surprised to know that many black men have secretly wished they were white. And I have thought that many blacks, having come to the realization that they cannot be white and cannot ever escape this fundamental condition, have gone on with their lives not wishing to think about such things as power and politics, never caring about voting, seeing it all as too overwhelming, too useless, and they have gone to work wherever they could find jobs, shoving these thoughts deep down somewhere that is too personal for any other man to reach, and have sweated out their days and nights in this fashion. I have thought that still others have despaired and turned on themselves, perhaps even unconsciously, and have spent lifetimes of slow, creeping death, lifetimes of dying. And others, I thought, have lashed out blindly. They have lashed out to steal, to kill, to rape, or to break merely small laws as a way of fighting back (but not really fighting at all, just racing about in the night, or lurking in alleyways, striking out and trying not to get caught, but losing anyway, whether they get caught or not). I have tried to think of these things and have seen with a part of my mind some small corner of that which is called black rage and, beyond that, black pride. And for brief moments I have understood something of deep power and beauty.

I have understood in a small way that despair can lead down to hell, to rage, to the smashing of the soul and finally to the discovery that, wait a minute, I am still alive, still a human being, I can still think and feel and move about—I am myself! And, yes, I am *black,* that *is* what I am and, yes, I am *glad* to be black because, yes, this mind, this soul, this *blackness* is just as good as, maybe better than, whiteness. I have tried to think of this and have come to understand that once a man goes this far, that once he jumps off the outer edge of his frustration and despair he is free. That like Martin Luther King, he has been to the mountaintop of his private soul—forced there by white racism— and has tasted the freedom that comes from accepting his identity, from *embracing* his identity. I have thought that this might have been what Richard Hatcher meant when he said that he could not, nor would he wish to, reject his blackness. ("And so I turn what the white world has attempted to make a handicap precisely into its opposite.") He would not reject his blackness because it has set him free, within himself. And then I have thought of Carl Stokes and wondered whether he would make such a statement. Or would he make it but not mean it? For Carl Stokes, I thought, had not been plunged into that private hell of total despair and had not come out accepting the condition of blackness in a white nation. Stokes had known the experience of blackness, of being black, but he had *overcome* it instead. And to overcome something was not necessarily, maybe not at all, to accept it. To overcome blackness was *to be accepted by others, by whites.* The distinction between Stokes and Hatcher was not made in order to infer that one was wrong and the other was right, but nevertheless it was a distinction. It occurred to me that Carl Stokes *would not mind* if he were white, that he had never been forced down into hell and forced to *cling* to his black identity in order to survive, that he had never come back up to the mountaintop as one who would never give up his blackness under any condition, just as most white men would never give up their whiteness. Stokes, in my view, instead had discovered that in this period of time it was almost *fun* to be a black man, he had learned to use the fact of his color to advantage, as one would use one's height or his strength or whatever. Carl Stokes had proved himself as a man, to whites and to blacks alike. But unlike Hatcher, I think he has gone beyond the reach of the "little people"—that many of them must see Stokes as they might have seen Jackie Robinson or Nat King Cole. They look at him through a window, so to speak. He is inside, being accepted for his personality and qualifications and all that, but they are still out there on the street, looking in. "The white world has embraced Carl Stokes—maybe we, too, can be embraced." But I do not think that this comes to grips with the condition of blackness, with the need, at this time, not for being embraced by whites but for embracing oneself. Stokes would reply, no doubt, "But *I* embrace myself." Yes, and so did all the Negro athletes and musicians who had "made it" because of their abilities. Stokes's ability was to be a good politician. He was the mayor of Cleveland who happened to be black; Hatcher was a black man who happened to choose politics and become mayor of Gary.

(On the other hand, the case could be made that no matter how "black" Stokes might become, he would face more difficulty than Hatcher in pursuing policies and programs because of the fact that his black base of support is smaller. It is as if the political base determines not only what kind of candidate can be elected but also the effectiveness of the politician once he is elected. It is possible that the "whiter" the district or city, the less-militant the black candidate must be, and the less-effective will he become once in office.)

2.

It is precisely because of the distinction I have made that Carl Stokes has a much better chance than Hatcher of becoming America's first black Vice-President. Or a better chance than Julian Bond, for that matter.

(I do not believe that any black man or woman has a chance of becoming President, simply because white people are unwilling to elect blacks to positions of great authority or responsibility. This was why some of the black candidates for the City Council of Detroit received many more white votes than Richard Austin received in his campaign for mayor. It was why Basil Paterson, although able to defeat his opponent in the Democratic primary for *lieutenant* governor of New York State, probably could not have won the nomination as a candidate—or at least not the election—for the governorship itself. Also, the same white folks who helped elect Austin as Michigan's secretary of state probably would not have helped to elect *him* governor, if he had run, either.)

The problem is that the more "acceptable" a black politician is—acceptable to white people, that is—the less effective he seems to become in using his office for blacks. One of the supreme ironies of the new black politics is that those who are "less-black," so to speak, have more chance of gaining high political office. Richard Austin has much more of a chance than John Conyers has of becoming the first black United States Senator from Michigan, for the same reason that Edward Brooke was able to become the black Senator from Massachusetts.

Brooke is the ultimate example of the Negro politician whose entire political future lies in the hands of white voters, who comprise something like 98 percent of the electorate in his state. (As high a position as U. S. Senator is, I think that Brooke would find it much more difficult to win election as governor.)

"I am not a civil-rights leader and I don't profess to be one," goes the typical Brooke response to those who want to know his position. "I can't serve just the Negro cause. I've got to serve all the people of Massachusetts."

There is nothing wrong with this position; it simply implies that Brooke is just another liberal politician.

The harshest criticism of Brooke comes from the black radical: "I was willing to let a cat like Brooke slide. I wanted to see how he performed. Well, he's performed dismally. He's not only a token, he's a jerk. He's a white man's nigger. He's not a personal victory for anybody. He's a disgusting defeat. He makes it very difficult for other Negroes of a different bent to aspire to his kind of office, because people realize that the Brooke image is the kind of image that people are going to have to mold themselves into."

"I was a happy child," Brooke has recalled. "I was conscious of being a Negro, yes, but I was not conscious of being underprivileged because of that." And that was precisely the *self*-image that a Negro politician needed in order to be elected by white folks in the first place. Electing Brooke was a way for whites to lessen the burden of conscience.

John Conyers told me that Brooke refused even to meet with the black Congressmen. "He's in a very difficult position," Conyers explained in his most tolerant, pragmatic, and objective manner. "He can be idealized by whites who like to see a black guy in a high position but it's clear that he can't do a great deal— with exceptions—on the major questions of race. We understand the political realities of his position, and therefore we don't *expect* much from him."

On the other hand, it was better to have Brooke as a senator than not at all (although the "black radical" quoted above would vehemently disagree), just as it was better to have a Carl Stokes in Cleveland than some totally insensitive white politician. The thing was, such men by themselves would mean nothing to the masses of black people. Isolated Negro political victories were one thing; a black-oriented political movement, one springing from the thrust of the civil-rights movement and from the concept of black self-determination, was another thing again.

3.

There is a fundamental paradox at the root of the new black politics. In most cases, blacks are being included in the System, not because the racial situation is getting better, but because it is growing worse. The ever-growing list of black elected officials, the sheer statistical aspect of the current phenomenon, would appear to a casual onlooker to mean that blacks and whites in America were finally coming together, when in fact the statistics are the result of a greater division or separation between the races than ever before. The progress is political, not social. The greatest "progress" is occurring in the cities, and that is because of the white middle-class exodus to the suburbs, an exodus that is expected to continue until at least 1985. By that time, the outlook is that 70 percent of whites dwelling in metropolitan areas will be living in the suburbs, while 75 percent of the nonwhites will be in the central cities. The paradox of rising black political power was expressed this way in the U. S. Riot Commission Report:

> The acquisition of power by Negro-dominated governments in central cities is surely a legitimate and desirable exercise of political power by a minority group. . . . But such Negro political development would also involve virtually complete racial segregation and virtually complete spatial separation.

The prospect that ten or fifteen of America's largest cities will wind up with black majorities and therefore with black mayors and black governments represents the same kind of hollow victory that Charles Evers pointed to when he said, "We won the whole school without firing a single shot."

4.

The new black politics, then, would be based upon a cynical realism—or a realistic cynicism, if you will—which was summed up by Julian Bond in his speech to the black elected officials in Washington. We must assume, he said, that

> social, economic, educational, political, and physical segregation and discrimination fill a very real need for the white majority, that appeals to justice and fair play are outmoded and useless when power, financial gain, and prestige are at stake, and that positions of segregation and discrimination will be adhered to until change is forced through coercion, threats, power, or violence.

The new "movement" of political involvement was therefore to be grounded in an almost total lack of faith or trust in white people. Bond went on to define a few basic "rules" for such a movement:

> Initiative for black political education and organization must come from within the black community and must be sustained on a day-to-day, year-round basis; the geographical distribution of Negroes makes Negro-white coalitions desirable,

but only when based on racial self-interest and genuine equality betwen the coalescing groups; and racial self-interest, race-consciousness, and racial solidarity must always be paramount in the deeds and words of the black political animal. For when self-interest is forgotten, organized racism will continue to dominate and frustrate the best organized political actions of any black political unit, and will leave it powerless and defenseless.

This was not the same as "going it alone," not exactly, for Bond was well aware that it would be suicidal for blacks to turn inward and refuse support or assistance. Bond himself was the author of a much-quoted analogy that went, "If your house is on fire, and a man runs up with a bucket of water, don't ask him who he is, or where he got it, just make sure that it's not gasoline, and then pour it on." In calling for blacks to exercise their full political potential as "our major strategy for the seventies," Vice-Mayor Maynard Jackson of Atlanta suggests that the black community, once united, should "act in political concert with every available ally we can find, including, and maybe especially, poor whites. We should not turn down anybody, regardless of their motivation." John Conyers agrees, "but with this new distinction—*we will lead*."

5.

Within the context of such a philosophy, it seems to me that the model black candidate would present himself along lines such as the following imaginary speech: "I am running for office in order to fight racism in all its forms and to relieve black people of their many oppressive conditions. I will work on the problems of education, employment, housing, health, law enforcement, and so forth. I am not running merely to hold office but to use that office as a means of extricating my people from their degradations and deprivations. If I am successful to any degree, there is no doubt that white people suffering from similar conditions will benefit as well, for white people are the victims of racism also. I shall not compromise. If anyone wants to help me in this task, I shall accept his support but not for a price. I shall make coalitions only on terms that are consistent with my goals for black people."

Such was the philosophy of Dr. Cashin's Eagle Party in Alabama. The NDPA was black oriented, but it accepted the support of "anyone who wants to come along." And such was the strategy of Ken Gibson's campaign for mayor of Newark, although the candidate himself did not go around "talking black" in front of white audiences. Gibson didn't have to do that, or rather he could afford to become a "man for all the people" because he had the organization and grass-roots support behind him. As far as I know, he did not compromise his position in order to gain the support of Newark's newspapers or business establishment; instead, they saw his strength, found they had nowhere else to turn, and then went to him.

It is interesting to compare the elections in Los Angeles, Detroit, and Newark. It is my opinion that Bradley and Austin could have won if they had paid special attention to the black community in the way Gibson did. However, each was a special case.

Bradley had the most trouble, since he had the smallest black "base" from which to work. "I think he would have won," writes Shirley Chisholm, the first black woman in Congress, "if he had not forgotten that he is black and therefore more vulnerable." John Conyers agreed that Bradley could have made it: "Clearly the black community could have given him the balance." But Conyers added, somewhat humorously, "If he had recognized that he was black, they would have wiped him out! White people aren't used to voting for a guy who's asserting his blackness to them."

Most people who analyzed the Los Angeles election said that Yorty was able to win by running such a highly charged racist campaign, that he brought out the conservative voters in droves by appealing to their fears and prejudices. I tended to take the most cynical view—that the reason Bradley did so well was because Yorty was such a poor candidate. In my opinion, many of the whites who voted for Bradley would not have done so if they could have had a white candidate less embarrassingly, less ostentatiously racist.

Bradley had had a registered black vote of only 18 percent with which to work, while Austin in Detroit had at least twice that percentage. If Austin had run against Yorty instead of a "moderate" candidate like Gribbs (who was not an incumbent with a poor record, either), surely he would have become mayor of Detroit. Austin also lacked Gibson's grass-roots strength in the black community. The incredible statistic was that 10 percent more blacks in Detroit had gone to the polls to vote against Goldwater in 1964 than went to cast votes in the 1969 mayoralty election. Clearly, the Austin campaign hadn't aroused the enthusiasm and self-interest that were absolutely necessary for full black-voter participation.

Gibson, on the other hand, had all the necessary ingredients for victory. He was running against an incumbent who had let Newark decline to the brink of near-total collapse, a man who was under indictment for corruption, and this made it relatively easy for whites to vote for the black candidate. Gibson wound up with a sixth of the white votes. The amazing thing, to me, was not that he had gotten so much white support but so little. It demonstrated just how difficult it was for a black man to trust in the fairness of white voters under any circumstances—for if five sixths of Newark's white voters went along with Addonizio, it meant that under few conceivable conditions would they ever have voted for Ken Gibson. However, with the strength of his independent, grass-roots, black-oriented strategy behind him, the white vote proved enough, more than enough, for victory.

6.

The rejection of traditional party support—especially in cities like Newark and Detroit, which hold nonpartisan elections—and the growth of independent or third-party organizations to promote black candidates undoubtedly will become the trend of the seventies, in the North as well as the South. In most cases, black candidates will be elected from predominantly black districts, while others will forge coalitions around economic issues. Thousands of blacks will gain public offices at all levels of government during the decade. And yet, after all the campaigns, all the election parties, all the headlines, there will come a time when politics, by itself, will not be enough. Black control of Southern counties and of Northern cities may prove to be futile in the long run, primarily because the black-controlled counties and cities will be (and are) economically bankrupt. "The black movement," said Richard Hatcher, "must more and more doggedly direct its thoughts and energies to the problems of *economic* power." "Intelligent and responsible use of political power," adds Dr. Kenneth Clark, "is the basis of meaningful economic power. 'Black capitalism' and 'black economic development' will remain merely titillating words if they are not part of the total pattern of solid political activity among Negroes."

It becomes increasingly clear, then, that once blacks have "gotten themselves together" politically, that once they have closed the gap between the political power they now hold and that which they deserve according to their numerical strength, the burden of responsibility will still rest on white America to create a truly equal and open society. There is a point where political power must be translated into economic power. One has only to look at Fayette, Mississippi, where black political control has relieved the citizens of basic injustices, humiliations, degradations, and intimidations. Those changes are substantial, but only when the *economic* base of Fayette is altered will real changes occur in the conditions of black folks' lives. The new black mayors of the North have discovered the same thing—that City Hall does not have the power necessary to make fundamental economic changes, and that the answer lies at the state and Federal levels of government, which are white-dominated.

As the political advance of blacks across the nation continues, it will become increasingly clear that politics is not an end but a means to put pressure on white America for a national commitment to solving the race problem. The key word will shift from "control" to "leverage" or "muscle." While the development of a black political base seems necessary, the cultivation of alliances will have to follow, if the white majority is to be moved to action. Once the black minority has developed its political strength, having been driven to its "blackness" by white racism and by the sheer physical separation of the races, the best that can be hoped for is that America's 25 million black people will have a strong bargaining position in dealing with the rest of society. (If poor whites and other minority or dissident groups continue to awaken to their commonality with blacks, the emergence of such a bargaining position will be hastened.) Power comes from the bottom, but real change, real moral leadership for the nation as a whole, must be directed from the top—and that means it must come from the Congress and from the office of the President of the United States.

The prospect of 55,000 black elected officials throughout the country (including twelve black Senators and fifty-five black members of the House of Representatives) means that blacks have the potential capability to alter significantly the pattern of American politics as a whole. As more and more black Congressmen are sent to Capitol Hill, especially from the South, the old bipartisan, conservative coalition which has blocked so much progressive legislation will be broken up.

It seems there are a dozen pitfalls in the road ahead. There is the possibility that regional governments will be established to include cities where blacks have gained control, so that their newly acquired political power will be taken away. There are dangers to the black political movement if reapportionment is used as a tool to dilute the black population's strength. There is also a more subtle but perhaps more harmful trend to regard the nation's cities as "hopeless" and "not worth saving," now that those same cities have become identified with black people. And yet it would be suicidal for the nation to "sit back" and "let the blacks go it alone," for it is precisely at the moment that the System begins to work for blacks when the rest of America needs to make its biggest investment to insure ultimate success. Ultimately, the challenge will be for the white majority to spend billions of dollars on the urban and rural slums which it has abandoned, and to carry out a strong Federal policy on housing integration. Special attention—"going a long distance out of our way in order to come back a short distance correctly"—is needed. There is need for black economic development, not only for full employment and decent housing but for black ownership and control of production and distribution, so that the masses as well as the few benefit from capitalism. When blacks become economically as well as politically competitive, on all levels, the American Dream will have come into sight as something more than a promise.

Postscript

It may seem anticlimactic to wind up in vague generalities about economics and capitalism, but this book has been about black Americans who are still committed to America, and the path to liberation in America leads directly to—or springs from—the achievement of economic independence. And politics, to borrow Julian Bond's words again, has a great deal to do with seeing "who gets how much of what from whom." If politics fails for black people this time around, if they find themselves unable to make the System work for them as it has worked for others, then they will continue to be strangers in America. "If we fail," said Richard Hatcher, "there may be no way left for us to live in this country." The fact that most black Americans haven't despaired is the single reason why we do not yet have to face the horrible finality of what Hatcher suggests. He, too, is committed to success within the System, assuming it can be altered in the process. "Millions of Negro Americans, the overwhelming majority," said Roy Wilkins early in 1971, "have chosen to work within the framework of the American system." Has it ever been otherwise? Haven't we been blinded by acts of crime and violence? Indeed, was black violence in the form of urban disorders or "riots" ever a planned strategy? Was it not rather the expression of a frustration? In making a "reporter's journey" was I not merely rediscovering the basic faith and hope that black people have always had in this country? And in themselves?

The fact that I have discovered such enthusiasm for politics during a period when national leadership in behalf of the black struggle has been so negligible only reinforces my conviction that the "race problem" is on its way to being solved. The leadership in the White House had virtually excluded blacks from its calculations for political victory. The President made it "perfectly clear" that black Americans were on their own. Despite this, blacks have begun to make their greatest political gains. Now that blacks and their allies are "gettin' together," the movement toward equality is inescapable and unstoppable. This progress is not as dramatic as violence, and the importance of the lone charismatic leader is no doubt diminished. The real story is in community after community, large and small, all across the nation. And once political and economic equality comes into sight, we shall begin to reap the enormous additional input—social, cultural, scientific, spiritual, and so forth—that black people have always been willing and able to make.

It was impossible even to approach covering the full scope of "black politics in America" or some such all-encompassing assignment. Instead, I approached things somewhat intuitively, stopping when I had run out of time, money, and writing space, and when at last I felt I had come to an understanding of blacks in politics that I hadn't fully grasped before. I acknowledge the many omissions, including the absence of any female politicians in this book. However, I can only hope that the very narrow, or personal, quality of my report will not obscure the widespread, diverse nature of the "black political movement" itself.

What, I am asked, was it like to be a white man traveling in so-called black circles? To be honest, I am somewhat embarrassed at having to come up with an answer, since there was no occasion when I felt any sort of sharp discomfort. Blacks are extremely used to white people in America, and my presence probably was viewed quite often as that of just another white man trying to exploit a situation. Well, nothing new about that. For my part, I am grateful for having made some friendships.

—L.H.W.